T0129207

AN INTREPID TRAVELLER

Book 2

An Olympic Year

BY

MARK JACKSON

Order this book online at www.trafford.com
or email orders@trafford.com

Most Trafford titles are also available at major online book retailers.

Printed in the United States of America.

ISBN: 978-1-4669-6513-3 (sc)
ISBN: 978-1-4669-6514-0 (e)

Library of Congress Control Number: 2012919985

Trafford rev. 11/09/2012

 www.trafford.com

North America & international
toll-free: 1 888 232 4444 (USA & Canada)
phone: 250 383 6864 ⋅ fax: 812 355 4082

List of Chapters

Chapter 1. Good Morning Vietnam 1

Chapter 2. Happy New Years 47

Chapter 3. Back on the Road 95

Chapter 4. The Procession of the Olympic Flame............ 131

Chapter 5. Beyond the Great Wall.................................. 169

Chapter 6. There and Back Again................................... 221

Chapter 7. South for the Winter..................................... 267

Cast Of Main Characters In Order Of Appearance. 311

List of Poems

37. Warm Hearts in a Cold Winter....................................23

38. Sapa 22/12/07 (Sapa)...44

39. Hanoi and beer hoi 26/12/07 (Hanoi)........................45

40. Hanoi 26/12/07 53

41. Tourism 13-18/01/08 (Hanoi/HCMC) 54

42. Return to HCMC 18/01/08 (HCMC)............................74

43. The Time Travellers Wife 21/01/08 (HCMC) 75

44. Mekong Market River Cruise 23/01/08
    (Mekong river boat) 79

45. The Coast Road 24/01/08
    (Long Beach, Phu Quoc Island)................................80

46. Untitled 04/02/08 (Hua Hin, Thailand)........................90

47. The end of backpacker alley 08/02/08
    (KS Guesthouse BKK) 91

48. Lost on an Island 08/03 (Shekou) 110

49. Traveller...111

50. My Friend Mr Hai and his friends 17/04/08 143

51. Cat Ba Beach 1 18/04/08 144

52. Cat Ba Beach 2 18/04/08 145

53. On leaving Vietnam 17/04......................................145

54. A Picture Window 05/04/08 (Xin Jiang) 204

55. The end of the Great Wall 27/05/08 (Xin Jiang) 204

56. On the Silk Road West 03/06 (Xin Jiang) 205

57. Untitled 06/06/08 (Xin Jiang) 206

58. Departure Cities 09/06/2008 (Kashgar) 206

59. From Chongqing to Chengdu 20/11/08 (China). 294

60. Temple Street Market 26/10/08 (Temple St, H.K.). 295

61. Goodnight Kisses 03/11/08
    (Camellia Hotel, Kunming) 296

62. Bus Kunming to He Kou 4/11/08 (He Kou). 297

63. At Blue Note Bar 11/11/08 (Blue Note Bar, Cat Ba).... 300

64. A passport to Paradise 11/11/08
    (Blue Note Bar, Cat Ba) 301

65. Madness 15/11/08 (Nanjiang Hotel, Liuzhou)............ 302

66. Just for a second 27/11/08 (H.K. apartment)............ 302

67. Sapa 05/11/08 (Sapa). 306

68. Hanoi 4/12/08 (Bus to San Jiang). 307

69. Superhero 28/11/08 (H.K. apartment)...................... 307

70. This most beautiful view 1/12/08 (Cat Ba Beach). 307

Chapter 1.

GOOD MORNING VIETNAM

"After the rain, good weather.
In the wink of an eye,
the universe throws off its muddy clothes."

Hồ Chí Minh

My flight ticket from Beijing to Hanoi still hadn't arrived. UPS Beijing office didn't speak any English. The reception at the Harmony helped and passed on the message that my ticket may arrive today, or tomorrow. I'd bought it two weeks earlier, so there should not have been a problem, and I was flying at 10am the next day. After a couple of hours I was wondering what to do next. Thinking about purchasing back-up tickets, texting the Irish Girl, Mary to say that I might not be in Hanoi when I'd originally planned (yes, there was more than just a trip riding on this). She had texted me with a 48 hour plan of sight-seeing, things to do and how she was looking forward to seeing me. When I didn't reply (because I was busy), I got the "have I scarred you off?" text message. I think we both know she's a bit weird. I did the old "Dong" joke about her arrangements for the "local payment" and scarred her off even more than she did me. The tickets finally arrived around 7 o'clock. I got Jim's bag out of storage for the following days trip (nice guy aren't I, I'd said I'd transport it to him). He had left it there when he started doing the Vietnam trips eight months earlier and had only been back to Beijing once I that time. Then I went out. I found Steven in the usual Hostel Bar and we drank until very late. At around 4:30am I texted the Irish girl asking her to ring me at 7am to wake me because otherwise I would probably not get up. I was priding myself with my pre-organisation and getting clever at being a serious drinker, but there is always one major failing with these plans. No-one else is up at 4:30 to receive text messages, let alone 7am to ring me back.

I've no idea how I managed to get up and to the airport on time. I was cutting it really fine but had a taxi waiting for me and had organised a wake-up call with the front desk. They looked at me quite puzzled when I'd asked them for a call, only two hours later than I was heading to my room. Jim's bag was heavy, so heavy that I thought I might not be able to carry it through the airport and I actually dragged it most of the way, huffing, puffing, sweating, and being pointed at by all the "well to do" Chinese travellers. At the bag check in, they would not allow me to take Jim's bag on without paying, I'd expected as much, but didn't expect that it would cost me 610 Yuan to get it on the plane. Considering the beer consumption from the night before, coupled with the bag carrying fitness test, I kept thinking I was going to pass out. There was no way that I'd pass one of those customs health inspections with my red sweaty face and panting. Nevertheless, they waved me through. Farewell to China, which had been my home for almost a year, bye bye Beijing, I didn't know when I would be seeing you again. I was off to Hanoi.

Vietnam has such a different vibe to China. I leave the airport and there is a lot of English speaking touts trying to get me to take a taxi and sell me a hotel, it's a lot more slick with the tourists. I know where the public bus stop is and it is less than one tenth of the price that the tout with the van is trying to extort from me. Out from the modern airport and into the surrounding countryside. It is still a hotch-potch of paddy fields and "flat houses". These houses can be built three or four stories, like thin towers, sometimes in complete isolation of each other. Their facades painted in cream, or sky blue or yellow, all with balconies. They look very pretty, all part of the French influence. Then, you look at the sides of the tall houses, no paint, only grey concrete. The reason being is also from the French colonial time, and a taxation system where a house-owner paid tax proportional to the amount of road frontage, so they were built with a narrow front, tall, and extending far back. Many of these were now cheekily constructed, just so to have a smaller frontage, whilst the main body of the house was technical the "side". The houses in the small villages are surrounded by fields. Next to these, the new expressway from the airport to the city still looks out of place. Cutting through the ancient patchwork of small paddy fields with the new grey concrete and black tarmac ribbon of the road. The massive advertising hoarding look like they're out of an American 1950's movie, advertising a "welcome" and some product to buy. There are motorcycles and white taxis, everywhere. As we approach the city, the clusters of tall houses grow into terraces, but no two houses are alike, not even the same size or colour. The advertising hoardings on the road are now also on every building. Hand painted signs, the width of each house advertising what business they are doing, what food they are selling, what paint to buy. This would be a sign painter's paradise and everywhere is open for business, doing something. Doors open to the street, people standing looking out of their shop fronts, people going in, coming out, hanging around, chatting, smoking, playing cards, drinking tea, maybe doing nothing. Maybe watching the endless stream of traffic that we are part of, the taxis, motos weaving in between and lorries carrying goods in a constant, pushing, horn beeping, stop-start moving traffic jam.

When I got to the Victory Hotel they had no rooms. They had two solutions, wait until 9pm and a room would be available in one of the hotels close by, or get on the back of a motorbike and scout the locality asking for rooms. I went for a third option and asked Irish Girl, who was waiting for me in reception, if she'd mind sharing (all rooms are twin), she was delighted. We went out into the old Town for food at Le Pub (Western owned, I'd had enough local stuff for a while) and afterwards we were walking around before the Water Puppets started when we bumped into who else but Monkey Jane. This was extremely random, but not a complete surprise as I knew she'd left Yangshuo for the winter to travel and look at setting up a new bar in Cambodia. Well, this was going to make for an interesting few days. I introduced the girls to Bia Hoi Corner before we went to the Water Puppets.

Mary hadn't checked the time on the tickets (and hadn't told me either) so I was a little puzzled that we were the last ones in and the brevity of the show. We still got a feel for the "punch and Judy in a pool" show, but afterwards I found out we had been half an hour late arriving. The Water Puppets are a traditional form of entertainment. Many years ago, when the rice paddys were flooded, some villagers perfected a way of performing mini plays, with puppets acting as the performers. The puppets were controlled by the "bottom up" method. Instead of having strings, these puppets rode on sticks and their movements were controlled by wires from below, Just how Kermit the Frog on the Muppets is controlled and all of this cunningly concealed in the flooded rice paddy. The puppeteers were hidden behind a screen with all the action happening out in front of them. All together I think there were nine mini shows, but we only got to see half of them. It is definitely not high brow entertainment, with the badly made wooden puppet boy bouncing on the back of an over-stylised water buffalo. Or the story of the turtle and the sword. Or the fireworks spitting from the fake dragon. Or the comedic "tiger" that runs up a tree after stealing the chickens. The plays were all about traditional life and goings on, bringing some of the folk-lore to life. What was truly impressive to me though, is the music, played on traditional instruments and the way that there are voices, as part of the incidental music, calling across the paddy-fields and giving the theatre as sense of the village life that is represents. I know of no other art form where there is actual calling and conversation as part of the music. I had seen the show before, but for Mary, it was her one chance and she had missed half of the show. I like the Irish girl, but she always gives me that feeling that she's going to walk into a door, fall off a rice terrace whilst hiking and taking a photograph, throw her air tickets away when clearing out her handbag sort of girl. I was going to have to be very patient on this next trip.

I stopped at Hoan Kiem lake. It is the lake in the centre of Hanoi and very pretty. It is where young couples go to stroll in the evening. There are two islands on the lake, one is a Temple and you can get there via a footbridge. It is a fine example of a Vietnamese temple but has the eccentric addition of a preserved turtle in a glass case. The other island is known as the Turtle Temple and is inaccessible. The whole turtle theme is very important for Hanoi. As the legend goes, Hanoi was founded when a young prince "Ly" (Ly Thai To) who in the year 1010 saw a multi coloured dragon flying above the place, so Ly decided that this would be his new capital. Ly went on to gain autonomy from the Chinese Song Dynasty court, which finally recognised Vietnam as an independent vassal state rather than its most southern province. Four hundred years later, his successor, named "Le" just so that there is no confusion (Le Loi) was out on a boat on Hoan Kiem Lake, once again contemplating his armies' struggles against the Chinese Ming Dynasty overlords who had re-invaded the country. A turtle swam up besides his boat and offered him a sword with which he could defeat the Chinese. In true Arthurian legend style, Prince Le took the sword, defeated the Chinese and years later, came back to the lake to return the sword to its rightful resting place. Hoan Kiem Lake translates into the Lake of the Restored Sword. People still say that the turtle lives in the lake, every year there is a sighting, but amidst all the pollution of a city of over 4 million people, there is little chance of anything much surviving in the lake. Rumour has it that the zoo puts a turtle in there every few years, just to keep the myth alive. But that is all that it will keep alive, the turtles undoubtedly suffocate or are poisoned in the polluted waters of the lake.

Jim was at the Victory Hotel. Over the last month we'd spoken a lot, about my leading trips over the winter and about his plans for the future. He'd met a girl in Sapa, her name was Phong and she was one of the hotel receptionists and they had fallen for each other. On my previous visit to Vietnam, one month earlier, he had been telling me how they had planned to open a café bar, or something similar, in Sapa. Things seemed to be going ok, but there was one problem. Phong had previously been seeing a French bloke, who now lived in Cambodia. It had been difficult for her family to approve of this. They were a traditional family and relationships of any sexual nature before marriage were frowned upon, relations with a foreigner were even worse, but to move from one foreigner to another one was tantamount to asking for your family and community to disown you for being a whore. The French bloke had not been to visit in over a year and so she was going to tell him that the relationship was over and that Jim was prepared to marry her. There would be a "don't ask, don't tell" attitude towards her previous relationship and things should then work themselves out. Jim was having his parents visit over during the next month, he had run his last trip as a tour leader and was looking forward to a new life.

The next evening I met the new group. Four absolutely stunning girls. Why oh why did the Irish girl pick this trip to join me? All four had been travelling for six months and nine months in their pairs and were heading back to England after this final leg. I quickly found out that they were quite skint and most of them had done all the adventuring they wanted to on their previous travels. Before we headed off for our first night dinner, I got my backpack out of the storage room, which I had placed there one month previously and saw that it had broken with a large rip down one side. One of the more challenging aspects of this lifestyle is living out of a bag, constantly. It is just about my most important possession, without it I cannot lead a trip. It also meant that I only had that evening to get a new backpack. I had to rush through dinner and get to the area of the Old Town, close by the Water Puppet Theatre where they were selling backpacks and haggle. I hate haggling, but this was my only chance of getting a backpack, it was late, not long before the shops would close down for the night and I didn't want the shopkeeper to see that I was desperate. I was very happy to come away with a 100 litre backpack, complete with detachable mini bags, for $35.

We had an 8 am start in the morning, our own minibus to Hai Phong City and the public ferry to Cat Ba Island. It was the first time that I'd done this, but the trip notes were surprisingly descriptive when they told of a rust bucket of a ferry, that was often dirty and overcrowded and that the Tour Leader should try to keep the group calm, as they often panicked and complained when they first saw the ferry. My group were no exception, saying "we can't be going on this, is it safe?" For the girls who had been travelling in South East Asia, it was their first real experience of travelling with local people on local transport. The rest of the trip was going to be one hell of a shock for them.

At Cat Ba Island we were met at the public ferry dock and escorted to our hotel. I had been here before, with Jim and Esemray to watch the sunset from its roof top bar. I took my group on the short walk, down the cliff stairs and to the beach for a late lunch. It's a beautiful introduction to Cat Ba Island, looking out to sea, with the smaller islands dotting the horizon. The cliffs on either side of the bay, with the wooden walk ways more or less saying "come and explore me". After lunch we went to see the local tour operator; Mr Hai. He gave the spiel about activities on the island, hikes into the forest, visiting the Hospital Cave from the Vietnam War, lunch in a village, visiting mangrove swamps, kayaking, secluded beaches and boat trips, but only the Irish girl was interested. The others said that they had done all these things elsewhere on their travels and were running low on cash, so opted for a cheap day of beach and walking around. That sort of set the tone for the rest of the trip. So I went hiking with Mary and a local guide called Lang. We took the walk to Frog Lake, through the forest and climbed the sides of a limestone karst. Mary said that the scenery was like the film "Pans Labyrinth". We stopped in a village for lunch, the only non-villagers there and our guide had to do all the translation. Then we went on a junk boat cruise back to the Cat Ba Town. It had all the ingredients for romance, Mary was saying that she was trying to stop herself from thinking that way, that this was just a trip, a well-deserved break and that I just happened to be the one guy she'd slept with. Back at the hotel, we waited for the rest of the girls to join us on the top floor bar to watch the sun go down over the boats in Cat Ba Harbour. This is one of my most favourite views. Since seeing it one month earlier I had not got it out of my mind, but the other girls did not come, so Mary and I watched the sunset together before I went out to join Mr Hai who had invited me to dinner. The others didn't do anything.

Mr Hai had been calling and he picked me up on his motorbike, we drove to his house. Jim, Steven and Philip had all told me about this hot pot experience. Mr Hai's hospitality was legendary, as was his rice wine. I was a little surprised with where he lived; it was just a one room flat house, looking onto a small courtyard where Hai parked his moto. The house was made from concrete and large enough for the bed, some chest of draws upon which stood a small T.V. and floor space where we would eat. He hung his suit up on a peg above the bed. Hai was always immaculately dressed and that is why I'd been expecting a more expensively furnished apartment. His sister had been cooking, she lived next door and Hai was technically her guardian whilst she was his cook and cleaner. Hai had got divorced a couple of years earlier and he had a son. His ex-wife and boy still lived in one of the hotels in the town that he once owned. We sat on the mat on the ground around the electric hot plate and Hai's sister brought in the large bowl of sea food hot pot. I don't really like sea-food, but I had decided that I could not turn down Hai's hospitality, so I would give it a go. Into the bubbling stock went some small fish, complete with heads and tails. In went some squid, some small octopus, some prawns, all in their entirety. Hai then took out the plastic bottle that he had previously decanted from one of the demi jars that were in the corner of his room. The demi jars contained rice wine and other things, such as the alcohol bleached bones of Geckos, or some tree bark, or a snake. He poured me a small glass, looked me in the eye and invited me to raise my glass to his. We clinked "cheers" and as he continued to stare into my eye, then knocked the alcohol back. I followed. If anything deserved to be called fire water, this was it. As soon as my glass hit the mat again, Hai re-filled and we said cheers and knocked another one back. By this time, the hot pot was bubbling again, it was time to eat.

Hai's sister helped serve, but she didn't eat with us. Hai said that he usually had friends around and that next time I came I would meet them. Hai put things into my bowl to eat, the fish, the prawns, everything. I took time peeling the prawns taking care to remove the head, as Hai just removed the shell and ate his whole. With the squid, he showed me how to take out the internal cartilage, then dipped it into the marinade of lime juice, salt, pepper and chilli that acts as a multi-purpose condiment in Vietnam. Then eat whole again. As soon as I'd finished one, then another arrived in my bowl and the glass of rice wine was replenished and we said "cheers" again. In Vietnamese, this is "Choc Di" or "Choc Si Quay". Or you could chant "one, two, three, yo!" or "mot, hai, ba, yo!". The other tour leaders had said that these dinners around at Mr Hai's house could get really stupid, I could see why and I think that as it was my first night, and there were only the two of us, I got off lightly.

I then met up with Monkey Jane. She had joined a tour group from Hanoi doing the Ha Long Bay and one night in Cat Ba thing. Her fellow travellers hadn't got the measure of her, not sure what to make of a crazy Chinese girl. As for me; I was feeling the effects of Mr Hai's dinner and had to go to bed earlier than planned.

Day four of the trip took us on a four hour boat cruise around the bay, a visit to a cave and a lunch of sea-food. This was heads and tails again and the girls hardly touched a thing. The cave we went to was "Surprising Cave", so called because when it was first discovered; people were surprised at how big it was as it is actually three magnificent inter-connected chambers. We don't get a guide in the cave, we just walk through ourselves but I listened in to the other groups and their guides. Most of the information was about the strange stalactite and stalagmite formations in the cave and what they looked like. A guide with a laser pen pointed out a Buddha. Then a woman looking in a mirror, an elephant a lion and then there was another Buddha. Amid all the gaudy lighting, it wasn't too difficult to see the outlines of the shapes, but it was all in the name of entertainment rather than education. I wondered when we would be told when the cave was actually formed, how it was formed, was it part of some massive underground river system before the land was broken into these islands? Instead we were shown another Buddha image and en route around the caves, a dragon. "What does this look like?" he would enquire to his group as we encountered another in descript rock. "A turd" I thought to myself. This guiding lark was just a whole heap of bullshit. To get to the second chamber, we had to pass through a narrow entrance and one guide suggested that it was like the female genitalia, with a peculiar rock above the arch way that could have been a clitoris. Then came the rock formation that we had all been waiting for, "the happy finger". This rock was an outcrop from a larger stalactite and stood proudly at 45 degrees like an erect penis. Everyone was crowding around to take pictures. As we wandered on through the rest of the cave, on the concrete path beneath the multi coloured lights, with the surround sound speakers appearing every few meters, I thought to myself, that this was not responsible travel at all, it was a theme park, but the Vietnamese and Chinese tourists were loving it and my lot were also taken aback by its actual beauty. It's a pity that it could not have been better preserved, but the "keep on the path", "don't climb the rocks" and "don't graffiti" signs were pretty much ignored.

According to my research, Ha Long Bay had been a shallow sub-tropical sea around 400 million years ago. This is when the limestone was laid down as the dead fish sank to the bottom of the sea and in turn were covered by more dead fish and sea life, mixing with the silt, their bones being compressed over time to form a rock. A great geological event was the detachment of "India" from east Africa and it went hurtling over the now Indian Ocean and ploughed into southern Asia, lifting the Himalayan Mountains. This took millions of years and the Himalayas are still being lifted by this action today. Our part of South East Asia was also lifted and the limestone at Ha Long Bay came above the water in a series of hills. Over the next 200million years, these have been weathered, by rain and sea, to form the karst island landscape that we see today.

The Vietnamese have a different version of events and it's all tied up in the history of the founding of their country. Around 1000 years ago, Vietnam was a vassal state of China and the Vietnamese were fighting for independence. The Chinese had sent an army to quell the rebellion and were invading by sea. A dragon saw the Vietnamese plight and flew off to defeat the

Chinese army and in so doing either spat jewels at invading boats, which became the mountains in the sea or churned up the land with his mighty tail, depending on which version of the story you read. Thus, the karst scenery at Ha Long Bay was created.

The bus came to meet us as we docked at Bai Chai and took us on the four hour journey to the border. The scenery changed and changed again, from the karsts of Ha Long bay, to the flat shores with the inundations and fisherman's huts raised above the water. A farmer here was also a fisherman. Then we went through the villages that almost constantly lined the road. Wherever the highway took us, there would be a house built every ten meters or so. Behind these, were the rice paddys, with the irrigation channels. The rice had been harvested, so the fields were lying barren. The road took us past factories, industrial complexes and out into the countryside again. In the distance as we headed north, we could see the chimney stacks of the brick kilns. Then less and less buildings as the land around us became open paddys, then the hills of limestone began to rise again and close in the road on either side. We were heading to the border town of Lang Son. This was going to be my first big test, negotiating a border town that was billed as having little or nothing of merit and only one listed restaurant. The hotel we were in wasn't up to much and located on the wrong side of town. I had a map and just set off on a 40 minute walk, with the girls following dutifully behind me across town. True to its billing, there was little of interest here and it looked like we were the only tourists staying in town. We made it to the hotel with the restaurant and the next problem was going through the Vietnamese menu and trying to feed them. I was glad to only have a group of five. I sort of pulled it off and we all went back to the hotel and found internet before I started feeling ill. There had already been an issue with the girls not wanting to eat chicken on the bone, and I was the only one to tuck in at this meal and it had given me food poisoning. First I was feeling ok, then I was vomiting for the next two hours. Luckily, Mary had found me on the bathroom floor when she came over to say something about a map. I was worried. Border crossings, travel days and a trip I wanted to do would all go out the window. I would have to contact the office and try and get someone else to take over. So much for the Irish girls plans. Somehow I would have to look after myself in a third world country where I didn't know the language, with no-one to help me. Well, the odds were always going to mean that I'd get ill at some-time. It was annoying that it was now. Luckily, I slept, with Mary watching over me.

I don't know how, but the following morning, I was fully functioning. No-one else had been ill and so we were off to the Chinese border. The Vietnamese side was a porter cabin with plastic chairs, whilst the Chinese border control was an impressive modern building of polished stone and glass. We were met by a driver, as the local operator cum guide was not available

I managed to convey to the driver that we needed to change money, my Chinese has improved and it needed to have as no one in this part of China spoke any English. Then he drove to our first night accommodation in China in Butterfly Valley. An astoundingly beautiful place, where we all stayed in individual huts, built on stilts in a traditional style, but without anybody to speak English or guide us it was a bit of an unfortunate loose end. I could organise food and the time to take the boat to see the Hua Shan painting, but that was as far as it got. The countryside was limestone karst scenery again, with the "Zuo Jiang" or "Left River" taking us on a boat journey to see 2000 year old cliff paintings. It was a bit of a non-event, we had a hand-out that briefly described the paintings, but to sum it up, nobody knew precisely who, why or when they were painted. The information was badly translated, talking of "menstruation", rather than a time "period" amongst the many mistakes. The up side was that the river cruise itself took us through scenery that was as beautiful if not more so than the Li river at Yangshuo. In the afternoon I'd wanted to go on a hike as there was supposed to be a route around the karsts that took in some maple trees, but we didn't really have the time. I didn't know that there were maples in China. That night it was cold and I met the local operator, Grass, who said that the trip would get colder as we continued through Guang Xi province. We'd had the offer of kara-oke at the guest house, with the staff, on their prized machine but no-one was up for it and by nine o'clock we were all turning in for bed. I also turned down Mary's offer of staying in her cabin with her. It would just be too obvious to the rest of the group or to the Guest House owners.

Jim, Lyn, Philip, Snow and Steve had all told me that the trip was different from the others that we had done, in that we didn't go to places with a specific activity at the destination. There was no Xi'an Terracotta Warrior, no Chengdu pandas, not even a Yangshuo bike ride or "backpacker paradise" as the main focus. For the next few days, there would be few activities beyond walks around villages and a hike through the Long Ji Rice Terraces. There was a lot of down time in each place with no specific itinerary for what to do in "free time" and yet we were up and moving nearly every day, on public busses early in the morning and for half day long journeys. I'd done as much preparation as I could, but the next 48 hours was hard. I had to get the group on a bus to Ninming, then at that bus station, get the next bus to Nanning. Once there, we had half an hour as I got another lot of bus tickets to Liuzhou. The girls were asking where the toilet was and why couldn't we stop anywhere for lunch, then realising that there was nowhere for lunch as western style cafes are in short supply in South West China. There was a KFC at Nanning bus station. They could even get chicken without bones. All this was in places that I'd never been to before and the bus station attendants were not used to foreigners buying bus tickets either. When we arrived there at 4:45 I had to take a look around to see where about I was in the city. Somewhat fortunately, I'd checked this part of Liuzhou out for half an hour whilst waiting for a train about a month earlier. My last Essence of China trip had us taking the bus from Yangshuo to Liuzhou and the train from Liuzhou to Yichang and the Yangtze River. Otherwise, I'd be completely blind on this trip for over a week. Once I'd figured out where I was we walked the 10 minutes to the hotel, everybody staring at us on the city street. Checking in was thankfully easy, then I was off again to find the other bus station where I bought tickets to San Jiang for the following day. OK. I suppose it's what I'm paid to do, but the language barrier is immense and the actual hassle of getting a ticket with the push and shove of a Chinese non-queue is near impossible. Doing all this whilst finding places in new towns as your passengers keep wanting to know where *they* are going and when *they* are going to eat when these are questions that I wish I could answer for my own satisfaction. Well, we ate at around 7pm at UBC Coffee (a Taiwanese chain with a picture menu in English) and that was good enough for me. We also took a look around town and decided that it really wasn't worth stopping there for the night. Liuzhou has the reputation of being Guilin's bigger uglier sister, an industrial and transportation hub with only a couple of karsts in the park in the city as redeeming features. You could get a cable car up these karsts, if you set off early enough in the morning, but no one did. We don't stop in Guilin on any of our trips, so why visit her sister?

Mary had got her own back that night by turning down my advances. I shouldn't be too sure of myself, should I? I wrote the morning off too and only surfaced in time for a pot noodle breakfast and the taxi to the central bus station and then the bus to San Jiang. I've got to tell you about the baggage scanner at this bus station. (All transportation places have a baggage scanner). This one is at the top of a staircase. Let me elaborate. I'm quite an expert at putting my two or three bags on the conveyor belt of the baggage scanner, in sequence (big bag first, so I can get it off and put it on whilst the others come through and I'll have free hands to pick them up) and getting out at the other side, minimum of fuss. The only real problems to date have been the Chinese who fall over themselves in the rush to get their bags on and off, or fruit, that falls out of bags and rolls all around and off the conveyor belt. Well, today was a completely new Kripton Factor of a baggage scanner. On they went; no problem. I walked around the other side, and there was a staircase, leading down. The conveyor belt was propped in the air. Somehow, you had to walk down the steps and pick up your bags at the same time. OK, fair enough for me with a bit of a shove to the on-coming Chinese, but for the girls it all ended in one large pile of ruck-sac's and shopping and Chinese ladies looking for lost children. I'd know better for the next time.

As we entered San Jiang four hours later I said to the girls, "I bet you're happy you didn't grow up here?" It was a small concrete town with nothing that looked like it would give you hope. We met Tim, our guide. A lad of around 25, who took us by mini-van to our guesthouse 30 minutes away in Cheng Yang. He was wearing a white spots jacket and shades he was the best dressed guy in town. This would have been a beautiful spot, if only it wasn't covered in mist and drizzle. It was rural China at its best, wooden village houses, water wheels, stone pathways that wound between the houses on the hillsides. Then there was the Rain and Wind Bridge, unfortunately covered in too much rain and wind to give us a good impression, but it was there. This area was another ethnic minority prefecture. The locals were called the "Dong" people. Dare I say more?

We stayed in a wooden two story house, built in the local style, where we could pay an extra Y20 for heating in the rooms. It was bitterly cold once the sun went down, with little to do but play cards. The girls had invested in some cold weather clothes in Liuzhou, but this was cutting into their already tight budget. They had no idea that China would be this cold in winter and only had their holidaying clothes for Thailand and Australia. The guest house was cold. The common room was a big, open place and the windows would not close properly. In China, there are no fire places. I find this astounding in a country with over 5000 years of civilisation, but instead, there is a small metal bowl into which is put charcoaled wood. The heat from the bowl is minimal and the only consolation was that the food cooked by Tim's mum was ample and hearty.

Then Tim's Dad, Mr Wu arrived with a kettle of Bai Jiu. This is the rice wine that countryside people distil and it can get to a leathal 60% proof. Mr Wu had already been sampling some of his own produce and was a larger than life figure, huffing and puffing and shouting out "I am Mr Wu" and "drink" in an almost "Father Ted/Father Jack" style. We all had to join him in a drink, but it wasn't to the girls taste and Mr Wu wasn't taking 'no' for an answer. I tried to teach the group mah-jong, learned from my many boat trips with Amy and the Yangtze River guides, but Mr Wu was getting involved here again, playing the girls hands and they could not follow what was going on. This we did until 10pm, then bed. I was just getting warm when I got a text message. "You must be freezing, my door will be bolted in 5 minutes". It was an easy decision.

Tim took us for a walk around the villages the following day, firstly going across the "Wind and Rain Bridge" that the village is famous for. Wind and rain bridges were originally built, according to legend when a baby was rescued from drowning by a magical fish. The Dong people then built the bridges, for river crossing, but also as a gathering place for the women villagers. As part of their construction, there are benches along the length of the bridge and a temple to one of the preferred spirits or gods. This particular Wind and Rain Bridge was made entirely of wood and without nails in 1912. The central temple had been removed during the Cultural Revolution as it was "a fire hazard" and had not been replaced, but otherwise, the construction was true to its traditional architecture, high sloping roof and overhanging and upturned eves. We continued the walk through the village and onto the next village as they merged into each other. Mary is quite a photographer, having replaced the camera she lost at the Terracotta Warriors months earlier and was clicking away at everything we passed. Tim and Mr Wu asked if she could send copies of some of the photographs, as for many villagers, they had no photographic record of their family. Older generations would die, young children would never have pictures from their youth. Mary was happy to oblige and I said I would be returning to the villages in only one month. I was also surprised at the number of pictures she took of ducks, paddling in the streams, waddling along the stone pathways. Then there was the wooden houses, the rice terraces, the people at the market. The whole village life scene was literally, as pretty as a picture. Each village centre would have a "Drum Tower" another wooden construction, communal space for the men of the village to sit and play cards. They are identified mainly by their pyramidal high roof. In the front of the drum tower is usually a village square, where meetings are held and performances of song and dance. Many of the drum towers have an inventive way of funding their upkeep, in that there are stone tablets around them each with a name of a sponsor and their donation. As my Travel Company have been coming here for a number of years, I could see the names of some of the other Tour Leaders that I knew and their donation. There was Bruce and Tracey, both now my managers along with Jim, Philip, Steve and Lyn who did these trips over the last summer. As we walked on to another village, we passed through the barren rice paddies, filled with rain water and just the burnt stubble of rice showing through. We crossed another wind and rain bridge, smaller, yet older than the first one. This time with an intact temple to the Green Man; some devilish spirit figure who you had better give reverence to and offerings of incense.

It just happened to be 'Harvest' festival. As a result there was a lot of activity going on and we went to one of the family temples to watch the village elders perform some ritual. Mary was clicking away with her camera, there was no one else there to witness and preserve this vanishing tradition. The three old men, dressed in robes, took offerings of fish, chicken and a pig head to an altar. There were lots of incense and speeches. Behind the altar was a painting of a mythical beast, not unlike a Qilin, a mixture of horse, lion and dragon with scales. People from all the villages were crowding into the small temple. Outside, was cold and drizzle, but the festivities were only just getting under way and had a song and dance show from the different village troupes that lasted a couple of hours. They all wore traditional costume with silver head dresses and pleated skirts. The men wore some type of black "sailor suit" or even "pyjama" style costume and played a local variation of pan pipes, called a lusheng, which came in various sizes from hand held to larger ones needing a stand. For some dances, there were parasols, in others, there were depictions of daily life, picking tea, sowing rice, fishing in the river. Unless you know anything about China, you would not know that there are ethnic minorities in the country, with their own traditions, language, dress and local songs and dances. To stumble upon these Dong people celebrating their most important festival of the year, the way they have done for thousands of years was quite amazing. Unfortunately, the girls didn't see it that way. They were cold and didn't like it when all the fire-crackers were let off next to them. We did join in with the final dance as the local ladies pulled us into a circle and we moved around and around with them. For the grand finale, one of my girls got thrown up into the air three times, but apart from that, you could tell that the girls were not impressed with the cold and the rain. Tim also looked bored with the whole thing. He's just about the only person in the locality with a university education and he's stuck there working for his family.

After we left Cheng Yang, we took the local bus up to Long ji. I've been there once before and had Farmer Tang as a guide there last time as well. I'd been looking forward to this part of the trip because it meant I could take a back seat whilst Farmer Tang did the local guide stuff. The one hour bus journey from San Jang got us to Long Shen where Farmer Tang was waiting for us with gifts of fruit and hot dumplings. The previous year, I had read in my notes that the bus ride took four hours, but the road we travelled on was newly constructed, it was another part of Chinas rapid development and the 10 year plan to construct a country wide major road network.

Farmer Tang had organised for us to drop off our larger bags at a hotel in He Ping village which we used as a bag store. The idea was that we would be hiking the next day, from one village to another and could pick up the big bags the day after that when we passed this way again as we headed off to Yangshuo. All we needed to carry with us was the overnight bag or a day pack for the hike. The issue was, that it was so cold, in summer this was not a problem, but in winter, our overnight bags and day packs were almost the size of our normal ruck sacks. We took a while to organise ourselves, I should have pre-warned the group about this bag drop off, but it was the first time that I'd encountered it. We put our bags in one of the rooms of the hotel owners' apartment. I noticed how empty and bare the place looked, no soft furnishings, no carpet, but a massive television and an ornately carved wooden sofa, with no cushions. I still hadn't been in many Chinese peoples' houses but this was the first time that it had dawned on me that they were all sparsely furnished and "hard". Not because they didn't have money, but because that was the traditional way. It was the cold temperature that had got me noticing this difference, along with the lack of a fireplace and the way that everyone was now wearing layer upon layer of clothes. Mary had also noticed this from her time in Shanghai where she had been learning Chinese medicine. As the weather got colder, people were coming for treatment with up to six layers of clothes. She had already noticed that most women over thirty wore a type of body stocking, to sort of hold everything in. Now, in the winter, it was layer and layer of body stocking with almost no easy way of removing them in order to give diagnosis or treatment.

We were back on our way again and by mid-afternoon we were in the guesthouse at Ping An. On the way up there were some market stalls and the girls had decided that they could get some traditional garments, for presents for their family as they were going home soon. I mentioned that they would have to carry them on the hike; I mentioned that they could get the same stuff in Yangshuo and they had also been trying to save money as they were at the end of their budgets and would be emailing home to get more cash to finish off the trip. Over the last couple of days, they had decided against the "group meal" as it cost around 30 Yuan and instead were getting their own food. This was a false economy, if ever there was one because it led to them having a basic dinner, then being tempted by the pancakes that Mrs Wu and now Yi Beng's wife could make in the Li Qing Guest house. Farmer Tang was encouraging us to do a hike up to scenic point two. I went, although the weather was not so good to view the vastness and beauty of the rice terraces. Still it killed a couple of hours before sunset and the onset of the freezing night. Once again, we played mah-jong and gathered ourselves around the small metal bowl with charcoal in it that served as a fire place. We were all wrapped up in our bed duvets, but it was still cold and none of us stayed up past nine o'clock again. Mary had noticed the way that the women who had joined us by the charcoal bowl were knitting with four needles. She hadn't seen this before and was intrigued with how it was done. After a while, she had it figured, but I can't remember the intricacies of how it was done.

The next day was a four hour hike to Da Zhai village, which is another fantastic day out, but it was a bit of a struggle for a couple of the girls. You have to have a decent level of fitness to do these walks. I'm not fit, and I like it when the passengers are slow, because it allows me to walk at a reasonable pace at the back of the group. The Yao minority women were hassling Farmer Tang to tell us to buy things from them, then getting annoyed when he wouldn't. Then they would hassle us directly, but we didn't want anything, certainly not a picture of their long hair, but Mary in photographer mode got one anyway. It was a tough climb in the drizzle, but when the clouds broke, it was the magnificent rice terrace scenery that is worth the discomfort of a little rain. As I'd predicted, Mary nearly fell off a rice terrace, as she was trying to kick me for something that I had said to her in jest. We got to the second guesthouse around mid-afternoon again and like the previous day, Farmer Tang encouraged us to go on another hike to another scenic point. There was no chance this time. Then it was the much needed hot showers before the onset of the cold winter night.

37. Warm Hearts in a Cold Winter

(A) Into the cold of Winter 09/12/07

North across the border
And into the hills of winter
Along the half concrete road
That winds besides the river
The big houses on the valley side

Askew with age and rain soaked timbers
Stilts that prop up a veranda
The family homestead of the rice terrace farmers

A dozen buildings in concrete
Pushing up from the roadside
A foreigner,
pushing tradition aside
The market on the ground cloths
In the shadow, selling the local food
Brought up the stone pathway
On the backs of the double bent and old

I see a spirit that laughs at me
Looking at me from the aged face
There is more to this than my money
There is much more to this place

(B) 09/12/07 Chen Yang

In the street market in the Big Village
A women chooses the biggest fish

The Harvest festival
Old men in the temple
The family eats together
Buying fruits and sugar

A priest in a trilby and shades
Beckons all into his courtyard temple
we all push together in the hustle and bustle
Foreigners mixing in with the locals

In the village square, the women make ready
In their traditional dress for the dancing display
The procession of the silver crowns
Silver leaves, silver birds and coloured pom-poms

The fire crackers fill the courtyard
With a deafening attack
That has the tourists cowering
Then moving back

I peer over the huddled crowd for a look
Smokey dust settles on my notebook

The village elders gather
In the old wooden barn with an alter
Long coats and the symbol
Of the maze in a circle
3 incense sticks and 2 candles to the alter
Behind is a picture of some Chimera
Part horse, part fish-scale
Walking on the water, head of a devil

A pigs head, a duck and a fish
3 foods in a procession on a dish
Then gunshot rattles the air again
Before the priest beginning the dedication

10 bamboo pipe players, swaying with their swinging tune
Joined by the girls with the pink parasols,
Then the formal dance begins
Pipers play, kneeling, parasol girls encircle
Then a chant goes out
Drinking songs, courtship songs and dancing together
Till we get wrapped up in the festival
And we're dancing until we get tossed in the air

(C) 09/12/07

Tiptoeing back to my cold room
Before anyone wakes me for breakfast
Trying not to get too carried away
Knowing each stolen moment won't last
For being there whilst I vomited
When I slept and when I awoke
For making me believe I could go on
From my night in the desert, it makes us even

(D) 11/12/07 Long Ji

Walking the stone pathways
Upwards between the rice paddies
Built on terraces that clothe the hillside
The mist that swirls away in the valley
Revealing an enchanted world as we look
A picture discovered in a dusty old book

We look out over this Shangri La
Then into the fairy-tale village we walk
Along the valley side, to follow the river
Past the bamboo water-wheel, spilling everywhere

Chickens cross the pathway, the ducks gather together
The women that want to show you their long hair
And carrying their baskets of market-wares
Local fruit and bracelets in silver

Chatting and pointing and always laughter
This warm hearted place, enchanted against winter.

The following morning we set off for Yangshou and I headed straight to Bar 98 for a late lunch. The following couple of days went as they usually do in Yangshuo, although there were no leaders around for drinks. On these winter trips, I was going to be on my own a lot and pretty isolated compared to how it had been with all the camaraderie of the leaders meeting up in Yangshuo and elsewhere. We went to Monkey Janes, but the roof top bar was freezing as soon as the sun went down. Bar 98 had Ton Ton in charge as Snow was having a break. The four girls in the group were not interested in any activity beyond massage and were on Skype to their parents asking for money. They were down to their last £20 until the end of the trip and that included a day in Hong Kong. So it was me and Mary hanging around together while she contemplated getting a teaching job.

We did the usual bike ride to moon hill, but in the cold weather for the first time and I was ill prepared, wearing shorts and a t shirt. George was our guide and he was telling us his usual jokes and stories, but they weren't interested. As it was New Year, he had another story for us, all about the Chinese New Year and how each animal was selected to represent each year in the cycle of twelve.

A long time ago, the Buddha decided that he would give each year a name and announced that the first ten animals that would come to him after sunrise would each have a year named after them. There was much excitement and discussion about this. The mouse and the cat said to each other "if you wake up before me, can you make sure that you wake me up also, so that I can get to the Buddha and have a year named after me?" They both agreed and fell asleep. Before first light, the mouse woke up and he decided to see what was happening and forgot all about waking up the cat. It is from this time that the cat and the mouse have been enemies as the cat never stood a chance of having a year name after him. The mouse ran to where there was a big commotion and all the animals were trying to get to the finish line where they would cross and be given a year. In amongst all the big crush, the mouse was able to run and climb onto the larger animals and he sat upon the ox as the ox muscled himself to the front of the pack and crossed the finish line. As the ox crossed the line, the mouse jumped from the ox's nose and was the first to be given a year in his honour, the ox was given the second year. Next came the tiger, who'se speed had got him to third place and the rabbit then squeezed in between the bigger animals to hop over in fourth. Next came the dragon, who flew across the line and then the snake who stretched himself across in sixth place. The horse and the ram were chasing each other across the line in seventh and eighth, then the monkey swung from a branch above all the other animals to come in ninth. Last of the animals to cross was the rooster, who amid all the confusion, strutted proudly across the line in tenth.

The agent of the Buddha shouted out "enough" but that was not the end of it. The animals had not been counting, or had thought that the Buddha had changed his mind for some reason and had called for the dog because "enough" in Chinese sounds like the word for "dog". So the dog crossed the line in eleventh place and was also granted a year. Now some of the animals were protesting, whilst others were starting to go home and the pig was only just arriving as he was so slow and lazy that he had not got up in the morning and he had missed the race. When he got close to the line, he heard the agent of the Buddha shout out "zhu le", in exasperation, which sounded like the word for "pig" so the pig wandered across the line and became the twelfth year and recognised as the luckiest animal of them all. This is why the lucky pig is the shape of your childrens "piggy-bank" bestowing good fortune on the saver.

We had decided to visit Farmer Tang for lunch. No one climbed moon hill and none of them ate the whole chicken cooked by Farmer Tangs wife as it came complete with feet and bones and they decided that it looked a bit pink. As George ate, he chewed the chicken bones in his mouth and spat them out on the table, to the disgust of the group, though it is perfectly normal table manners in China. On the way back to Yangshuo one of the girls that didn't ever ride a bike got saddle sore so we had to walk back 5K and as I said, I was not dressed for a walk in the cold. Only Mary did cooking school, so we had to join in with another group. This was my first experience of the

Gap-year travellers of South East Asia. I'd made allowances as they were at the end of their trips, but I was beginning to wonder . . . could they all be like this?

The train to Shenzhen is never on time. Always an hour or so after we are supposed to arrive I look out of the window for the tall shimmering buildings of the new city and I know that I am nearly there when we pass the statue of liberty holding a microphone in front of the karaoke bar. We have to walk across the border. From our corridor crossing the stream between what was Red China and the British Empire and the free west, I can still see the barbed wire stretched across the concrete embankment. Sometimes we can queue for over an hour, carrying our backpacks before we can be processed and get on the KCR train to Kowloon and finally to the West Hotel. Knowing that this was all coming to an end made it all the more awkward and intense. The girls ate at McDonalds for lunch. They were bored of the Light Show before it was over, so we did the final night dinner in the Eight Fine Irishmen, rather than Blues on the Bay, because it was the cheapest option. British food, even though they would be back home in 24 hours. They had just had the trip of a life-time, but didn't appreciate any of it. I managed Sunday Roast in Murphey's bar with Mary the following day. I wanted to spend some valuable last time with her, but I had another trip to start the following day and had to take a look at the bus stop where I bought tickets for the border crossing with my new group. I had a fair bit of preparation to do; this was a completely new trip to me. Back at the hotel I took out the last of my body piercings and gave the bar to Mary. It was something that had been part of my body for so long and I thought that I had nothing else to give her, nothing that could compare to what she had given me. Another goodbye and another trip over as I waved her off, probably for the last time, probably forever, watching her leave on the red Hong Kong double decker airport bus.

In the afternoon I moved from the West Hotel to the YMCA to start my next trip. I only had three female passengers in this group so I wrote a note for each and placed it under their doors. Tamsin 35 from Hastings quickly got in touch. She'd been on an Essence of China trip already and had spent the last 10 days in Hong Kong (I wouldn't wish that on anyone). Then she told me that she'd just noticed that her visa for Vietnam didn't start until 25th December, and we crossed the border on 21st. "Maybe I'll wing it at the border" she said. I explained that this was impossible, you can't just "wing it" between China and Vietnam. This was going to be another one of those trips. The two other girls on the trip were Claire 31 from Leeds and Kelly 22 from Melbourne. Claire was just finishing a Roam China trip, so we joined that group for dinner and the leader was my old room-mate from training, Jay who I'd only run into only twice during the whole of the season.

He walked us to his chosen restaurant in Temple St market along the market streets which had everyone getting lost as they stopped to browse the market stalls. Some of these were stranger than others as there is a section of Shanghai Street that you have to walk along to get to Temple Street Market that has stalls selling sex aids. Right there, out in the open were dildos and vibrators standing proudly erect as we passed by. He chose one of the street side cafes where the staff hastily put together enough tables and chairs for the group to squeeze themselves around. Then he ordered dinner, Hong Kong Specialities that only a few of the group wanted to try. Spicy Crab at an open air street café, sitting on plastic chairs was not what they wanted for their end of trip meal in Hong Kong. They preferred to get their own individual meals as it was the first opportunity to do so. He was complaining about them to me, their attitude, their lack of interest, lack of culture, that they only wanted to drink beer. It was his last trip and he was glad to be out of it. He didn't like the passengers and he said that he needed to earn more money. I understood where he was coming from, that the people on his trips were not that interested in China and many had only added it in as part of a "Round the World" tour. He wanted to give them a cultural experience that they didn't want. He would be better suited in a different travel company. I headed off back to the hotel, leaving the girls with the other group as I had to stay up until around 1am, finishing off my accounts for the previous trip and emailed Bruce in the office about Tamsin's Vietnam Visa situation. The next morning at 7:30 we were off on a bus to Shenzhen and the plane to Guiyang

This was another blind trip for me. The only place I'd been to on this trip before was Kunming. Luckily it was just a 10 day trip, so however much of a cockup I made of it, It would be over and done with before too long. This was also going to be rural China, in winter, so some of the trip was going to be hard. There were three long treks included and I didn't think the girls had known what they had booked up for. It soon turned out that for Tamsin and Claire it was more a case of getting from H.K. to Vietnam than the trip of a lifetime. Both were in the middle of Round the World trips. Kelly had picked the trip because it worked well with her Australian University summer brake, she hiked regularly, so would probably get the most out of the trip.

It was a hectic start to the trip. Beginning at 7am, we walked to the bus stop for a cross border public bus to Shenzhen airport. Once there I had to find C-Trip to check in, they were expecting me, even without the paperwork that I had not been able to print off. We had enough time for food at KFC. Claire was a bit surprised as she told me that Jay would refuse to take them to any western or fast food joint. He had run his trip like a boot camp and the group were afraid of crossing him at any point. He'd had a go at them for drinking too much coke, lecturing them on diabetes. It had got to the point where the group would discuss what they were going to do, and wonder if Jay would approve. With enough time for lunch we had a flight to Guiyang in Guizhou province in the hills of south west China. From the airport we had a pick-up and a four hour journey by bus to the town of Kaili, where we would spend the night and meet out local guide.

The bus journey through the hills to Kaili really showed us where we were. The highway was modern; it could only have been a couple of years old and was almost deserted as it cut a swathe through the barren hills and moorlands. There was the occasional farmstead and forested hillside, but otherwise, this place was remote. The remoteness gave it a wild beauty that only the highway brought to civilisation. It was early evening by the time we had arrived, checked in, then was greeted by the local operator, another Mr Wu, who I had to meet for payment. He said that our guide would meet us in a couple of hours, we had been travelling all day and the girls were not impressed with where I had taken them. This region was also an ethnic minority area, for the Miao people. "Minority women" hung around outside the hotel trying to sell things to the few guests, or to beg. It was colder than I'd expected again, caught off guard by the sudden shower of sleet.

Kai Li as a city wasn't much to write home about. It reminded me a little of Zhongwei, on the opposite side of the country. I think most Chinese towns, when they were re-developed in the 60's and 70's were done from the same standardised government plan. There was a round-a-bout in the centre of town, where our hotel was. A few modern buildings, then, away from the centre was the old 1970's style mass produced concrete of the pre-modernising China. It was a dirty concrete mess. According to the guidebook, the temple on the hill was worth taking a look at, so we wandered up there and back. It was cold, close to freezing once the sun went down and from now on it was going to be guesthouses all the way. We met our guide 'Fox' a very likeable 24 year old who tried to please at every opportunity. He took us to a roadside cafe for our dinner and the girls were in shock at the basic facilities. The "cafe" was just a room with some plastic chairs and tables and the cooking was on a gas burner and wok out the back. Vegetables and cuts of meat lay out in the open, cats scampered in and out; "well," I thought, "at least they won't have mice". We took a look around the town after dinner, but the cold and the dark were off putting. We went into the underground market that was the subway for people to cross beneath the main road system by the central traffic round-a-bout. They did a spot of shopping because the girls didn't have much in the way of winter clothes. Then I had a look around before it was time for bed, trying to find if there was much else to come back for in this town. I wasn't out for long, but I did get an unexpected message from Bruce in the office who texted to say he was on the case about the visa to get into Nam.

Day three of the trip was a private bus ride to the countryside and then a trek through to Xi Jiang. Once we were away from the city we were back on the road that cut through the mountains. It was a road that seemed to connect nowhere with nowhere, a modern highway with bridges and cuttings between the dark towering mountains with only the odd tumbledown farmhouse that it could serve. It was obviously part of the National Road strategy, but to serve what purpose, I could only guess. I began to appreciate why this trip was called the Rural Colours of China. It was truly fantastic scenery again. We wove up mountainsides, then down and through valleys. Rice terraces covered some of the hillsides, some were forested.

We got out of the bus where there was a dirt road cut into the hillside; this was to be the start of our trek. We had to Hike for four hours. Up and down, a bit cold and slippery, crossing a few streams and having to get our feet wet. We managed an open air lunch break by the side of the trail as it drizzled. When I looked out over the valleys, I saw that the hills were covered in what looked like Christmas trees and as we were in the middle of December, this seemed quite apt. Fox was quite chatty once we got him going, he seemed shy at first. He talked about the lives of the villagers in the places that we hiked through. Some were from different ethnic groups, not only Miao, and some Han Chinese too, who had come to live in this rural idyll. He told me that 10,000 Yuan would build me a house, all from the local wood. Older houses don't have treated wood and don't last too long, maybe 20-30 years. Wood treating is a new concept, as is brick and concrete and they are also starting to make an appearance. The typical Chinese way of thinking, that everything old is bad and everything modern is good, has meant that those with money are now building concrete houses and the wooden ones will be gone in a couple of decades. Fox told me that it was tradition for the oldest son to build a new house for himself and his new wife to move in to. Why have wood when you can have concrete?

Xi Jiang itself was an ethnic minority village for the Miao people. Fox told me it was "the biggest Miao village in the world", which he seemed proud of and was obviously true as there were not so many Miao communities beyond these hills. It nestled in the valley sides between terraces and mountain top. A cluster of wooden, two-story big houses, similar to the villages that I had visited around Long Ji, but not quite the same. We arrived around 4pm. We were given a warm reception by the Li family which included two shots of rice wine, one for each leg according to tradition. Then singing and fire crackers. We were given a boiled egg on a string; it is supposed to be a good luck charm for the onward journey. You are supposed to keep it for as long as possible without breaking it. The record according to the trip notes was as far as the border with Vietnam. Then we were told that there was no electricity. So the warm welcome was about as warm it was going to get. We were told that there was internet in a place in the town, but without electricity, it was pointless. We would also have to wait to be fed, because even though the stove was powered by burning charcoal logs, there was no light to see by to cook, or to eat. We were told that electricity should be back on in the village at around 7pm. We had a walk around the town and Tamsin asked why everyone was wearing pyjamas? She was correct in her description and I had also seen this in other towns, but it had never registered with me until now. Most of the women were wearing matching pyjama sets, many of them with cartoon prints that only a child would wear. This was some sort of modern twist on the traditional single dark colour pyjama type dress of the southern Chinese tribes. It didn't look right at all and it brought to mind something that a Liverpudlian passenger had mentioned on a trip the previous year. That the fashion in Liverpool had been to walk around in your pyjamas as a sign that you didn't need to go to work. It is still bad fashion, wherever you are in the world.

We sat in the main room, there was a metal stove which we huddled around, above this, suspended on the ceiling was meat, being cured. This was a specifically done at this time of the year, with the onset of winter, making sausages that would keep through to the spring and drying meats for preservation. Every once in a while there would be a greasy drip from a hanging sausage on to the metal arguer. A regular conversation stopper as you looked ceiling-ward to check that you weren't in the way of the next globule of fat.

There is one thing that we could do to pass the time, and also keep us warm. The local brew of rice wine was produced. I knew that this would come out at some point, as the trip notes I had mentioned a cultural show put on by the locals, which usually got people drinking, singing and dancing. We were not to be disappointed. The rice wine started to flow; dinner was served, with more rice wine. We had a cultural show of singing and dancing, similar to the songs of the other hill tribe minorities that I had seen over the last year, the Dong, the Zhang, the Yao and then got involved ourselves. We did the Hokey-cokey for the locals as our 'gift of a song'. We played fox and chickens. We played another game where everyone was sat in a circle and a handkerchief was placed behind you. Whoever got the handkerchief had to run around the outside of the circle and place the handkerchief behind someone else without them knowing. The object of the game was to do this and complete a full circle. The person who didn't realise the handkerchief was behind them had to 'sing' as a forfeit. Lots of singing, dancing and drinking. What an unexpectedly wonderful place with wonderful people.

Fox was drunk very quickly, he kept asking the girls to put him on Facebook. He was such a nice lad, but somewhat shy, then over-eager in trying to impress, then becoming also quite effeminate in his mannerisms and in a western culture I would have marked him as possibly being gay. I don't think that is acceptable in rural China, he may be gay, but this would not stop him from getting married and living a conventional life. Actually, being a guide was not conventional, he had trained as a teacher and this was a better paying job, but he wanted to travel and meet people so took this lower paid and irregular guiding job. His mum, his girlfriend, all wanted him to go back to teaching, earn more money, enough to put his sister through university, enough to get married, but as I said, he just wasn't that sort of lad.

We left the valley the following morning with the steam and smoke from the kitchen fires rising as we did, up the mountain side. More spectacular scenery again. A couple of hours in, we stopped at Da Feng Dong village, a town where there was a market. We were obviously the first westerners that had been here. The staring was more apparent than it usually is in China. There were all sorts of market life going on. Charcoal logs were for sale, all sorts of fruit and veg and people going about their business including a roadside dentist. I've seen similar things where dentists in buildings conduct their practice in the shop window. This is supposed to give the public the surety that the dentist operates in a clean and modern environment. This dentist was definitely missing the 'clean and modern' aspects of the practice as trucks and cattle rumbled on by, food was at every stage of preparation and rubbish collected in the gutters where whole families urinated together. Still, the dentist conducted his practice, surrounded by onlookers and well-wishers. A short journey later, down a bumpy dirt-track (free Chinese massage was the phrase coined by Fox) and we were at a small river dock at Ping Liang. We were going on a boat trip, and what a boat. Almost as old as the Ark, this wooden longboat had a pole man at fore and aft, We got in between them and set off. Again, this was fantastic scenery, which was a thrill only added to as we descended through a series of rapids. I wondered if the RNLI operated this far out. 75 minutes later and we were docking at Ao Chang. A small village with only two guest houses; both of which vied for the title of "worst accommodation used by our Tour Company" according to my old trip notes. Our place had no running water. The toilets had to be flushed by bucket anyway; they had never been plumbed in. I was told there was a shower outside, but there was no point in me checking it out. Electricity was sporadic; the rooms had never been cleaned. The girls were not happy, but, there were no options. The other guest house used to be used by our Tour Company, but was deemed to be so bad that we had moved to our present accommodation.

I thought the town was quite quaint, with the series of communal water wheels set up on a weir on a man-made island in the river. Villagers would paddle a boat over to the water wheels to mill their rice or corn on the ancient wooden structures. This was not enough for the girls to win them over. As far as they were concerned, the town was a dump. We had a walk around that evening but there was little to see or do and we tried to amuse ourselves again with Fox guiding us the following morning, but we were off before mid-day. We left our guide en route and ended up in Guiyang again; the provincial capital. This was a place with very little merit as it was just another identikit Chinese City. The highlight here was a 'pizza buffet all you can eat' that we found. So we did. Our next 24 hours was almost all travelling. First an overnight train to Kunming, then a 12 hour bus ride to the border with Vietnam.

For our time in Kunming the trip notes say that we can explore the delights of this wonderful city. We arrived at 6am and the first thing was to try and get taxis in the mad rush of the typical Chinese taxi rank. I was glad that there was only the four of us and glad that I knew where I was going. I'd kept a hotel card from my last visit to the Camellia hotel, six months earlier. I'm glad I keep all this information, along with all the other stuff I pass around for the interested people in my groups. We had just long enough for breakfast and a crap at the Camellia Hotel, where I picked up the bus tickets from Local Operator Pauline and printed off the email from Bruce that had the information for us to get a visa on entry in Vietnam. So much for the delights of Kunming. Before long we were on a 12 hour bus to the border. I had still never seen any more of Kunming than the hotel block and this was my eighth visit there.

The road got progressively worse. Up and down and winding around hills. Chinese passengers were trying to outdo each other in the throwing up competition that always takes place on these kind of journeys. As a westerner, we are brought up travelling in cars, so by the time we have got to our teenage years, we are usually immune to travel sickness. This is not the case in China and unfortunately, lots of Chinese get travel sick. There was a toilet stop at 12 o'clock, then a food stop around 2 o'clock. The choice was not so great and of course, we were the only westerners. There was a bain-marie selection, and a metal tray with compartments. The easy thing was to just point at what you wanted to try and up it was scooped and on it went. No fuss, no bother, I told the girls that it was a bit like prison food as a joke, especially with the metal tray thing. They were not happy with any aspect of this journey. The scenery in Yunnan province is legendary. This is where we see Tiger Leaping Gorge, the ancient towns of Da Li and Li Jiang and the rest of the province is also full of dramatic views over valleys with ancient field systems, traditional villages and beautiful countryside. We are skirting the Himalayas and then heading southwards to the more tropical scenery of the Red River Valley and Vietnam. There were roadside stalls along the way that now bent under great bunches of bananas. There were over-filled lorries buying up the produce for transport and there was the scent in the air of something more "tropical" than Chinese.

We finally got to He Kou. It looked a pleasant enough place with a few palm trees and restaurants along the river that bordered it from Vietnam. I found the very basic Ming Feng hotel, but we were used to this level of accommodation by now, at least I could say it was a real hotel and the rooms could have accommodated an entire family, they were so big. There were girls hanging around reception that were attentive to my bad mandarin at check in, giggling and pointing at my three travelling companions, but I hadn't seen the obvious. The Lonely planet says that "you have to be a fan of border towns to find anything to keep you here". That evening I found out why. We had a simple dinner at what looked like the best road-side cafe in town, then, after being approached for "Xiao Ji?" on a number of occasions whilst I had a beer, it became obvious that this town was possibly the biggest brothel community in the whole of China. I had been watching girls coming and going into the covered market, some were dressed like they were going out for the night, so I assumed that there must be a bar or nightclub or something similar in there. What I discovered surprised me. On the second and third story of the market building, every shop-front was lit up by pink or blue neon. There must have been forty "massage" parlours, or "hairdressers". As I looked up and up to the sky filled with pink neon, I could only coin the phrase "whore heaven" to aptly describe what I saw. I had a quick look around, it had to be quick, because any longer and they would all have ganged up on me. I was grabbed and pulled at every opportunity by girls and Madams into the shops. However, the looks on the faces of many of the girls said that they didn't want anything to do with a foreigner. I asked "how much?" and each time said that it was too expensive, but they dropped the price to 50 Yuan on hearing that I spoke Mandarin. I'd heard Steven mention that the cheapest street prostitutes in Guangzhuo were known as "Yi Bai's" because they only cost one hundred Yuan. In the other cities that I had visited I had heard that in the "hairdressers" and "massage" places the prices started at 150, 200, 300 Yuan. I'd had the occasional phone call in the hotels for "ao mo" or "massage", all at these sort of prices and if you went to the special kare-oke places in Beijing and Shanghai, prices got considerably higher. I went to bed, took the phone out and double locked the door. I was easy pickings in this town.

Now came the interesting bit. Crossing the border with Tamsin and her visa with the wrong date on it. I'd actually received an emailed letter from Bruce in the office (I was gobsmacked and impressed that he'd managed to sort this out) that was supposed to allow her a visa on arrival in Vietnam. The actual difficulty was in leaving China. We were checked, and held, then the three of us were waved through without Tamsin. "No", I told them that we were staying with Tamsin. I knew that without the rest of the group, they'd just not let her through. The letter we had was written in Vietnamese. None of the Chinese border guards either seemed to understand the language or what was exactly written. We were told that without a visa in the passport to enter Vietnam, they were obliged to not let us leave. I called Bruce, he suggested I called the Travel Company Office in Vietnam. (Gobsmacked and unimpressed, back to normal with Bruce). The Vietnam office didn't pick up the phone. This looked like it was going to be a long haul, but I'm sure having three girls in the group helped as a young official finally stepped up. He 'warned' us of our actions and said that if he let us pass into no-mans-land, and that if the Vietnamese would not let Tamsin in, she would be stuck between the two countries. There would be no coming back to China, as that visa would be spent. This is the point that Tamsin bottled it, but, there was no alternative as far as I could see but to trust in the piece of paper that she held in her hand. We walked across the border. The Vietnamese side kept us waiting, but they knew what the letter was. They also charged Tamsin $40 to enter when it should have been only $25, but no-one was arguing any more. Well, that was the difficult bit out of the way. Or so I thought.

The next part of the journey was to get a bus to Sapa. This is a scenic spot in the mountains less than 40K from the border. A girl at the exit from the border said she could organise this for a round $2 each, which looked like a bargain. After a 10 minute wait, we were on our way. Or so we thought. The bus stopped, we were joined by more people. Then off we went again and stopped again. Here we stayed for 20 mins whilst the bus owner swaggered around the street trying to pick up passengers. He told me his name was Spy. He was an arsehole. He was trying to drum up trade, whilst trying to impress everyone with his antics and it wasn't happening. Even the bus driver was getting annoyed with him. We set off again, only to go around the block and stop again. 10 minutes later we were off again, but only as far as the first pick up point, back at the border crossing. The girls had been relieved to be leaving China for the relative civilisation of Vietnam. There had been English spoken at the border and everything was re-assuringly back on the tourist trail. By this time Claire's frustration was about to burst into tears as the bus owner chatted to a couple of blokes with some bags of grain. Finally we were off. The bus owner hanging out the window in typical 'White Van Man' mode and annoying whoever he saw fit. Welcome to Vietnam. I tried to tell the girls that it wasn't all like this. The bus started its' long climb up the switch-back road to Sapa. There was not so much traffic on the road, but we were trying to overtake and be overtaken at any opportunity. The driving in Vietnam was one thing that had not improved since crossing the border from China. Then there was a crowd of people gathered by the roadside, overlooking a steep drop down the mountainside. Someone had driven their motorbike off the mountainside and over the edge. The bus owner came back shaking his head and gesturing that there was very little left of the guy. The journey could not be over with soon enough.

Sapa was worth the wait. It is situated at 1,600m in the mountains and only gets 100 fine days a year but we got two of them. Amazingly, for the first time on the trip, we were warm. The town is a French colonial settlement set amongst the rice terraces. It is a fabulous mixture of European architecture with the ornate three and four story buildings, complete with balconies, all painted in yellows, pale greens and sky blues. There is a shopping street complete with French bistros and cafes and a town square, with a park, overlooked by a small neo gothic Cathedral. Being Christmas time, this was decorated in all its finery, with the imposing frontage covered in a white banner proclaiming "Joyeux Noel" and the equivalent in Vietnamese.

This place was a virtual beacon, with all the neon light adorning the front of the building and the bright white light coming from the interior. Once inside, the place became even more surreal as pumping rave music was blasting out a medley of Christmas carols. Not the thing you would associate with the locality. Outside the Cathedral again, the local people, tribeswomen from the Black H'mong and the Red Giay tribes clustered around bemused tourists, trying to sell shawls, blankets, silver jewellery, pipes, all home spun and worked.

It is most likely that Sapa was first inhabited by highland minorities of the H'mong and Dao (pronounced Yao) ethnic groups, as well as by smaller numbers of Tày and Giay (pronounced Zai). These are the four main minority groups still present in Sapa district today. The Kinh (what the lowland Vietnamese call themselves) never originally colonised this highest of Việt Nam's valleys, which lie in the shadow of Fansipan a 3143 meter giant of a mountain and the highest peak in the country. Along the main street, the women followed us again at the slightest interest in any of their wares. That evening we ate western and went to a bar. Just next to the Mountain View Hotel where we were staying was a bar with a dart board, pool table and a reasonable selection of music. The two English girls kept me company until around midnight. A couple of very small H'mong girls were also in the bar, they were obviously local guides and with a couple of tourists. I couldn't figure out their age, they could have been adolescent as they were so petite and acted so child-like with enthusiasm for playing drinking games and flirting with the much taller western tourists.

The following day, Kelly didn't feel too well so dropped out of the hike. This was after her first western food, in a real restaurant, in over a week. Our local guide was Doung, from the Black H'mong, she arrived in her traditional dress and we were suitably impressed. The H'mong are an ethnic group, who are originally from China and related to the Miao. Their clothes comprise of a pleated skirt and gaiters, all embroidered. Then a shirt and type of waist coat. This is topped off with a head scarf turned into a small hat that sits jauntily on the top of the head. The black H'mong dress is based on a black cloth, as opposed to Green H'mong and White H'mong who are named after the core colour of their dress. The Flower H'mong have the most colourful clothes, though for celebrations, even the Black H'mong would wear more colourful clothing. That is not to say that the clothes are not colourful, the embroidery is in geometric shapes and dots in yellows, greens, and every other colour, set upon the black material. I had read that the H'mong were one of the few peoples left in the world who still made their own clothes in their entirety, from spinning the cloth, to dyeing and the embroidery and batik work that they were famous for. They also produced their own silver jewellery and this adorned them in bangles, necklaces and ear-rings.

We were doing a four hour hike to Ben Bo village. Doung started off well and chatted for a while. She showed us the plant that died the H'mong clothes, told us about the limestone used for "fixing the dye" and pointed out another plant that was poisonous. This was used if someone wanted to kill themselves and she gave the example of someone who had been cheated on in love or through adultery. Soon we got on to her life and she told us that she'd been married at age thirteen, then left her husband soon afterwards to move back with her mum. It turn out her stepsister had been married off at age nine and Doungs' return wasn't greeted with open arms. After a year or so, she moved into Sapa Town and picked up enough English language to start guiding. All this and she was just 22 years old. Unfortunately for us, that is where the interest ended and we got little more than the ins and outs of her love life after that, which boyfriend she wanted to get married to and a lot of time on her mobile phone. Just like every other 22 year old. The hike was a bit much for the girls and Doungs' reaction wasn't good, especially when they decided they didn't want to stay at the homestay that Doung had recommended because it looked like one of the children had a chicken pox infection. Then Doung described symptoms that sounded very much like she'd just got over the virus herself and the girls were near frantic, while I tried to calm the whole thing down and we asked if we could stay somewhere else. We moved across the village to a place owned by a Red Giay woman, took the rooms and Doung started to cook our dinner.

We were in a village populated by both Red Giay and Black H'mong tribes, both got along well together but we had moved from a H'mong homestay to a Red Giay homestay and we could tell that Doung was not so happy. The striking features of the Red Giay is that the women wear red turbans and shave their eyebrows. It was around this time that Tamsin had exclaimed "oh, they are all wearing little Santa hats for Christmas" and I suppose, they did have the appearance of the jovial pointed elf style hats. She was actually being serious and we had to point out that this was nothing at all to do with Christmas and more to do with Red Giay traditional culture. They often shave the front of their scalp too and above the ears. This is supposedly a fashion from a time many hundreds of years ago, when in China it was considered beautiful to remove the hair and have a clean complexion. Both the Red Giay and the H'mong were two of a number of ethnic minorities that originated in China and headed south during the persecutions of the Ming and Qing dynasties. Doung had lost interest in us. She was moody and constantly on her phone. She wanted us to be more fun, but the girls just wanted to read and not want to try the rice wine. She took us to see a waterfall, a place that according to my notes had seen fatalities every year. There was a legend that a spirit needed to have a death there every year as a sort of offering or sacrifice. Doung was not happy by our lack of enthusiasm for swimming and when I told her that I knew of the waterfalls reputation, she said that as someone had already died there this year, then the spirit would not let us drown. I wasn't going to risk it, she was in a mood again and try as I might, I couldn't get her to cheer up, she even asked me if I was boring. I thought at first that this was a mis-translation, of bored, but I think she was genuinely asking me if I was a boring person. I'd done so many outrageous acts, lived life on the edge, and to the full before I travelled across the world. I didn't even know where to start to tell her that I'd done so many things.

It's not as if she would even understand the nightclub scene in London and here this village girl was asking me a question like that. I was pretty much taken aback with her attitude.

I took in our surroundings from the waterfall back to the village. It was a scattering of wooden built, two story houses, each with their own land surrounding, dotted across the gently sloping hill and across the valley. The trek back the next day was in worse weather and we hit cloud level and the cold swirling mist before mid-day. We were thankful of the bus that drove us back to the hotel and warm showers and dry clean clothes. I had just enough time to check out the Sapa town again. Walking through the traditional market with cuts of meat laid out on stone benches, and the once pretty street that looked far more eerie and Dickensian in the descending cold foggy cloud. That evening we got the bus back to Lao Cai town in the dark through the swirling mountainside mist to the border town where we caught a train to Hanoi.

38. Sapa 22/12/07 (Sapa)

Sapa church lit in neon
Playing hymns to a 'rave on rave on'
Sound system, lit up, 'Noel 07'
Out in the square, the Black H'mong
Busying around, selling blankets
And the striped embroidery
Sewing by their roadside
Selling armfuls of silver jewellery
That rivals the towns Christmas tree
Clothed in coloured lights and a big star
Queen of the mountains, mountain town
Where clouds sweep in turning summer to winter

Striking faces
Without eyebrows
Under a red
Cloth head dress

39. Hanoi and beer hoi 26/12/07 (Hanoi)

On beer hoi corner, kebabs to eat
Drinking for only seven p
Where all of life is on the street
Weaving all around me

Shop front crammed with bottles
Spilling out people on plastic stools
In front walks a conical hatted girl
Two open baskets across a pole

Walking along the roadside
Against that wave of motorcycle tide
Like birds in flight or school of fish
Somehow it all moves as one and they miss

Buildings stacked like ill-fitting blocks
Painted sign boards jostle for a look
Over the pavement, over run with a jumble
Of bikes and box's and stools and tables

Someone must have raised the signal
The street sellers move on
Then when the police van has passed by
They move back with their cooking pots as one

The sound of the city, a two stroke engine
The horns that blow from every direction
The laughter in every conversation
Warm hearts on this feast of Stephen.

The train had wooden panels and as a seasoned train traveller I was more than happy with the compartment and the night journey to Hanoi. The girls found the rocking and rolling of the train on the old tracks a bit much. They said they felt sea sick and unable to sleep. I was happily humming the tune to "Morning Town. Rocking, rolling, riding . . . ." We arrived around 4:30 am on Christmas Day. Claire's boyfriend had arrived at the

Victory Hotel hours earlier and booked a room for them both, so they were having an early Xmas present. We got a few hours sleep before having a wander around the city, catching the Hanoi Cathedral in all its glory, complete with outdoor nativity scene and thousands of people. We hunted around for a place that would do a Christmas dinner for us all, not that any of us was religious, but it's just something that you have to do. As Vietnam was an old French colony, there were a lot of places that had celebrated Christmas Eve with a feast, rather than Christmas day. We ended up in Le Pub that evening, turkey and trimmings and the end of another trip. Merry Christmas. In my full and varied life, I've had some good ones and some bad ones, but never one like this.

Chapter 2.

HAPPY NEW YEARS

"It's a dangerous business, Frodo, going out your door. You step onto the road, and if you don't keep your feet, there's no knowing where you might be swept off to."

J.R.R. Tolkien, The Lord of the Rings

The trip ended on Boxing Day. I moved to a cheaper hotel and two of the girls moved on. The weather was not quite cold enough to force me to wear a coat, but was grey and drizzly for the four days off that I had until my next trip. It is a strange way of spending Christmas and even though I'm not particularly close to my family, it is at times like this that you really realise how remote you are from everything that you once took for granted. There were emails from friends and I was missing being home. I arranged to meet Tamsin on a couple of afternoons. I enjoyed walking around these streets and visiting the places that I hadn't been to in years, some places that I'd never been to before. I was trying to piece together my memories and map my way around the old quarter. It didn't seem to have changed too much since my few days here in 2003. It had grown more tour agents, selling trips to various places in Vietnam, connecting bus services and maybe a few more cafes and guesthouses advertising for western trade, but it was not significantly different. There was still no obvious backpacker area. I had been told years ago that when a backpacker area was trying to establish itself in the street called Ngo Bao Khanh, near the North West corner of the lake, the government had taken action. Bars like the Funky Monkey had moved elsewhere in the old quarter and now there was a sprinkling of bars throughout this area, hidden in backstreets. I went looking around. Of the most peculiar things I was looking for; I remembered shops full of mannequins, all in a style of 1950's French school children, I couldn't find it, but the mannequins were in shops throughout the Old Quarter. There was also a row of shops selling grave stones that I looked for and found again, with the engraved pictures of the recent dead looking out at me. The original lay out of the Old Quarter was of individual street selling specific products, much like the East End of London of old, where you had "milk" and "bread" streets. Here it was everything from "Silver Street" to bamboo ladders. Another street sold pots and pans and another street corner was selling stationary items. There was a street selling decorations for Christmas, the New Year, birthdays, weddings and the up-coming Chinese/Vietnamese New Year festival of Tet. There were flags, which were a coloured square, inside a coloured square, inside a coloured square. I'd wondered what these were on my previous visits and now I was told that they were the old flags of the old royal houses of Vietnam and they were now brought out at all the ancient festival times. These streets were also named after the products that they sold, it is a fascinating place to walk around.

I took a look around the lake, checking out Fanny ice cream and then the Ngoc Son Temple, on the island on the lake. I love the setting of this place and although it is in the middle of a bustling city and there are always hoards of visitors, it still retains and aspect of religious other-worldliness and calm. The temple itself has a heady mix of towering statues and incense burning. There is a room that houses a dead leatherback turtle, found in the Hoan Kiem Lake in the 1960's and I explained to Tamsin the story and certain significance to this. Elsewhere on the islet, you can still find a space to sit and contemplate the lake with its' Turtle Temple on the other islet and the changes that this burgeoning city must have seen over the last 1000 years.

Just around the corner from the Victory Hotel is the Temple of Literature and as it is one of the major buildings in Vietnam, I had decided to visit there with Tamsin. It had been nearly five years since I had last visited this place and I knew it was on the itinerary of many of our tourist groups, so I had decided to brush up on my local knowledge and give it a visit again. The "temple of Literature" moniker is not the best way to describe it. The building is a mixture of a University, where students would study to sit the Imperial examination and it is also a temple dedicated to Confucius. The Chinese influence is more than obvious. The Vietnamese had been a Chinese colony for over 1000 years and even though they had thrown off that yoke around 1000 AD, their new capital city, had as its centre-piece a building steeped in Chinese culture and tradition. It was first constructed in 1076 and had had many additions and renovations, not least after the Vietnam War and again in 2000.

You enter through a Chinese style stone gate, into a series of garden courtyards. The third courtyard has low buildings on either side of you as you enter, these contain the "Doctors Steele" record the names and native places of 1,307 graduates of 82 triennial royal exams. 81 exams were held by the Le dynasty and one by the Mac dynasty, which were held from 1442 to 1779. Each Steele is set upon a statue of a turtle. The turtle is the animal that represents wisdom and longevity. The information on the wall states that the turtle s one of the four supernatural beings in Vietnamese (and Chinese) mythology and counts the others as the dragon, the phoenix and the unicorn. "Wrong" I thought. Although the dragon and phoenix represent the male and female, king and queens power, there is no unicorn in Chinese mythology. What this animal is, is a Qilin (sometimes pronounced or called a Kilin) which is an amalgam of animals depicted as having a few horns or antlers, green and blue scaly skin, or sometime with a fiery appearance. It has the hooves of a deer, the head of a dragon and a bear's tail. You couldn't possibly get one mixed up with a unicorn (though it is indeed quite a mixed up animal itself). As far as I could gather, the Unicorn resemblance is in its habits as being a wise and gentle creature, a symbol of peace; causing no harm to animals or even making tracks as it walks across grass.

Into the Fourth courtyard and along the opposite wall is the House for Ceremonies, used at auspicious occasions. If you walk through this building you immediately enter the Dai Thanh sanctuary, where Confucius and his four closest disciples Yanhui, Zengshen, Zisi and Mencius are worshipped. There are statues of the great sage and his followers along with those of the "Ten Honored Philosophers" and incense fills the air as it would in any other Asian temple, be it Buddhist, Hindu or Taoist. The final courtyard is the 2000 A.D. re-construction and houses a giant drum and bell along with a building on two floors dedicated to the ancient rector of the academy and the monarchs that contributed most to its establishment. Everywhere we walked there were groups of women wearing the traditional Ao Dai dresses. These long split dresses that they wear over pajama pants add an air of sophistication and elegance to the place. These groups of women were invariably having their photos taken; some on a day out, others looked like they were part of wedding parties as a bride in full traditional, western style wedding dress would strike a pose. I suppose my description of the ancient walled gardens, the ponds, the flower beds, and the gently rustling trees in the gardens would not do the place justice, so let's just say that this is the place where you would go to get you wedding photos taken. Even in the midst of the usual Vietnamese crowds, the place is a gem set in the heart of Hanoi.

Another place that I wanted to re visit was Hao Lo Prison. I wanted to visit this place again because of its recent history and I remember it as being an interesting and emotive place. The Americans called it "The Hanoi Hilton" when, during their Vietnam War, they were imprisoned there, but there is a lot more history than just their war. The French had originally commandeered a village that was built here and decided to construct the most modern prison of its day to hold the Vietnamese who were rebelling against French Colonial rule. Conditions were gruesome and there is a lot of information in English about how the inmates would live their lives, many dying of starvation or malnutrition or from the insanitary conditions. There are prison cells in their original state. Lifelike mannequins are shackled together and to long wooden benches that act as beds. It's all quite eerie in the twilight of the prison which as its centre piece an original guillotine. Beyond all the horrors, are the accounts of the prisoners from the "American War", these, we are told were housed in light, airy rooms and that they were well fed and catered for, wiling their days away playing cards and guitars. There is the photograph of U.S. Senator John Mc Cain being hauled out of his aircraft after being shot down. If this is all a little ironic, the fact that the site immediately next to the "Hanoi Hilton", which once constituted part of the prison, is now the site of the Hanoi Towers, one of Hanoi's most prestigious hotels.

Later that evening I'd arranged to meet Tamsin again at beer hoi corner. She texted back saying that she wouldn't be good company because she'd stupidly sent her ex-boyfriend a text and he'd replied saying that he was already with someone else. I convinced her to come out for a drink, we both needed the company. We downed a few of the seven pence beers in and amongst the westerners and Vietnamese, all sat on the low plastic stools and the fortunate groups using a stool as a table. It is real street life as a book-seller comes up with a stack of the travellers favourites, "Life of Pi", "Richard Marx", "The Quiet American" and "The girl in the Picture" about the Vietnam war and so many "Lonely Planets", all photocopied and you can haggle them down to around three dollars for a book. Women walk by with the baskets on bamboo poles with their home made Vietnamese "doughnuts". Others have a block of charcoal and a grill and will actually cook you up some shrimp on the road in front of you until the police come to chase them away. Once beer hoi corner closed (a watchful eye is never too far away and the police turn up around 11pm) we went to "Hair of the Dog". The "owner" is one of the few people who actually promotes his business by flyering, so he gets the trade. My first impressions of him were that he was a bit of a knob, riding single handed through the streets and having an "aren't I special" attitude about him. The long blond ponytail and pointed goatee didn't help and he oozed himself between every group gathered to find himself talking to the prettiest girls about his bar. We still went in and by one o'clock-ish were pretty drunk. Everyone was heading off to some bar called "Soulless". Before we knew it we were on the back of a motorbike with some drunk from the bar in charge whizzing through the back alleys of Hanoi again.

40. Hanoi 26/12/07

Getting lost in Hanoi Old town
Looking for something, just walking around
"Hello moto, hello banana"
A hand waves like a friend from every corner

The bursting shop-fronts
Carved and pictured head stones
Cafes for the westerners
Guest houses and tour centres

Menus in English, prices in dollars
In a peculiar way, we've taken over
Selling photocopied novels, pestering a shoe shine
Standing at the roadside, mesmerised for a time

Till it's time to walk into the on-coming flow
Swimming in this alien environment
Take a deep breath, take the plunge
And you're swimming with the motorcycles in Hanoi Old Town

41. Tourism 13-18/01/08 (Hanoi/HCMC)

Looking for their comfort
Looking for a restaurant
Something familiar
Tea, or eggs and bacon
Something that looks western
With a sit down toilet, then
I have to pinch myself
Because Now I'm thinking like them

Lost in the unfamiliarity
Of another foreign city
Thinking like a tourist
When I hate them with voracity

So I sit with my beer
Watch a bar full of westerners
Like on a day-trip to the coast
Arguing with each other
Making the biggest noise
Shouting at the waitress
Wanting to pick a fight
And slagging off the foreigners.

Tamsin had never been on a motorbike. Earlier in our trip she'd said that she was too scared to go on one. She'd refused to take the moto taxi's preferring the four wheeled variety. Well, there is always a first time for everything, but I reckon she wasn't actually aware of what she'd just gone and done. Soulless, was on a boat, moored on the great Red River that flows through Hanoi and it was filled with westerners and dance music. As far as nights go, it was good enough to get us drunk and dancing. We got back to the hotels by moto again around 3:30. When I met up with her again; Tamsin just didn't believe that she'd just done what she'd done. We went out again the next night, meeting at Beer Hoi corner, where we met a few other tourists and moved on to Mao's Red Lounge. Things got a bit heated here when one of the tourists stepped over the legs of one of the Vietnamese who was sitting on the floor. This is a big insult in South East Asian countries. Your head is the highest part of the body both physically and spiritually. The feet are the lowest and whilst many people have been told not to point the soles of your feet at a person, as it shows that you are lower than their feet, the stepping over someone who is lead on cushions in a western style bar was not anticipated to get the response that it did. It sort of brought the night to an abrupt and uncomfortable end.

My new trip started on 30th December. I'd been wondering what sort of losers would book trips at this time of the year. Every Tour Leader with sense had gone home for Xmas and New Year. The cold winter weather in China was only for the hardy, or foolhardy. So I was quite surprised to find that I had a full group of 12. I was even more surprised to find that this included two families. One with a son of 17, the other with son and daughter of 17 and 15. I was not looking forward to this. I don't like families at the best of times. I keep the one that I was born into at a comfortable distance and have never been convinced of the merits of starting one of my own. This was only made worse by finding out that the reason why I had two families was that it was the big school holiday in Australia, and who else do you get travelling at school holidays? but teachers.

In the first welcome meeting I told them about what to expect on the trip, mainly a lot of cold weather in rural guest houses and a lot of travelling on public transport. The English man, a teacher nearing retirement age from North Yorkshire called Joseph asked me if we were going to have the noodle soup with spit in it. I didn't know what that was, but evidently, they'd been given it somewhere on their trip. They had been travelling for a while and were now doing their last two weeks on what I now found out to be a "trail of the Dragon" trip from Bangkok to Hong Kong. I was taking the second section of this trip. A Thai girl called Gift had done the first leg and we had met in the hotel lobby, she said that the group were nice people, but were prone to asking a lot of questions and complaining. They had a couple of issues from the first part of the trip, namely the long drive from the Laos border to Hanoi. I told them there would be more of the same. There were murmurings from the group.

The only person who seemed less impressed with the group was Nina 24 from Australia. She'd been hoping to meet a few people her own age whilst travelling and along with the two families had just the other two couples, one British, one Aussie, both in their fifties and sixties. These two couples had already been travelling together on the first part of the trip through Thailand and Laos. They had a lovely time and thought their guide was excellent. I had to break the bad news to them. From now on, it was going to be cold, possibly freezing. We were going into rural China in winter, so don't expect western food, western toilets, western standards of cleanliness or service, or even continuous electricity or water supply. We would be travelling on public transport with the locals and whatever they brought with them, be it noisy phlegm clearing, chain-smoking, or livestock. We would have no local guide until half way through the trip. I also explained to the vegetarian family that food would be a problem for them, but I'd help where I could. I don't think they actually understood exactly what I meant. One had put on her form that she'd eat dairy, but in a country with virtually no dairy production, where 30% of the population is lactose intolerant, that was neither here or there. I later found out that some of them contemplated leaving there and then. The older Brits and the Aussies had left the first night dinner at KOTO and gone for a beer and were just about convincing themselves that they could do the trip when a rat scuttled through the bar.

As we waited to depart the hotel, I ran into Jim. He was unshaven and looked ill, so I asked him what was up? He had just come back from Sapa where his girlfriend had been told by her family that she should marry the French guy and she had agreed with them. A month earlier, Phong had called the French guy to say that it was all over and that she was going to marry Jim. A few days earlier the French guy had turned up in Sapa and said that it was not over. The family had backed the old suitor, rather than Jim, even though he was the one who had originally said that he would marry Phong, whilst the French guy had not been on the scene for over a year. Jim also had plans, the idea of opening a café, the background as a business analyst and he seemed on the whole to be quite a gentleman, whereas the French guy was, in Jims words "a douche bag". The French guy had flamboyantly picked up Phong and carried her off to his room, a sign for all the family to see. Out of respect for tradition, they had to tell Phong that she had to marry the French guy. Jim had tried to petition her brother and friends, but they said that he just didn't understand what had happened. She had to marry the French guy. It would be the best if he went away and forgot about her now. So, here he was, in the lobby of the Victory Hotel, about to do just that. He saw no other option. After I listened to him, I asked him if he really loved her, if she really was the one? We had both talked about ex-girlfriends and relationships and Jim had more or less said that his whole world had been turned around over this last year. Coming to work in China, then being placed in Vietnam, then finding the girl of his dreams. There was nothing else, she was "the one". So, I told him that he should go back to Sapa. If he wanted her, he should go and get her. She should see that he meant what he had said and no doubt the French guy would move on before too long, he didn't have a good track record as it stood. He still said that I didn't understand what he was up against with the family asking him to leave. I asked him what else he had to lose? With that, I had to leave with my group to Ha Long Bay and Jim returned to Sapa.

It was New Years Eve when we got to Cat Ba. The weather was not warm, but warm enough for us Brits and still warm enough for us to have to negotiate the dogs, flopped out on their bellies in the middle of the road, soaking up the winter sun as we passed by in the mini van. Once we had checked in and met Mr Hai who had given us a run through of what activities were on offer; all the Aussies went on a hike through the centre of the island, whilst the Brits lazed. I found them at the Koala Bar, eating spaghetti Bolognaise and sharing a bottle of red wine. They said that they were not the people for hiking; the flat was ok, but not hills. I said that we would be hiking the Long Ji Rice Terraces and that was all hills. It hadn't occurred to them. Then they told me that their Spaghetti Bolognaise wasn't real spaghetti, it was really just noodles and the red wine wasn't up to much either. Well, it was only going to get worse. Cat Ba Island did not let us down with a fantastic sunset viewed from the balcony. Mr Hai invited me out to dinner with him as usual, but this time there was a twist. He asked if I liked massage, or sauna. I replied truthfully, that I'd never indulged. I've always said that there is a time and a place for me to be semi naked with a girl kneading my flesh, and that was the bedroom. To be truthful, I have a lack of self-discipline in this department. I've avoided these sort of places, because I know what I'm like and apart from anything else it is a sackable offense if I was caught (literally) with my pants down. Nevertheless, after a couple of shots of rice wine, Mr Hai convinced me that it would be unacceptably rude for me to decline his offer. We went to the 6th floor of the Prince Hotel, Mr Hai paid some money, and there we were in a changing room. Then, the next thing occurred to me. Me and Mr Hai. Mr Hai and I. Nobody else. What if the offer that I couldn't refuse was something that I was just going to have to refuse? This was a very delicate situation and he was already naked. I quickly changed into the sky blue shorts that were provided and followed him into a steam room. I tried to talk about work, the weather; it all seemed a bit too awkward to just act natural in this situation. We didn't steam for long. We crossed the floor and into a Jacuzzi. Mr Hai and I in a Jacuzzi together. This was no easier than the steam room but at least the bubbles and underwater jets (at least I hope that's what they were) were a distraction. Then came the grand finale. We donned robes and were shown to separate rooms. Inside mine was a cute girl about half my size. She didn't speak any English. I spoke no Vietnamese.

This was a very awkward situation. Apart from the obvious, I was wondering what I was supposed to do next. She was gesticulating for me to get onto the massage table. I was looking around, probably confusing the girl every bit as much as I felt confused. I gestured that I could do with a hair dryer, the one hanging on the wall. It was the only thing I could think of. I lead on the bed (complete with circular hole cut into what acted as the mattress, um . . . , I wondered), she dried my hair. Then the fun really started. The massage. I'm ticklish. In some ways, that was a good thing, because I was constantly trying to compose myself in order to stop myself from squirming around and bursting into laughter. That wasn't the perfect antidote to my problem though. Soon, I was having to think about my accounts, border crossings, ordering food in different languages, anything to stop me thinking about the girl who was now rubbing herself up and down my semi naked body. It came to an end just as I was about to give in and rip her clothes off her and have her up against every surface in the room. Mr Hai, knocked on the door and said my time was up.

We went off for more rice wine, then I joined my group in the Noble House/Koala Bar, and then on to Flightless Bird for New Year. There were gangs of other tourists, roaming between the few bars and wanting something to happen. They were drunk and obnoxious. As I stood at the bar, the door opened and a dozen or so young Brits came in and flooded the bar, all shouting at once at the waitresses to be served. One was shouting "I was here first, me, me!" and I heard one complaining that she wanted "the same drink as last time . . . I can't remember what it was, you served it to me, I was here before I went to that other bar". The bar waitresses couldn't cope, it was obvious that they were not having a Happy New Year. Outside the bar, away from the appalling young tourists, the British couple, Nina and I sang Auld Liang Sayne, Scottish style with folded arms crossed. I haven't done that for years. This was definitely the strangest New Year I'd ever had.

On New Years Day I ran into Tamsin from my last trip, who was now on another trip, she wasn't looking forward to this section as most of the group were in their sixties and the two other girls of around her age didn't drink. That evening, I had dinner with the single Australian girl in the group, all the others wanted to hang around in their families, I guessed this might be the case for us for a lot of the trip. Then, I thought that with the food situation in China, the lack of western menus, eating in the guesthouses and the like, we should at least have a few group meals and hang out together afterwards. The next morning we were heading back over to the mainland and I had my first problem of feeding the vegetarian family when it was a sea food lunch. I had advised the boat galley in advance, but the vegetarian option was not what the family expected, it was more of the stir fried vegetables, a serving of tofu and an extra serving of chips whilst they were expecting some sort of "real replacement" for our fish, stuffed crab, tiger prawns, fried calamari and clams. In China, it would only get worse.

I knew that my group were going to be difficult as nearly every adult on the trip was a teacher. That meant ridiculously difficult questions that no-one apart from local experts can answer and lots of disappointment. The questions that I got on the boat, heading to the mainland included "what is that boat?" followed by "what is in that boat?" All I could give was an educated guess that it was a coal barge, probably on its way to China, as, without my x-ray specs, there was no better answer that I could give. Whilst travelling on a bus, heading towards the border, the pointless questioning continued in the same vein and I did actually get asked, as we sped along "what is in those green bottles, what, didn't you see them?" With the onset of winter, there were a lot of farmers pickling vegetables and they were on sale by the side of the road. In other areas, there were root vegetables, sliced and drying, ready for pickling. They took up kilometre after kilometre of the roadside, so our bus had to drive constantly on the central white line so as to avoid running over the carpet of drying sliced roots. I found out it was some sort of cassava or tapioca. This would be pickled and stored over the winter. Then, I would get the questions of "what are they going to grow in that field?" As they were rice paddies, there was an easy answer there. When the older Aussies started asking questions, I knew that I was really in for it. It felt like it was some sort of competition between the teachers as to who could ask the most, usually pointless, questions "Mark . . . What are those people doing?" as we just passed a group of workers on their way home. "How do they get a water supply out here?" when the answer was simply wells, some reservoirs and small pumping stations. "Where do they get their electricity from? Is it hyrdo-power or coal?" To which the answer was both, as Vietnam has both schemes in operation. "How much does petrol cost?" as we drew into a petrol station. "What crops are grown here? Is that sugar cane in the fields?" It turns out that the older Aussie bloke had worked in a sugar refining plant all his life and what he didn't know about sugar wasn't worth knowing. He talked about the burning of the stubble, now outlawed in the western world, but still happening here. He was surprised that when we passed the sugar refinery, on the way to Hua Shan, how big it was and how much was going on. Cart after ox-cart was weighed down with cane, each local producer bringing it to the factory. The smell of it was thick in the air.

In Lang Son, I had another food poisoning, or whatever it was; episode where I threw up for two hours then was all right in the morning. My only real concern once again was weather I'd poisoned the entire group or not. Maybe it would have been better if I had. For some reason, it had just affected me again. At the border we had an issue as the guards checked our passports and looked for the exit stamps from our own countries. There was no exit stamp from Australia, most western countries just don't bother to issue them but for the Vietnamese in this quiet border crossing, they had to see a stamp. It took a phone call to sort this out. A bus pick up later and we arrived in the rural idyll of Butterfly valley. I allocated the cabins. It was a bit of a surprise to most as they expected a hotel of some sorts and not the individual huts on stilts. I quickly got asked about the whereabouts of the towels and how to turn on the gas boilers under each of the huts for any hot water. These had a habit of hissing and half of the group was convinced that the boilers were unsafe, they would either be gassed in their sleep, or the whole thing would explode. Then I was told that the towels were not big enough. We were given a traditional Chinese farmers lunch, the first of many and the first time that the group had to share a meal. Once again, I had explained in email to our local operator and guide "Grass" that we had vegetarians on the trip, so the hosts were prepared. It's a pity that the vegetarians were not prepared. Even though there was Aubergine, fried pumpkin, tofu, beans and a whole vegetable smorgasbord of other dishes, they were unhappy that we were all sharing from what they saw as "their food". We went on the trip to the Hua Shan cliff paintings, a bigger boat than last time and more tourists. Aussie teacher and mother; Elaine was asking about the fish, the plants, and the history of the paintings and the area even though there was an information sheet given out by Grass which she had failed to read. "So, how big is this?" She asked as she looked at the cliff face in front of her. How much I wanted to point and say "it's that big".

Back at Butterfly Valley, it was suggested by Grass that we could walk into the countryside which we thought would be a nice way of exploring and passing some time. I was given the impression that to get to the Maple Forest would be an hour or so round trip and we set off with the waitresses from the guest house and their friends as our guides. Soon we were surrounded by the rice paddys and sugar cane plantations. We passes an old grave, decorated with the bleached out paper and hung with small charms and gifts, it looked a little bit like something from the Blair Witch Project. It's one of the most beautiful walks I'd done and there was the feeling of a trek of discovery, what were we going to see next? We rounded one limestone outcrop and it was like entering a lost valley. A couple of the group took a wrong trail, so we had young Mark shouting out "cooo-ey" in his best Australian orienteering scout voice. There were high grasses and a coppice of enormous "flame trees" that some of the group had wanted to wander over to. It was all very atmospheric. Then we were in the forest on a trail, then we were climbing. We were going at quite a pace and the Brits, who had already told me that they "didn't do hiking"; especially up hills were looking unhappy and a little red in the face. I asked the waitresses again how long the hike was and got a different answer than previously, this was not an hour long walk but three, or four hours more and it all looked like we wold be scaling the limestone karsts. The Brits were never going to do that and I was concerned about the lack of actual guiding, more like guessing. I had to call the whole thing off, taking a while to convince some of them that an unguided walk in uncharted countryside was just not a good idea.

The following morning, we were on our journey into China. As we travelled on the highway, the older Australians were the first to exclaim that they hadn't expected to see six lane highways with manicured lawns. As we entered Nan Ning, they said "Their towns are like our cities and their cities are like our capitals. I wonder what Shanghai and Peking are like". They were stunned with the mass of new buildings. They didn't like the high rises and said so, but I had to bring them back to reality. China is a country not so much bigger than Australia, but with over 50 times the population. We quickly go on to "who owns what" and "how do you buy a house?" I had to talk about the pressure on the land with such a big population and that this population had been here for thousands of years, not a few generations as in Australia. This land had been owned by some feudal lord since before Australia was discovered by the white man and it was the Communist Party who had seized this land and then turned it over for the benefit of the population, building these houses, roads, schools, shopping malls and everything else that they were wondering at. They didn't like the idea of Communism; they were brought up during the Cold War and only knew of the idea as something "evil". They just couldn't understand where all the money had come from if this country was Communist and "everyone was made to be the same". They were asking me, how much the people earned, how they could afford things, how much a house cost. I had already given the example of the sugar cane factory that we had passed on the way to Butterfly Valley, where a set price was paid for the cane grown and the state acted as marketer and sales distribution. Now I was telling them that the Chinese economy was a lot like a very big sugar factory, but producing everything, much in the way that companied in the west like Glaxo-Smithklein, or Unilever produce a multitude of products. I reminded them of the old days when companies would provide accommodation, maybe healthcare and crèche facilities. Much in the same way, China "the company" provided these along with roads, power, anything you could think of. To which I had to explain how all this was paid for, as the group couldn't understand where all the money had come from. I started from my model of China as "the company", it was the easiest way and although there is a lot more "free capitalist enterprise" in the country now, it was the principal of the state Communist system that I was trying to get across to them. At home, the company would pay you a wage, the government taxes you and then spends your money on public services. You live on what is left, buying your house as the single biggest payout.

In China, instead of paying and taxing you, they just pay you that percentage less and keep the difference. For example, if you paid 40% tax in Australia, here in China, they just pay you 40% less and keep the rest to build your house and hospitals. It means that there is more control over the countries purse, capitalists can't squander the wealth on luxury items, people can't avoid paying tax, as there is no tax to pay and there is no inefficient tax collecting system either. It sort of means that people work for less actual money, but get the same quality of life, as long as the government is doing its job properly. Considering that I had a group of teachers, I was surprised how all of these ideas were completely new to them. They had never considered that our western governments or free market systems could ever be questioned or engineered. That maybe there was another way of doing things that was more radical than the Labour Party had ever tried to do, or that the world as they knew it was maybe wrong in the way that it did things and could even be replaced by a completely different system.

When we got to Liuzhou, the group that had been travelling in South East Asia were asking for maps and what there was to see in the town, maybe even a good bar. I told them that there was none of this, but I would show them to the central park, with its karsts and cable cars, then go for dinner. I took them around town, pointing out options for dinner such as small local cafes and the street food stalls then said that the only place with a menu in English was U.B.C. Coffee. We entered and were greeted by the staff saying "good morning" as it struck seven o'clock at night. We got a private room and sat down with the picture menu and badly phrased English descriptions. The vegetarians were not so pleased with what was on offer, then a waiter entered, "Would you like beer?" he said, in well-practiced tones. Vegetarian dad was straight in for the kill (so to speak) asking what ingredients were in some of the menu selections and if they could have something similar, but without meat. The bemused waiter looked on again, practiced his smile and said very clearly. "How many beer?" It was the only English he knew. What's-more, if it wasn't on the menu, there was nothing that I could do about it. Dad removed his family from the restaurant, saying that he would find somewhere else, I didn't hold out much hope for him. In the morning, I asked him how he had faired, "it was crap" he replied scornfully. After that, the father hardly spoke to me again.

We moved on to Chenyang. On arrival, I got a "wow" from young Mark, looking at the wooden guesthouse nestled in the hills, overlooking the stream. So, some people were coming round to the wonders of travel, but the vegetarian family were still not talking or listening much to what I had to say. It was cold, a few degrees above zero and definitely not the weather that the Aussies were used to. The guest house could provide heating in the rooms, at a cost of Y40, but as vegetarian dad wasn't listening to me, the family had to suffer a lack of heating as a result. Compared to dads stubbornness, the rest of the family were coming around and the kids played Mahjong. The daughter was winning every game and becoming a bit of a spoilt brat. The British couple were now keeping their distance from the Vego's, and as long as they could have a drink every night, they were fine with the weather. We chatted and I found that Joseph and especially his wife Joan really missed home and family. They had both taken redundancy from teaching, the job had changed so much in the previous years and new upstarts were giving them a hard time. They had come up with the novel idea (probably over a few bottles of wine) that wouldn't it be wonderful to travel the world and at the same time do a blog of each place they went to. A sort of educational thing that could then be used as a teaching aid. I liked their idea and was asking how it was going. They had their nephew who was "good at computers" doing the blog, but he just hadn't been updating the website for them. They were months behind and the schools that had initially shown interest were no longer following them. To be honest, it was an ill thought through venture that would have needed much more research and expertise. They were a couple of middle aged northerners, finding anything outside their small world odd and weird. They were definitely, typical, salt of the earth people, much like the families that I had grown up with. They were northern folk and in a comical sort of way, for some reason they reminded me more of "Hobbit Shire" than Yorkshire. Out on a great adventure and struggling in this big wide world. They even told me that when they met the Australians, they were puzzled about their lifestyle. They had got on to talking about houses and the Australians did not have a fire place. "Well", said Joan, "without a mantel piece, where do they put their ornaments?" A day later and another conversation. As much as I explained to Joseph that the water from the wash basin was supposed to empty out over the bathroom floor, he wasn't having it and kept harassing Mr Wu to call a plumber. Sometimes they were trying, but they were at least, trying and finding good amongst the bad, with the attitude that it would all turn out right in the end. Mr Wu was on good form, staggering around with a silver kettle full of bai jiu rice wine until veggi dad had enough of him and went to bed. Then Mr Wu got involved in the mah-jong, butting into the plays, causing havoc and having everyone shouting out at him when he interrupted. At least veggie annoying brat of a daughter was not getting it all her own way.

We had a tour of the villages, walking on the stone roads, between the rice paddys, through the street market selling the few seasonable vegetables from mats on the ground or low tables. There were frogs in nets, some fish in a plastic bowl and cuts of meat at the open air butcher. We entered "Da Village" where Tim told us that the people there were not friendly, as they thought they were more important, living in the self proclaimed "big village". In the village centre was the usual drum tower and stage area with a lot of old men playing mah-jong cards and smoking. Tim told us that they would ask for money if we took photographs. The houses along the village were like a traditional terrace, made of wood and two stories high. They had balconies from the second floor, from which hung some corn on the cob and some water spinach; it all looked very rustic and quaint. There was an old building opposite the drum tower with a sign asking for money for restoration and the stone slabs for engraving your name. For some reason, I decided this was a more worthy cause than the drum towers and wind and rain bridges that everyone donated to, so, very out of character for me, I chipped in. Then we wandered out through the village on the dirt road between the straight lines of houses. We went to see the performance by the Dong villagers' official and government sponsored dance troupe. This was a similar performance to the dances and songs performed the last time I was here. Men and women in traditional dress and playing lusheng. There was a welcome to the village dance, tea picking, bai jiu drinking and a sort of hop scotch-cum sword dance between two long bamboo poles. For this, the village girls would get one of us as a partner and would have to skip over the four moving bamboo poles in order to get from one side to the other. The grand finale was the circular dance that ended with our youngest girl being thrown up into the air. Our tour of the villages ended with a visit to drink local "oil tea", which to me tasted a lot liked sugar puffs. It is local tea, with local tea oil, but the cups also contain wok fried rice and sugar. My business head saw this as a great possibility, especially with all the "Eastern Medicinal Properties" that we could bestow it with.

After another night of Mr Wu's bai jiu fuelled entertainment around the dinner table and mah-jong game, we were off to The Long Ji rice terraces. We were on a crowded public bus and it was the most uncomfortable of the journeys for my group. More people got on the bus as we passed through a village, cramming the aisles. Someone got on with a container with live fish in it from the village market. Another man got on with his cage of chickens. He stood in front of a man with a large bag of grain on the floor in front of him, there was other stuff piled high on the roof of the public bus, going between the market and the villages. As I watched, I saw the chickens poke their heads out from in between the bars of their cage and start to peck at the bag of grain. A few minutes later and the owner of the bag noticed that the chickens had pecked a hole in the bag and were getting to the grain. Then there was an exclamation and outburst from him towards the owners of the chickens who only saw the funny side of things, as did I.

We were met by Farmer Tang and he took us to the Rice Terraces. Only doing the first half hour climb to the guest houses had me wondering if the Brits could make the hike the next day. Even though for some of us it was hard work, especially for the Brits, we made it up and down rice terraces with Farmer Tang. At one point Joseph was being pointed at by the villagers, who were saying that he was so large that he was about to have a baby. He laughed it all off, it wasn't as if he could run after them. Then it was Yangshuo again and on the bike ride we had the usual good time cycling to Moon Hill and back. I also got most of the group out for sunset at Monkey Janes' and then on to Bar 98. The group had sort of side-lined Veggo dad and daughter by now, even the mother and son were more inclined to join the rest of us. The Brits had really taken to young Mark, he'd been such a contrast to the other two kids and I got him a morning rock climbing with Ton Ton. We all got pretty plastered on the last night in Bar 98, it didn't help that we came second in their quiz and won yet another round of drinks. Joan found a mannequin on the way back to the hotel. All the jokes about stealing it, or finding a new man, being "legless" were "armless" until the arms of the mannequin fell off in the street, so we laughed some more.

We finished in Hong Kong with a final night dinner at Blues on the Bay. Joseph and Joan had composed a poem about travelling with Australians. This went along the lines of them wanting to walk up hills when the alternative was to have a lie in and there was a perfectly good bar to go to instead. They had also bought some "prizes" which had Mark unwrapping a willy warmer in front of mum and the rest of the group. Well, some people had a good trip. The vegetarians would go home, none the wiser for the experience.

By the time that we had arrived in Hong Kong I'd already decided that I was heading straight to Hanoi to join my Tour

Leading friend Jane on her trip before sorting out my new passport and visas. A curry in Chungking Mansions and a trip across the road to Shoestring Travel was all I needed and I flew the following day. One of the reasons why I was joining Jane's trip was to give her money. She had no way of accessing funds to run the trip, as she was still on report, still without a credit card. It was decided by the management of my tour company that I could take out Chinese Yuan and Hong Kong dollars from the cashpoints along the way during my last trip and transport it to her. It was only as I passed through customs that I realised that I'd more than tripled the limit of $5000 that I could transport between countries. Now, that would have been a little difficult to explain.

Another issue was starting to gnaw at me. My passport only had only two blank pages left. I had filled it in six years. I couldn't risk leaving the renewing of it until my next time off. At this moment in time I had two weeks off in between trips for the first time ever. I was allotted more time off after completing my next two trips, but with all the schedule changes there was no guarantee that this would ever happen, so I had decided to get it done now. I had a few choices of where I could get a new passport. With my trips ending and beginning in Hong Kong and Hanoi, they were the two obvious choices. I could also get passports and multi entry visas in Beijing, but that was at the other end of the country and it was minus 15 degrees. Also, I had no scheduled trips there so there was no reason to go to Beijing. Hong Kong is ridiculously expensive. Rooms are at least HK $200 per night and food and drink would mean that all the money I'd saved over the last year would be gone. Hong Kong was experiencing its worst ever winter and the prospect of two weeks of grey skies and cold in this city was depressing. It looked like it was going to be Hanoi, but as I'd just spent Christmas there and the weather hadn't improved, I didn't fancy two weeks on my own there either. There was also going to be one major stumbling block with getting all of this done. Chinese New Year fell on 6th February (also known as "Tet" in Vietnam) and just about everything in this part of Asia grinds to a halt for a week. Getting things like Chinese visas would be impossible unless I had my passport back at least a week before the holiday started. I needed a plan, a good plan, and a hell of a lot of luck.

I met up with Tour Leader Jane and went with her and her group over to Cat Ba. This is the first time that she had done this trip and was more than appreciative of me coming along to give her some money and a few pointers. She had a bit of a strange group too, a hippy couple in their fifties and a very straight laced couple, it was obvious that there would be friction, especially as the hippies wanted to go singing and dancing to karaoke on their first night on the Ha Long Bay boat whilst the other couple went to bed at nine o'clock and complained about the noise and smoking. Once on Cat Ba Island I was chatting with Mr Hai as I stayed on an extra day and came up with an idea. It turns out that Ho Chi Minh City would also renew my passport at the British Consulate. The weather would be in the 30's, my friend Jim had decided to move there to look for work and it was now on the cards that Phong was moving from Sapa to be with him. From another email I saw that Tamsin from the last trip would be passing through with her group on her way to Bangkok. I remembered having good times on Backpacker Street in a bar called "Guns 'n' Roses" about four years previously. Mr Hai could arrange transport to fly me there for $85. It seemed like the perfect solution. Before I flew, I checked my emails again. Jim should be back in HCMC soon and I really wanted to find out what had happened with Phong. Then I contacted Esmeray, I knew she was flying back to Bangkok from Turkey at the end of the month. Then I tracked down Lewis. He is a friend from my days at London Guildhall S.U. and I had been receiving updates from him about his travels in South East Asia. Maybe he would be somewhere near Vietnam and we should try to meet up if he could make it. As I checked again, I also found that I had received emails from John and Karen. These are two of my best friends from London. They were saying that their holiday in Kenya had been cancelled due to the government unrest after the disputed elections. Now they were coming to

Hong Kong. Dam, I'd just left there. But then they were flying on to Thailand. Now, I thought, just think if I could get all my passports and visas sorted in under two weeks then fly over to Thailand to surprise John for his birthday. A ridiculous plan, but hey . . .

Mr Hai had got his "friend" Miss Nham to pick me up on motorbike and take me to Hai Phong Airport which was a bit of a surprise, as it was closed when I got there. I had to wait for the security guard to open it up, put the lights on, then the staff arrived, set up the registration and ticketing counters then the snack shop, where the only thing edible was pizza flavoured Pringles. Then, arriving in Ho Chi Minh City was amazing. The weather had changed from the 10 degrees in the north of the country to 26 degrees in just one plane flight. I got on the back of a moto taxi and whizzed through the streets to a place I'd been to once before, four and a half years ago, which I couldn't pronounce. Sure enough though, after some knee cap risking, weaving and bobbing through the late evening traffic, I was dropped off just outside Guns 'n' Roses bar. I found a room above a launderette of all places and ate 'pho', the local beef noodle soup for dinner for less than a dollar. I tried to track some people down, but as yet, no one was in town. Probably for the best. I needed a clear head and an early start in order to get my photographs and then get my passport in to the British Consulate before it closed at 11am. The down side of this was that I needed someone to countersign my passport application. Preferably, this should be someone British with a professional qualification, otherwise a foreign professional who had known me for three years. This was going to be hard to find in HCMC. I texted Tamsin and asked if she minded me forging her name. Luckily, working for a travel company, I had all her details on file from her last trip.

This didn't actually go to plan. The photos took three hours to develop and I arrived at the Consulate at 11am dead on and they refused me entry. Tamsin still hadn't replied, but I'd forged her name and made up a company where she worked (1066

Accountancy in Hastings, it might just exist). I was the first through the door when it re-opened. The woman behind the counter looked at me, looked at my documents and said. "We can't accept these" I asked "Why?" then she replied "Did you read all the information concerning these . . . . ?" She pointed at my photographs "Your head is not large enough" So, there you have it, officially, from no higher source than the British Consulate in Ho Chi Minh City. I do not have a big head.

The trouble was; what to do about it? The office would close in a couple of hours and I needed the forms to be sent off like yesterday. She gave me the address of a photographer and I left, jumped on the nearest moto and shot off through the city traffic again. The photographer was a man of his profession. He assessed the light, my positioning, and his equipment meticulously. He took his time, when all I wanted was snappy snaps. Nevertheless, within the hour I was on my way back to the Consulate with an envelope of photographs. At the counter I passed the pictures over. "Which one do you prefer?" she asked as I saw them for the first time. I looked on them in disbelief. In my haste to get to the photographer on the back of the bike, I'd never even considered what I may look like. Now, the pictures were in front of me and the "back of a bike look" was all too obvious. Hair was swept around my head and flying off at all angles. Well, I'd be supporting this picture for the next 10 years, and it was certainly an individual look. I just visualised the amount of curious inspection that I would get every time I passed a border checkpoint, and that would be often. The woman behind the counter smiled as she accepted my passport application. Hopefully, it would be processed, hopefully within the 10 working days that the Consulate had stated.

Tamsin got in touch at last. She was ok with me forging her signature and I bought the drinks as a way of a thank you. The thank you continued until the early hours of the morning again in Go2 bar. It's the "in place" on the corner of De Tham in the backpacker area and has foreigners sitting there drinking beer with their breakfasts as much as it has people drinking until the wee hours. Once again we were drinking and dancing before I dragged her off to bed. The following day, I was ill. So ill that instead of eating dinner that night, I threw up and instead of going out for drinks we had a night in front of the T.V. Tamsin had yet another new group to join the following day. For her it was a nightmare scenario. All the others had already been travelling together for the last two weeks. She nearly decided not to go. For me, I was at a loose end. I had to wait until my passport was returned, or did I . . .

Technically, it's illegal to travel in Vietnam without a passport. You have to submit them at every guesthouse and hotel (or on the boat when we stay overnight on the boat) and they keep them until we leave. I'd made photocopies of my passport, visa, and letter requesting visa on arrival and the word on the street (especially from the travel agencies that were trying to sell me a tour) was that this would suffice. So I booked a tour through the Mekong River Delta, with an onward connection to Phu Quoc Island. This was going to be a little bit of a holiday for me.

42. Return to HCMC 18/01/08 (HCMC)

(A)

I love the buzz of these cities
I arrive on an evening flight, 26 degrees
As I leave the airport, a hail of taxi's
'Where you want to go?' I haggle down the fee

Then I'm off on the back of a moto
To a place that sounded vaguely where I want to go
As we weave and bob the whereabouts I don't know
Caught up in the night drive, go with the flow

More flash buildings than I remember
A sexy girl overtakes, I hope we follow her
A family of 4 squeezed between handle bars and back fender
We swerve left and right, no place for a nervous passenger

Back packer alley has broken its' levee
And flooded the surrounding streets of the city
Tourists cram into a hundred bars and cafes
Then, for the first time in a long time, there's only me

(B)

Greeted by a wave from across the road
Where do you want to go?
The most I do is politely say "hello"
And walk through the streets of a hundred echoes

This place has changed, buildings have grown
A dozen stories of polished stone
Surrounded by a manicured lawn
I notice that all the cyclos have gone

(C)

Offers to shoe-shine your sandals
Wondering who actually buys from the stalls
Full of non-descript food, or sunglass hawkers
Or the girls who walk with the baskets on poles
When all we want is all we get
Western food, souvenirs and the internet

43. The Time Travellers Wife 21/01/08 (HCMC)

Strange how the Time Travellers Wife
Has turned up out of nowhere
To be my partner
In some shifting of the reality of my life
Never knowing who's out there
Just around the corner
Change time and space and bump into each other
A parallel world, a parallel lover

Just a minute away in cyberspace
And hopping from country to country
Meeting people from another time, another place
And mind maps I must dredge up from memory.

I'd been through the Mekong delta a few years earlier whilst on one of my summer holiday tours with Intrepid Travel. This was quite a different trip. We were a group of 20 or so travelling on a big bus. All were strangers or couples and most happy amongst themselves not to talk to anyone new. It was the scenery that impressed me most. The jungle on either side of the river, on the flat islands that made up the land here, was as green and forbidding an environment as you could imagine. The trees looked impenetrable. Then, you would see the road that was being built through them. Just cutting away through the thick mass. Then the bridges. These were alien constructions in every sense of the word. They looked so out of place with their half built concrete towers soaring high above the flat river and surrounding jungle. They looked like immense see-saws, precariously balanced and reminded me of the alien craft from "War of the Worlds" or that little remembered sci-fi T.V. series "The Tripods". This part of Vietnam was jumping from third world to first, from jungle to superhighway in one single span of a suspension bridge.

We visited one of the islands. I remembered that the last time I was here, there being a community of weavers from an ethnic minority, living life as they had done for hundreds of years. Progress had removed all this and along with the construction of roads and bridges and with it brought modernity and tourism. We were a crowd on the newly paved pathway through what was more of a garden than jungle, until we came upon a small community making sweets and covering peanuts with toffee. This was all for sale and we sat in a bamboo tea house afterwards as other tourists filed in and out. We drank tea as others purchased the sweets and got photographs of themselves holding a large snake. What would Intrepid make of this I wondered? We had a lunch with the option to buy a better lunch before we actually knew what our included lunch consisted of. We were told we could "look around"; half hoping to discover the weavers or rice paper making of my last visit but all I could see were the glass cabinets filed with souvenirs, snacks, strings of pearls. We crossed back over the rivulets and more islands and finally took a ferry to the other side of the delta where we stayed in a town for the night.

The following morning we went to the floating market. This was boat after boat, anchored in the river, all piled high with produce. There were fruits and livestock. Most boats were doing quite a trade with smaller craft offloading bags and baskets and transporting them to the shore. Here, they were accepted by a jumble of ramshackle huts with jetties that acted as warehouses and wholesale shops. There was so much activity going on and we were always close to colliding to one of the craft that darted between the bigger vessels. All this was serviced by other boats selling snacks or cooking breakfast, it truly was a village market on the open water. Back on land again and we saw a place that made rice paper, the kind that you get on spring rolls and it was just as I'd remembered the process from my last visit. Rice being pummelled by hand, the husks being separated and then the rice itself ground into a flour. This was then added to water and the resulting mixture spread on a hot plate, not dis-similar to a crêpe. Then the round papers were left to dry on little woven bamboo mats. Next was the rice mill. Here the local people would bring bags of rice to be de husked and processed according to size and quality before being bagged. We also saw rice being made into flat pancakes. I wondered about this machinery, simple though it was, being pivotal to the local economy and essential for the local way of life. It wouldn't take much for this to completely change by just the removal, or introduction of a bigger better machine. I asked how much the rice cost, 6000 Dong per kilo or about three times the price of the rice in China, that difference in price surprised me, though 6000 Dong is still only about $0.30. Our group split and I went on to Rach Gia, where I had problems getting accommodation without a passport. In the 3rd hotel I simply got a room because an American couple had just refused to pay the asking price and I said that I would and the girl on the desk was happy to make a sale before realising that she should have checked my documentation first. Well, what her boss didn't know wouldn't hurt her. There is not much in Rach Gia, a nice town square, some food stalls where I ate a fabulous pork and rice dinner and then there are docks for the boat to Phu Quoc and elsewhere.

In the morning I headed to the dock by moto taxi. I tried a couple of offices and got waved on and on with my receipt. Finally, I got to the right office and I was cutting it fine with the boats departure time of 8am. They didn't speak a great deal of English and looked puzzled when I produced my receipt but no boat ticket. They dealt with some other people who had tickets and the time ticked by. Once again, something had gone wrong. The girl on the desk was on the phone, bare in mind that this was 7:50, I didn't hold out much hope for her, or me getting the result I wanted. As the time got closer to departure time, she handed the phone to me. A booming voice on the other end said. "Your ticket is in Saigon" . . . . "But, the captain will let you travel". Phew, now to get to the boat. The moto outside realised I was in a hurry, so much so that we hit an oncoming bike, which brought us to a stop. He was so concerned about his possible broken hand and screaming at the other moto driver in the accident that he didn't look at me for the money. Not that with broken fingers he could easily accept any, anyway. I was in too much of a hurry to wait for the outplay of this drama so I scampered up the gang plank and onto a crowded boat to Phu Quoc Island

A moto at the dock took me to a hotel in the vicinity of the main place for tourists to be based, according to the Lonely Planet. They accepted my photocopy passport, so I was happy with the price. Then I went off to explore. The only town on the island was a 15 minute walk away along a road running parallel to the coast. It wasn't so big and had that ramshackle charm of a place still with one foot in the third world. It had a few local amenities, and a sprinkling of shops and cafes with western goods and food. On the other side of the river was the old fishing village with its extensive market and no foreigners at all. Then I headed back past the hotel and down to the beach. The whole of the 17Km stretch of beach is being developed for tourism. The 300m wide plots of land between the road and the beach, is resort, after resort. As yet they are not full and the development not too obvious from the seafront, but each resort would accommodate over 1000 people and there is more construction on the way. It wasn't hard to imagine how, only a few years earlier, this place was a deserted paradise and also how it was going to look in a few years time. I saw a billboard for a new casino being built, what would be a golf retreat and there was also mention of developing an airport where at the moment only local planes could access the island. As I wandered around I saw that there were not too many people visiting the resorts, but already there were German and Russian families and the evidence of package holidays. You can see exactly where it is all going. I'm glad I came when I did.

44. Mekong Market River Cruise 23/01/08 (Mekong river boat)

Floating market, hotchpotch of wooden boats
One serves hot coffee for a 5000 dong note
Others laden with pineapple, pomelo fruits
One man tucks into his pho' noodle soup
Long-tail boats and paddles
Skit between the larger vessels
And the river bank houses
And landing pontoons all a jumble

In the distance, watching over, like some alien invader
The part built bridge that rises from the river
A towering see-saw of an unbalanced structure
To cut a road into the jungle that it will soon clear

45. The Coast Road 24/01/08 (Long Beach, Phu Quoc Island)

There is a place that no one knows about
Further up the coast
It's just like paradise
Further up the coast
A tropical island,
Where a clear mountain spring
Reaches the sea,
At a sandy white beach
Just up the coast

You can watch the deer go down to the beach
At sunset
And the fishermen in the bay
Cast their nets
This undiscovered Eden
That I have a claim on
This home by the sea
And it belongs to me
And I haven't started yet

They call it 'development'
Means you can do what you want
Now that you've bought a piece of land
Don't know who you bought it from
Didn't think it belonged to anyone
That's the way it should have stayed, sea and sand
You put up signposts to keep trespassers away
Because this is your part of the bay

The man by the water
Said he used to fish here
Another let his cattle on the beach
But they don't have a permit
And you've bought a government writ
So you can keep them safely out of reach

Now you can sit on your piece of paradise
Without a care in the world
Why not sit, and don't think twice
Without a care in the world
Not a care in the world
But not a care for the world

So you found your piece of paradise
Why did you have to spoil it?
Why did you follow greed and avarice
Why not just enjoy it?
Why did you build another room on
Import cold beer and air con?
And where before it was you and a boat
It all comes to you on the new coast road

Now the world beats a path to your door
Built by the man who drove cattle before
Whilst the fisherman
Throws away his beer can
Thinks about the girl he would have wed
To raise livestock in their homestead
Now she wears a uniform instead
And for a price or a lie will share your bed

And this absurdity
That makes you buy a piece of the sea
Building hotels on sand
Of course it will slip right through your hands
But unfortunately
That will be too late for you and me
Because you don't want to understand
This paradise is becoming your wasteland

There's a place that no one knows about further up the
coast . . . .

That evening I watched the sunset from a beach bar, that was deserted as soon as the sun went down. Then went back into town, the nightlife was non-existent. When I got back to the hotel there was a problem. The manager had been asked to produce my passport for the police. He'd made up some story to fob off the officials until I returned, but once I explained that I didn't have a passport, he went quite pale. I was not allowed to travel without a passport, how had I actually got to the island? It seems that my problems over the boat ticket had meant that no one had bothered to check that I had a passport to travel. So here I was. I produced my visa documents, arrival card with stamps and that had to be enough. It's not as if I could actually go anywhere else. That was also going to be a problem for later.

Considering that I was temporarily marooned on Paradise Island, I made the best of it. I got along well with the hotel owner and helped him with his "marketing plan". His tag line of "Special service for you" was just never going to hit the mark. If the island becomes marketed with anything to do with an elephants head, I want a cut. A couple of the guests were also good company. The highlight of my stay was going SCUBA diving. I'd done this once before, seven years earlier, off the Great barrier reef and looked on it as a once in a lifetime experience. I'd loved doing it, but those sort of opportunities don't come around too often, so I'd just consigned it to memory as one of the most fabulous things that I've done in what was quickly becoming a very full and amazing life. This time was every bit as good as the last and I swam with the fish and saw the coral come to life with its varied plant-life and colours. That afternoon I got a return ticket to Saigon, without any hassle. All I did was point at the calendar on the wall and say what day I wanted to travel on. I checked out and set off early in the following morning, only to find that I'd got the dates wrong and the boat wouldn't take me back. The travel company hadn't changed their calendar on the wall. How was I supposed to know the date? I'm glad I only make these cock ups when only

I'm involved and not any passengers. So, back to the hotel and another day in paradise.

I made it back to Saigon the following day. Jim was in town and sorted out a hotel for me. Then we hit the bars. I'd contacted Esmeray and she had a date and a hotel in Bangkok. I had contacted my company mangers asking for a letter in order to get a China Visa, but the best they had come up with in three weeks was "it would be easier if you were in Beijing". I hadn't been anywhere near Beijing for nearly three months. They knew where I was because it was they who sent me to Vietnam and they were being no help at all. We had a new boss, it was Tracey, a leader who I had met only once in Amdo Tibet, and she had a good reputation with the other leaders. She had contacted me about my time off, new passport and visa runs but was pretty much new to everything. She was relying upon Bruce and the team that had been hired as the company looked to expand. All the management and new support staff were in the process of moving into a new office. I was emailing my friends from home who were supposedly travelling to South East Asia, but I was still getting no reply from either John and Karen or Lewis. However, my thinking had me heading more and more in the direction of getting a flight to Bangkok and seeing what happened. The following morning around 10am I was woken by my phone ringing. It was the British consulate. Amazingly and with perfect timing, my passport was ready for collection. By mid day I was in the Vietnamese immigration office trying to get a visa. Officially, with the cancelling of my passport, my visa was also cancelled and I needed one to reside in the country, or to leave it. Here we had another example of bureaucracy. I was told that to renew my visa, I would need a letter from the company that got me the last one. This company, just happened to be in Hanoi. (They didn't need to know that I'd got the visa through a bribe at the airport, I was using the letter that my employers had sent me). I was told that I should return to Hanoi and visit this company's office; they assumed I knew who I was dealing with. I asked instead for a tourist visa. It didn't make any difference to me. No, they wouldn't issue me one because I had a work visa (or not as the case may be). So I left.

I went back to De Tham Street in the backpacker area and walked into STA travel. Another very random occurrence happened as I bumped into another Tour Leader who I had met briefly in China, Maria; and we chatted. Then I asked about flights to Bangkok. Yes, I could go there, then on to Hanoi for $300. I mentioned my lack of visa and asked if they could sort me out. Yes, but it would take another day. I asked, what would happen if I just tried to leave. The girl on the desk said that I could get the visa as I left. No problem then. She sold me the flight, then said, "maybe" I could get the visa as I left the airport. Maybe wasn't good enough and she'd just taken $300 off me. Around this time I was joined by Jim. This was a bit of a farce. I said to the girl, "what happens if I get to the airport and I can't leave, will you give me my money back?" No, was the answer, but I could cancel the flight, for a fee. I decided that I would rather chance it. So far I'd managed to get into Vietnam without a visa, travel around the country without a passport, so getting out without a visa would only add another ridiculous story to my adventure.

That night, the three of us, Jim, Maria and I, went out. One peculiar thing about Saigon, that I had never experienced before was the way that the hookers operate from motos. You can be calmly walking along the street, Phan Ngo Lao and a bike with two girls will drive up to you. In one single movement, the pretty girl dismounts from the back of the bike and puts her arm in yours as you're walking. As you turn, she smiles and her driver asks you if you like the girl. From then, it's all about shaking yourself free and being on your guard against the next one. We ended up in Go2 bar and I stayed up chatting to Maria until around 4am, which is really stupid when I have a flight and passport problems for the following day. Nevertheless I saw Jim in the morning before his job interview. He had decided that all the crap with Phong in Sapa meant that he would definitely leave tour leading but was looking forward to Phong joining him in Saigon. I went looking for a moto to the airport and got offered dope, then opium, then a girl, then a boy, then a gun, then asked if I wanted to shoot a bazooka at a cow. It's not the same as flagging a cab in London. I was still at the airport for 2:30 when my flight was at 6pm. I wasn't going to take too many chances. As I passed the passport control, I was held back. The officer couldn't find my visa (of course) so I produced my old passport. He went off and I had to wait. I peered over the desk and could see the computer terminal displaying both my two passports, photographs and details. So at least it was obvious what was going on. When he returned, I was led off to another room where the whole "you can not leave without a visa" was explained to me. I did my best "oh, sorry, what can I do to catch my flight" routine and before too long I was paying $10, which turned into a 200,000 Dong bribe to be the proud owner of a Vietnam visa. What's more, it was a transfer of my old visa, so it was still multiple entry and valid until May. Not bad at all. Then all I had to do was get on the plane and I was in Bangkok again.

I've arrived in this city about half a dozen times now. The airport is a different one than it was 15 years ago, but the buses to Khoa San Road still stops outside and less than an hour later I was on that backpacker street again looking for somewhere to spend the night. Khoa San Road has just exploded in the last 15 years. There used to be half a dozen bars and cafes on the road, with a couple of others tucked up alleyways. I remember Stopping in P.B. Guesthouse and drinking in No Name Bar the first time I was here. Both of these were long gone when I returned five years ago, but even then there were still a couple of local places to eat Thai curry or noodles. Now even this had been replaced. P.B. guesthouse had been one of the scummiest places I'd ever stayed. The dormitory beds were right up next to one another and semi naked westerners gasped in the stifling heat under the one fan. The place was raided twice for drugs whilst I was there and I saw people being beaten before being carted off by the police. No Name Bar had been part owned by a young British lad (Giles) and it's where I met the other westerners who were making Bangkok their temporary home. That atmosphere no longer existed. Now the street was bars after bars with neon signs stacked higher and higher offering cheap beer, accommodation, local goods and tours. It was a little bit like some Spanish holiday resort, a Benidorm in South East Asia. It had also attracted the sort of people you'd find in Benidorm. From out of the bars you could hear cries of "Aussie, Aussie, Aussie" or Brits chanting football songs at the tops of their voices. There were Americans complaining about the standard of the service or the food and drunk girls staggering around or sitting by the roadside throwing up and crying into their own vomit. Everybody had already been everywhere. All pontificated about how great a certain beach or village was and how cheap they had got there. I didn't last too long on the street; bed seemed a much pleasanter option.

The following morning the first thing I had to do was sort out a visa for China. Without this I would be unable to do my next trip, which started in a weeks' time. The hotel could do this and get it back to me in five days. This was just about perfect again, because Chinese New Year was on the 6th and that meant everything closed down. It looks as though my impossible plan had actually come together. Later that morning I was at one of my old haunts, "Cool Corner". Even this place on Rambuttri was now at the hub of the tourist town, rather than being on the edge of the madness as it used to be. After breakfast I was interneting Esmeray, along with my friends from London, John and Karen, then Lewis again. Esmeray was supposed to be getting in the next day, but the weather was delaying her flight. I still wasn't getting any reply from John and Karen, but then Lewis suddenly got in touch as I was reading hotmail. Whats more he was in Bangkok for a few days. How about that for good timing? Just then, I looked up, and saw Tamsin, the girl from one of my trips, who I had last seen in Saigon, on the other side of the street. Now, things like that just don't happen too often. For a split second I thought about not calling out to her. With Esmeray arriving, it could get a bit tricky, but then I thought, "What the heck" and shouted out to a very puzzled

Tamsin who obviously couldn't believe that I was standing on the opposite side of the street to her in Bangkok.

That afternoon, I checked into the hotel that Esmeray had booked for us. She was definitely being delayed. Then I met up with Tamsin. We placed ourselves on Khoa San Road where I could see if anyone I knew walked by. These days, a number of stalls have set themselves up on the road and they sell bottles of beer and cocktails. The idea is that you sit on small plastic chairs on the street and drink plastic buckets full of "sex on the beach" until you are drunk enough to actually believe that you may be on a beach and try to have sex with someone just as mashed as you are. This had quite an effect on Tamsin, who, as the night went on, and nobody I knew walked by (Esmeray could be in the hotel room . . . .) got "friendlier and friendlier", as she put it herself. I walked her back as she was too drunk to walk back to her hotel. The upshot was that she got very emotional. She was on her period, so there couldn't be any sex, but she didn't want me to leave. I tried to as she nodded off, but she caught me and in the end I stayed until the morning, all the time wondering what sort of mess I had just got myself into?

I headed back to my place the following morning and was relieved to find that Esmeray hadn't made it in yet. That would have taken quite a lot of explaining, although nothing had actually happened, Tamsin simply wouldn't let me leave. I texted Tamsin, who said she was too ill to move. The best news possible. Then I headed off back to Khoa San to scout around again. On the way there I ran into Esmeray. Synchronicity had struck again. She'd been trapped in Jordan (the country) overnight and some of her fellow passengers had been detained at a military base. With all that going on and a story to tell, she didn't really ask me any questions, so of course, I didn't have to say too much. On Kho San Road we had a beer and tried ringing John, then Lewis. He actually replied and said he would meet us that night. Wow, my first friend from back home in nearly a year. That would be good. That evening everybody met up around Kho San Rd. Me, Esmeray, Tamsin, Lewis and his friend. Lots of pleasant conversation with me wondering what the hell was going to happen next. I thought I'd better not get too drunk and hoped that Tamsin wouldn't too. Luckily, she was still feeling rough and left early. She was leaving for Chang Mai the following day anyway. This was a total relief going on what had happened the night before. Then the rest of us spent the remainder of the night on the street drinking cocktails until they closed the stalls down at 12, then in and out of a couple of bars including a place that had just had a "metal" night that we decided we would have to check out again.

The next day, Esmeray was ill. She hardly moved all day. I got on her laptop and we looked at Hua Hin. This was a place that I'd never heard of before, but in John's last email, he'd said that he and Karen had booked in there for a week. They would have left Bangkok at some point the previous day and be there now. Esmeray was up for the adventure, so that was the plan for the following morning once she'd recovered. As we were two tour leaders, getting to Hua Hin wasn't going to be a problem; it was just the finer details of getting somewhere to stay for the night for cheap. We got a bus to the Southern bus station, then a public bus to Hua Hin that took around four hours. Accommodation sorted itself out once we had arrived in the shape of lads on motorbikes that met the bus stop in Hua Hin. We looked at the photographs of guest houses that they all held on cards and just picked what seemed to be a good place and went with it.

Hua Hin was a very nice place on the surface. We'd read some reviews on the internet, but they were not so inviting. People who had been there years earlier had said the place was spoiled by not being able to walk along the beach anymore due to the development of the private resorts, or having restaurants called Le Bistro, and the amount of girlie bars that had sprung up. To be honest, we didn't expect anything more. The accommodation we had plumbed for was a sort of wooden pier that extended out over the sea. There were a dozen or so of these next to each other, some with restaurants attached and they gave off a romantic "seaside of yesteryear" vibe. A pity, because Esmeray and I just weren't getting it together. Whatever we had three months earlier wasn't there now and we just decided to call each other friends. The town around where we stayed was peppered with small cafes and places selling seaside souvenirs. We quite liked its charm. We walked past the Chinese temple, past the five star hotel resort and up the beach. This was excellent again. There were resorts, as you would expect, but nothing too obtrusive. There was a bar shack on the beach, with a band murdering a rock classic. This place was run by long haired, tattooed Thai drop-outs. We walked further up to where they did para-surfing (the thing with parachutes and surfboards), then we returned to the beach bar for a beer. That night we ate in one of the best settings ever, on one of the peers that went out over the sea. It rained, but we had umbrellas and the weather was fine when we started walking home. When it started raining again, we were in the district of girly bars. One of them happened to be called Sparks Bar, so we just had to go in to take shelter. The Madame was a little surprised with this, but took to Esmeray when it was obvious that we were just going to have a drink and a chat. We actually stayed for a couple of bottles, and once Esmeray said that she was not with me, the madame tried to offer her one of the girls, much to Esmerays amusement, though for some reason the madame never offered me a girl.

We were in two minds about staying, or moving on, but decided that we liked the place and I still hadn't given up hope on John and Karen arriving and getting in touch, so we booked in the guest house again. Then we found internet and to my surprise, John had contacted me. He was in some hotel nearby and had been in and out of every bar the previous night looking for us. Three hours later, I spotted him and Karen crossing a road. Then we were in the Irish bar, catching up on what had gone on over the previous year.

It's so odd meeting your best friends on the other side of the world. I asked so many questions about what was going on and who was doing what in London. Each time the answer was "not much", but for me, a lot had still happened that I wasn't a part of. Esmeray was a bit on the side-lines for much of this. I stayed out far too late visiting the girly bars again (we just had to have a photo of me in Sparks Bar with the girls for the folks back home) and the next day I was suffering, so much so that even in the afternoon, after trying to eat, I puked and decided to keep off the beer for the rest of the day. We hung around all night from pub to night market to bar again. The next day, we did it all again and covered quite a distance as we walked around Hua Hin. As we sat drinking, looking out at the ocean from this little bit of paradise, the three off us just had to comment on how it was. We were over here, whilst our friends were at home. What's more than this, it felt a bit like our friends were paying me to be out here and I had never felt so lucky or grateful for them. All three of us rented out spare rooms in our houses to other friends who at this very moment were on their way to work in the cold drizzle of a February morning. We wondered how everybody was suffering in what was the worst winter Britain had experienced in living memory. Then had another beer whilst looking out to the sea. John said one of the most profound things I've ever heard him come out with. He said that there was no such thing as luck. Some actor had said that it was when "preparation meets opportunity". That was worth thinking about. None of us was here through luck. We also need the right conditions and the ability to make things happen, but yes, you make your own luck.

46. Untitled 04/02/08 (Hua Hin, Thailand)

Signs in every guest house
No Thais allowed under any circumstance
Elephant seal bellied old man
Walking hand in hand
With a child like Thai

One quarter of his size
Everyone has a new tattoo
Another box ticked on the list of things to do

Buckets of cocktails on Kho San Road
Staggering drunk, after fights and whores
All have arrived for their moment in the sun
All screaming out load about what they've done
Countries, buckets, sex, tattoos and opium
I can have it all, screams the me generation
That corrupts everything it touches
So I pack my bag and head for the beaches

To fall asleep, to dream
Listening to the sea

47. The end of backpacker alley 08/02/08
    (KS Guesthouse BKK)

It's the end of the night
On backpacker alley
And I wish I had put
Some bromide in my tea
Everywhere I look
The girls are so pretty
And the one I'm with
Doesn't want to be with me

The food carts move on
The last desperate moths
Cavort with the dying neon bars
Neon girls, or both
Some slowly shutting down
Into a slumber
And massaged until
We are all asleep in our beer

One is too drunk
Hits the floor like a putty ball

The girls trying to move him
Are just too small
Then out in the street
The empty cups and wrappers
Are piled high for the rats
Our international playboy signature

It's the end of the night
The end of backpacker alley
And as I move on
The end of you and me
The end of a one month summer
The best time with the best of friends
I turn my back on the backpackers
This time has come to an end.

That evening we sat in the Irish Bar again looking out across the street at the girly bars. One westerner was so drunk that he collapsed in the middle of the veranda and passed out. There was then the comedy farce of two or three local bar girls, all one third of his size, trying to lift him. It was an impossible task that had to be left to one of the local men who placed him on the other side of the street, away from potential customers, to sober him up. This still didn't deter the bloke from trying to go back into the bar, even though he couldn't walk. This is a sad and lasting impression of western men in Thailand. It also got me thinking, "was this my future?" For Esmeray and I it was time to start heading back to Bangkok, so we said our goodbyes to John and Karen and left in the morning. I still had to pick up my China Visa. The last weeks had certainly taken a toll on us both. Esmeray had decided not to drink for our final two days, which was unfortunate because the Bangkok night-life provided us with an excellent rock covers band in the place we'd found on Kho san Road. The Chinese New Year celebrations passed us by as we hung around the backpacker areas, too jaded to get involved and go local. The following day I met up with Lewis again before he headed off to Chang Mai and we watched a storm flood out Khoa San Road. The Last day I wasn't feeling up to much, but still went out because Esmeray had met another Tour Leader in town, who was meeting up that evening with some other Leaders. An American girl called Aaron and Tony who was now the China manager of Gap Adventures, both of whom I'd also met in the past, so we agreed to go out. There is a place off Khoa San Road that is a petrol station by day and converts into a seating area, right across the fore-court, selling food and drink. An explosive idea, if you consider the amount of people smoking. Aaron had recently been leading trips in Morocco and as Esmeray had also lead trips in Morocco she was trying to compare notes on which of the local guides and drivers was the best shag. Esmeray wasn't being drawn into the conversation and trying to indicate that they shouldn't be talking about it with me there, it took a while for the penny to drop for Aaron. Then the following morning at five o'clock, I said goodbye to Esmeray, maybe for the last time again. Then I was in a taxi to the airport and flying back to Hanoi and another New Year back at work in Vietnam and China.

Chapter 3.

BACK ON THE ROAD

"Our battered suitcases were piled on the sidewalk again; we had longer ways to go. But no matter, the road is life."

Jack Kerouac

Arriving back in Hanoi was strange for a number of reasons. Firstly, although I'd just had a fantastic two weeks in South East Asia, I was ready to get back to work. It looked like I was going to do one more Hanoi to Hong Kong trip then the return leg back to Hanoi. Then, the next month I would be heading back into China proper with a new trip taking me all the way from Hanoi to Beijing. The second strange thing was the weather. It was still winter here. It was bitterly cold. So much so that the trip the previous week had only got as far as the Chinese border before the passengers abandoned it and flew directly to Hong Kong. Another leader sent photos of the Long Ji Rice terraces covered in snow. She added that the snow had taken all the power lines down in the area too. It was absolutely freezing and the roads had been impassable so they'd never gotten to Chen Yang. Hiking in these conditions was also not advisable. Elsewhere in China there were reports of trips being cancelled. Or other tour groups were being trapped in hotels and at train stations. Indeed, 250million Chinese had been caught out with the worst winter in 50 years and 200,000 had been stranded at Guangzhou train station where a stampede had crushed people to death. The reason why there had been so many people on the move is also connected to the third strange thing I noticed upon my arrival. Everything was closed for Chinese New Year. People had all stopped work and gone home to visit their families. The effect in Hanoi was that it had turned from the vibrant buzzing place of motos and shops that spilled people and wares onto the street, into a virtual ghost town. I went to KOTO to book the group meal for the night and it was closed. I walked into the Old Quarter, not being hassled at all. Crossing the road felt like someone was about to play a practical joke on you and reveal all the motos that were secretly hiding around the next corner about to run you down. I was pretty stuck for options, so it had to be Le Pub again. When I saw Gift, who was passing on four of her passengers to me, she also commented on how the city had been such a disappointment to her group because everything was closed. Once again, they'd had a fantastic time with her in Thailand and

Laos. They were definitely not prepared for Arctic China. She also gave me the heads up on one of the passengers, Keith, 37 from Australia and an experienced traveller who had questioned her all the way about everything she did. She was mostly pissed off because he and a couple of others had walked out of their final night meal. I was so grateful for the warning.

At the initial group meeting, the four who had completed the first part of the trip, Keith, Mike (18 from Canada), Les (22 English) and Astrid (19 Norway) were joined by Kim (35 Aussie with a Chinese background) and Bronwyn (22 Welsh). It was Bronwyn who really got the ball rolling with tirade about how much the local payment was, where she was immediately joined by Keith, who finished off with 'tipping kittys', 'how much does all of this actually cost?' and 'I think we should only eat street food with the locals'. What a Gift from Gift these lot were. I somehow calmed them down. Groups can be so difficult because people have varying expectations of what they are going to have from a trip. What is good for one person, another one will shy away from. Some have budgets to keep to, some need western food, whilst others avoid it at all costs. In many ways, one mans' wine really is another ones poison. I told them that I didn't use a tipping kitty, if they didn't want to tip, they wouldn't have to. I would cover the drivers and, if need be, also the guides in order to ensure that they would continue to give me good service. Then I talked about the "local payment". About how it was actually a way to keep costs down on the trip. I said that rather than pay their travel agent in London or wherever, and have money passed through office and administration, each taking their own percentage, then on through the Chinese tourism bureaucracy with all its backhanders, this way, the money came directly to me and I paid for services. I put their money in the hands of local people and that was something that we should be proud that we were doing. I was getting listened to, but they were still feeling that they had issues. However, once I had described the conditions that they may be facing in China, they began to focus a little more on the task in hand. They had two weeks with me on what could be a very difficult trip. I also pointed out to Keith that, on my inspection of the groups' paperwork, his visa wasn't correct. On the one hand, this pissed him off even more. He started ranting that my travel company had not told him that he would need a double entry visa to go into Hong Kong then back into China to join his next trip heading up to Beijing. On the other hand, at least I'd pointed it out and I said I would come up with a solution.

It was a new year and with it, on the way over to Cat Ba Island there was a change in itinerary. We now got a boat and stayed overnight. They are beautiful "Chinese Junk" style vessels, which have been enlarged and converted from the traditional merchant and fishing boats to serve tourists. Where we entered, jumping on to the prow of the boat, there was a dining room deck, above which was a sun deck and below all this were the cabins. It was all wood and felt like it was something special, especially with the dining room laid out like a top restaurant and all the crew in waiter uniforms. We were welcomed with wet towels and orange juice, all with the approval of my group and we settled down to a meal of nine dishes, all of which were excellent, from the stuffed crab shells to the fried whole fish, to the almost crispy calamari. This was an excellent start. However, I'd done this with Jane's group and knew what would happen next. No one had purchased the $15 bottles of wine during lunch, much to the disappointment and surprise of the waiting staff so we were all pretty sober when the music started. We watched, cringing as the boat crew tried their best to get us to sing karaoke. That had been a disaster with Jane's group as two of the couples; one hippy, the other academics were quickly at odds as to what passed as a good way to start a trip. The hippies wanted to drink, smoke and sing whilst the others went to their rooms and complained about the noise. I knew what we were in for.

The boat crew had expected an exuberant group of friends on tour, ready to drink and have fun and didn't really know how to treat these quiet people who preferred to read a book and asked for them to turn the music down. At dinner we were moored by the sister vessel of the one we were on. The food came out, a banquet by any standards and everyone began to tuck in. At that point a Chinese girl crossed over to our vessel and said 'Spark'. It was Ching, another leader who had been swept up with all the new changes and new positions being created in the new office in Beijing and was now working in the office in Beijing. She told me that she was on a training mission to our Tour Company office in Indo-China to see how things were done here. I'd met her twice before, each time for only a minute, but she chatted away and asked so many questions that it was like seeing an old friend. Out of the corner of my eye I could see the food quickly vanishing from the plates. Kim decided to but a King Prawn on my plate, but otherwise, the whole lot had been devoured in the space of a five minute conversation. It was obvious where I was in the pecking order, literally. Luckily, Ching let me share her food on the sister boat. She was the only passenger with a crew of half a dozen. On our return to our boat, it was Karaoke time. Throughout the whole of S.E. Asia, this is seen as the best sort of fun you can have in a small room. Unfortunately, being westerners, this doesn't work for us. With four new people out of eight in the group, no one was ready to make a fool of themselves quite yet, much to the frustration of the boat crew. They can't understand it. Are we not on holiday? Are we not all friends? Why are we not drinking and dancing like all the Vietnamese and Chinese tour groups? We just sit around making polite conversation, reading a book, maybe a game of cards, but that is it. They turn the Karaoke up, we turn it down. They turn it up, we turn it off. In the end they assume that we are unhappy, but can't understand why and it all becomes a bit tense.

We arrived at Cat Ba in the morning and were met by Mr Hai who I'd arranged a hike with. Ching also decided to join us for a day, rather than sit by herself on her boat. We did the "Bike/hike and Hospital cave" tour. We all had a moto driver and sat pillion, whizzing off through Cat Ba town and into the limestone scenery of the islands interior. The "Hospital Cave" in question was used in the war against the Americans as a barracks complete with cinema, swimming pool, offices and of course a hospital. The guide who took us around was wearing a green army helmet, not an actual relic of the Vietnamese War, (or American War as the Vietnamese call it), but more of a fashion item, that many men wear as part of daily life. They double up as motorcycle helmets since the law about everyone wearing a helmet was passed on 1st December 2007. Some men still wear reproduction green uniforms too. The guide enthusiastically ended the tour with a rendition of "Vietnam, Ho Chi Minh. Vietnam, Ho Chi Minh" The old war song about the leader, now the National Anthem, was as popular here as it ever was. The group were turning out to be OK, I'd had a couple of stupid questions, the first as we were on the boat, slowly swinging on the anchor. One of the girls asked, as the sun went down between the karst islands what direction we were facing. We'll that was changing all the time, but the sun was going down as normal in the West. Then, when we were taking then hike, somebody else asked how high above sea level we were, so I just pointed.

We were back at the hotel by 1pm. This is when Mr Hai invited Ching and me out for a drink. It was 'Tet', we could not refuse. It is not as if there was anything else open on the island anyway and the weather was far too cold for beach. So off we went to see Mr Hai's friend "Hong" at his house where we ate a hotpot of seafood washed down with an unhealthy amount of rice wine. I remember my Tour Leader friend Philip telling me about how he was invited around to Mr Hais house for a few days and ended up running away because it was just too much drinking. He had also thought for the six months that he was doing trips in Vietnam, that the number four in Vietnamese was pronounced Yo! The reason for this being that every time we drink we say 'mot, hai, ba, yo!'. Which is actually "one, two three, yo!" and the number four doesn't get a mention. He'd spent so much of his time with Mr Hai, that he was still asking for "yo bus tickets", or "yo rooms" in the hotel. A couple of hours of this and we tried to leave, but the other Mr Hong (there was two of them, or were we seeing double) was not having it until we went to drink at his house, which we did. We entered the small one room house and drank, toasting each other as his wife and child huddled under the blankets of the bed in the living room. Mr Hai told me that Tet is the time of the year that your wife can not tell you what to do, so you can drink when you want. Tet celebrations last for two weeks in this part of Vietnam. Mr Hai is divorced. I could see a pattern here. In the afternoon I managed an hours sleep and met the group on the roof top terrace for sunset. Then Mr Hai had us out drinking at his house, with his sister cooking hot pot for us and half a dozen friends around for dinner. Ching and I were honoured guests again and utterly legless by the time we left.

Then it was North to the border and into China. The border here doesn't see many foreigners and the guards eye us suspiciously and enjoy trying to give us orders and point at where we should be filling in arrival cards and queuing. They don't like me talking to the group, they can't speak any English. The inspector will take a lot of time inspecting the pages of each passport, even looking at the stitching of the pages. Someone is always brought out of line and their bag searched with an attempt of questioning. At the end of the stamping in procedure, as you stand in front of the desk awaiting the return of your passport, you notice that three lights spark up on a machine on the counter. It is an electronic satisfaction survey. "Are you satisfied with our service?" reads the question. There are three cartoon faces, one happy, one with a straight mouth and one unhappy face. You have to select a face and press a button. Would anyone dare to press the unhappy face? Would there be a trap door mechanism and down you would go to the security dungeon. I wasn't going to find out, happy face it was again. We were in China and it seemed that the weather was improving all the time. We were lucky. Our stay at Butterfly Valley allowed us to complete the hike, with Grass as our guide this time. The hike took us less than three hours and we passed the red maple trees, though most of their leaves had been shed. Grass told me that most people would take twice as long to do the trek, even that most people never completed it and turned back as there was no signpost or map to follow. I promised that I would return with some paint and mark out the trail.

We went on to Liuzhou and managed to find ourselves in the backstreets around the market with the locals, having a beer as dozens of them played mah-jong in a roadside cafe. Having Keith and Mike on the trip was good as it got me out and trying more things than I would with the usual, less adventurous groups. We tried local snacks from the market, a Chinese pancake with spring onion, deep fried pork dumplings, fruits such as mango stein and permission. We saw how people amused themselves in semi legal mah-jong gambling dens as they all stared at us. We were the only foreigners that they had seen. In Chen Yang, during our walk through the villages, I noticed that the Old Building in Da Village was no longer there and the square in front of the drum tower enlarged. Tim told me that the building had been removed and would be placed somewhere else. So much for the restoration fund that I had contributed to. So much for the Chinese attitude towards anything old when it could be "improved". The dirt road that I had walked on through the town only one month earlier was now stone block paving. Another improvement, no doubt.

In Long Ji we were met by Farmer Tang who told me of some of the developments over the winter. The Li Qing guest house had purchased a generator when the electricity lines had come down and he assured me that we could have heating in the rooms now. Unfortunately, the only heating was the metal bowl with charcoal as the generator was only hooked up to the lighting. Farmer Tang also told me that the Guest House in Da Zai had no electricity and that the last group that went there complained about the service and the price of the food. He didn't want to use the place and when the group overheard our conversation, they started discussing the possibility of hiking all the way from Ping An to Da Zai and back again. In some ways I am glad that they had considered this. When we did the hike to Da Zai, we found the entire village "closed". No one was around, no guest houses open and nowhere to buy something to eat. Our only solution was to get the bus back to Ping An again. This became a bit of an issue. Farmer Tangs bus driver friend would not go all the way to Ping An. There had been some sort of dispute between bus drivers taking people on other bus drivers routs. Our bus driver would only take us to the bottom of the hill. We could either have a long wait, or maybe even there would be no bus to pick us up, or we could try and hike the hill straight away. Farmer Tang told me that when our tour company first stayed in Ping An, it was before there was a road there and the groups had to hike up to the guest house. I had a young fit group. "How long should it take" I asked farmer Tang. "To the car park, maybe one hour, then to the guest house, another twenty minutes" came the precise reply. We completed the whole climb in just over an hour and were warmly welcomed back by Yi Ben and his family. I'm sure the food here just gets better and better.

In Yangshou, we had the usual fun in and around the town, getting involved in the backpacker vibe and ending up in a late night bar on West Street. On their free day, my group who had been refusing to spend anything more than the bare minimum on food, or tip guides anything more than the tatty change in their pockets still took to the West Street shops. Here, they were haggling for all they were worth and one of the group came away with a mah-jong game, a souvenir of my teaching them how to play. However, they had been sold the carved bone set, not the plastic one. For the first time ever, the tables had been turned on the stall-holder, or rather, the unfortunate assistant. So often in the past people have walked away, only to feel "ripped off". I have even seen girls returning to clothes stalls, with other members of the group, complaining that "They got it for fifty Yuan, but I paid one hundred". This time, the shop assistant was trying to get my group to give the bone mah-jong game back, as it cost far more than she had sold it for, thinking that it was an inferior plastic model. They stuck to their guns, with only one problem. You can't take bone back into Australia. I had other groups who knew this and had always got the Chinese stall holders puzzled about them not wanting the "superior" bone in favour of the plastic. These, guys decided that they would risk it anyway, no moral dilemma for them. I don't get involved with the shopping. When I walk by with the local guides, I can overhear the stall holders saying to them that they should get our groups to buy, so they will get a commission. When the guide says that they want the correct price, the seller was asking "why do you help these foreigners, are you not Chinese?" It is impossible for the local guides to refuse; it will look like they are snubbing the shop holders if they don't play along. After my many trips to Yangshuo, I was now being asked if I too would get my groups to buy from certain shops. As I said, I didn't want to get involved.

Yangshuo is where we left Keith. I introduced him to my co-Tour Leader and good friend Tang, who was to be his next leader. She was in Yangshuo visiting her family for Chinese New Year then was off to Hong Kong to start the trip that Keith would join. Then, for the rest of us it was the overnight train to Shenzhen and over the border to Hong Kong for our last group diner.

I had to get a visa for China here again. Unfortunately, getting multi entry visas for more than three months is becoming impossible. It's something to do with the government not wanting too many westerners just turning up for the Olympics and causing havoc with the hotels and transport. So, now I would have to renew the visa every third trip so I would have to plan my time wisely in 2008. I spent one extra night in Hong Kong and the newly arrived Tang was gracious enough to let me share in the twin room. We had quite a long conversation into the night. We talked about family life in Yangshuo. Her mother was now blind and of a very different farming generation. She could not understand how her daughter had first gone to work in M.C. Blues bar as a waitress, serving foreigners, then went to the cooking school, then became a manager there then left this amazingly good job to be a Tour Leader. Tradition implied that

Tang should be at home and married. I asked about boyfriends, she said that she had one love, but it was unrequited, he had gone on to marry someone else, he was no good anyway, a play-boy. I asked what she thought about the western men on her trips, many gave her a lot of attention as they do with all the Chinese girl Tour Leaders. She said that she could never marry a foreigner it just would not be accepted. She saw her life as an amazing experience for a farm girl from Yangshuo, she would continue as a Tour Leader, maybe for that year, then think about returning to Yangshuo and setting up some sort of business. I was grateful for this insight into Chinese life and culture, I was learning all the time. I was also grateful as this saved me a hefty accommodation bill. This was definitely needed, because the last group, although a very good group who had definitely enjoyed the trip, had not tipped. This was the first time that I had actually received nothing at all from a group. I already had the inkling that they were not going to tip, but the annoying thing for me from a financial point of view was that my travels in South East Asia and my passport renewal had cost me money and I had not earned anything for that month. I also now had a week off before my next trip and I was going to stay in the apartment in Shekou. This also meant spending, whilst not earning and Shekou is the sort of place where you have to spend money in order to avoid going stir crazy. On my last night in Hong Kong I met up with the last two remaining passengers in Murphy's Bar and watched the Rovers stuff Bolton 4-1, the most flattering of score-lines. Then the following day, I picked up my new, Chinese, three month, multi entry visa and crossed over to Shekou.

I had received a letter from my dad at The West Hotel. Since I had begun my life as a Tour Leader, I had found it difficult to keep in contact with my family. Most of my friends have email and over the last few months Facebook had taken the internet by storm. No one but a couple of Americans knew what it was on my first "training" trip in March 2007, now everyone had an account and so did I. On my last visit to see my mum in Clitheroe, she had produced a lap top that she had purchased at some electronics store in Blackburn, for some astronomical fee. She had little idea about what it was and said to me, "make it work". After a few choice magic words I asked if she had bought a router, for the internet. She hadn't. The man in the electronics shop in Blackburn was going to make even more money out of my mum, but at least he set up the internet for her over the following months. We then began an infrequent conversation over Hotmail. With my dad, things were a little different. Technology has passed him by. He admits to being "bad on the phone" yelling into it and nodding instead of speaking, even before he started going deaf. If I call him, he knows that it is me, but can't get the gist of what I am saying. "I'm in Xi'an" I would tell him "I've just been to the Terracotta Warriors". "You've been to see the Rovers?" my dad would yell back at me, confused as to where I was, or why I hadn't told him that I was back in London. "Send me a picture postcard of where you've been" he wold always ask me. Throughout my travels over the previous twenty years I had sent postcards from all over the globe. He had kept them all and often, when I visited him, he would get them out and read them back to me along with other collected family memorabilia.

There are not so many postcards in China, like so many other things it is a "westerners on holidays of yesteryear" sort of thing. Apart from the tourist sites around Beijing and Xi'an or Hong Kong, postcards were in short supply. I'd written to my dad in the first month telling him as much, along with all the other new and exciting things I was doing. Then told him that the only way that he could get in touch with me was so send a letter to the Travel Company Office in the Hotel in Beijing where we started and finished most trips. Every six weeks or so, I'd be passing through and if we synchronised things, I'd be able to pick up his letter and reply to it. Now that I was working the Hong Kong to Hanoi route, I'd let him know that he had to send letters to the West Hotel, rather than the one in Beijing. This way I would get updates from him about his health, his wife, their dogs, the relatives that I'd not seen in twenty years then on about the state of the Blackburn economy and the Rovers. I would always be asked if I had been in touch with my brother, who also lives in the north of England, but is an infrequent visitor to either of my parents. Then he would marvel at what I was doing, though he didn't really understand my Tour Leading job, then tell me not to drink too much, then ask when I was going to settle down. My replies at first were a painstaking attempt to explain why everything was so different in China compared to Blackburn. Things in London are different enough from Blackburn as I remember my dad asking me about everyone playing "bar skittles" in the pubs as opposed to darts, then saying "though I think it's all wine bars now". He had visited London once, for the 1960 F.A. Cup final and decided never to go back because "folk don't stop when they see you want to cross the road". He and my granddad had been stranded on the wrong side of Wembley Way for some inordinate amount of time whilst trying to get to the football match. During my eighteen year tenure in London, it had never crossed dads mind to visit. As he was "bad on the phone" I had to do all the calling too. "I never know when you are in" came an excuse one time when I asked him why he hadn't called since Boxing Day 1995, because on that day in question, I had not picked up the phone.

So, I started writing him letters. Then one time during my second trip I was on the computer, sending emails to my friends and I hit upon an idea. I cut and paste all the essential details from the emails to my friends into one long story of what I had been up to for the previous month. After a little editing, I printed it out and posted it to my dad. I also decided to send this long account of my adventures in China to all my friends on Hotmail. I thought, "This will be a good way of keeping in touch" and sure enough, people replied to it. I titled the email "The Essence of China" after the trip that I had been doing. The next month I produced another one and then another whilst people were replying and saying "you should write a book". A book, a "real book" would take a lot more than just the musings and accounts of me "Flying by the seat of my pants" as I took tours around China.

I think I have said that Shekou was a nice surprise to what I thought it would be when I first went there. By my fifth visit, knowing that there would be no-one else around for a week, it had lost its appeal. A couple of nights in the Irish bar with Mind the Gap would be the only things to occupy a whole week off. I got to the apartment and it resembled a student house. Pizza box's everywhere, nothing was clean, be it the kitchen, or the used laundry. The computer didn't work. The T.V. was only useful as a DVD player and most of the DVD's didn't work. This was worse than I'd imagined. I thought to myself, that if I had known that it would be this bad, I would have organised going back up to Yangshuo, or somewhere. Then I wondered what I would gain, or lose, by doing that. I needed a plan for how to make use of my time so I went down to the place that Mill had told me did Mandarin lessons and booked a course. This cost me somewhere in the region of $600, well, it was either that, or I would just fritter it away on too many late nights and excesses. The DVD of the first two seasons of the T.V. series 'Lost' also worked. So there you have it. I spent my days taking Mandarin classes, then in the evening, a little homework and 'Lost'.

The only visitor in a week was Cherie, a Chinese Tour Leader who I'd met once before and who stayed just one night and we had the briefest of conversations about the leading life. She brought me up to date with the new management of Tracey and Max and the demise of Bruce. Max had been brought in with a great fanfare, he had been a Tour Leader a few years earlier and after a stint back in Australia and doing some work on the Commonwealth Games he had been welcomed back with open arms as the new manager for China with Tracey taking over the day to day operations. There was a new office, new staff being recruited. Cherie's' boyfriend Tony had moved over from Tour Leader to be a manager with our main competitor tour company in China. Things were not going as she had hoped in their relationship. Like most western men, he was holding off on the idea of marriage and she had got upset at the last night dinner with her group and spent $1500 Hong Kong and got so drunk that she woke up in one of the passenger's rooms. She was making a vow of not drinking any more and turning vegetarian. She thought that she had to make some sort of sacrifice to stop all the bad things happening in her life, her mum was also ill and even thought she was one of the most westernised Chinese that I had met, she was still reverting to the traditional ways. I'd been pretty much, literally "out of the loop" down here on the Hanoi to Hong Kong trips. For the rest of the week, my routine kept me out of the bars for at least half of the time. I was thankful to get back to work again.

48. Lost on an Island 08/03 (Shekou)

Somewhat lost
Brought here by fate
Trying to master my destiny
With choices and actions

Somewhat lost
Is it all too late
Trying to move things my way
And not just move in reaction

Lost in this island
Of ex pats and western food
And girly bars to early hours
The crush of stars inside my head
The fierce light that blurs and blanks out
Everything else is just shadows off to the side
And I need the fix that the night time provides
In my frustration in being trapped here
I'll try to fill the emptiness with another night of beer
And rock tunes in a fake Irish bar
Then the girls that I buy drinks for
And the three in a bed suggestions
And all the other temptations
Won't get that far

For a moment I thought I was lost
On an Island and trapped between sea sand and the hill
In the middle of the stairway to heaven
In the middle of Freebird I was standing still

49. Traveller

(A) 25/03/08 Long Ji

Early misty morning
And the daylight wakes me gently
Where have I been dreaming
Am I home again, am I far away?
Wrapped in another bed again
Another new room, another new day
Another new year
Time to get up and be back on my way

A new day, like a mountain view
So many possibilities under a clear sky
Places to visit and things to do
The old and the new, all of this my
land of golden opportunities
I swing my backpack on and get
that feeling that all I want to be
Is back on the road to places I've not been yet

(B) 19/03/08 Ha Long Bay

Another city goes by in the night
Sometimes I see those city lights
And dream of a place called home
But it's a place I've never known
As I travel on and on
In the morning it's long gone
Another dream of a fantasy
Another place I'll never be

From satellite to satellite
Mountainside to mountainside
City to city and every country
The horizons beyond the endless sea
To the island of childhood adventures
The dusty atlas and a map of hidden treasures
I have all this and more
I travel on, the traveller

(C) 05/04/08

Another letting go of dreams
Another early morning
Somehow, they're never quite the same
As I look in the mirror to shave

Sometimes, there's no mirror
and it's all done by feeling
Five senses all alive on a razor blade
Five senses reeling

A girl steps from between the wooden houses,
Stands in the alley that leads to the rice terraces
Shouts to her family, then bursts into a song
Picks up a child, takes it to where it belongs

This most impossible collage
Life in a picture, more than just an image
As the sound of morning
Echoes of the village awakening

From the fire cracker welcome to the rice wine and singing
Right through to these colours of morning
And out across the country, with a new day
Walking on the hillside pathway

Past the new rice being planted
By the family, knee high in paddy mud
Until I rest in the village, the first day in the sun
And watch a spiders web being spun.

My next group of six had already been travelling with Tour Leader Janie from Beijing to Hong Kong. I'd been in touch with her over the previous two weeks because one of the group, Zeb, didn't have a visa with entry back into China and she had been running around trying to get one on the one spare day in Hong Kong. Two others didn't have Vietnam visas. They were all young and fun and running around having a great time. So much so that when I had the group meeting only three of them turned up. Two of the others were in Macao doing a Bungie Jump. The sixth member of the group had now decided to drop out and would join us in Hanoi. The group was Sarah and Helga, both 19 and from Norway. Zeb, 23 and a British Arab, Mike 22 from England and Alan 28 from Australia. I met up with Janie and had dinner. She talked about her time off in the States, her holiday in India with Eugenie which had not gone according to plan because they are a bit like chalk and cheese, then the usual moans about how bad the Tour Company organisation is. I met the remainder of the group in Murphey's bar at around 10:30 and briefed them about the following day. We didn't have a proper welcome meeting, Janie just handed me their details and paperwork. Only when I took a look at Mike and Alan passports did I see that Alan's visa for Vietnam started the day after we were supposed to cross the border and Mike still didn't even have a visa. The Norwegian girls didn't need a Vietnam visa, Zeb had only just got his China visa an hour or so earlier on express delivery. I told Alan we could get a visa in Kunming through my contact Pauline at the Camellia hotel. This was the craziest start to any trip that I had done so far. I also had visa problems myself. The Chinese government were becoming concerned about the possible influx of foreigners for the Beijing Olympics, so would only issue three or six month multi entry visas which meant that I would have to leave the country every thirty days. This would be OK whilst I was doing Hong Kong to Hanoi trips, but what if my trip ended in Beijing? I'm all for travelling and visiting other countries but had never really considered twenty-four hour stopovers in Seoul or Tokyo as the way to see the world. There was also the added expense to consider.

My new trip was almost underway but there was already going to be a slight delay. Zeb had not collected his laundry and we would have to wait for this in the morning. No real problem, I thought that we would still have time to spare before we had to catch our bus. In the morning the launderette opened before 8am, but Zebs clothes were not there. In the confusion of the previous day, no one had the correct ticket and his clothes were no longer in the shop. They were somewhere in Hong Kong being tried on by some bemused Chinaman. We just had to leave, with Zeb wearing the only clothes he had and caught the plane back into the wintery mountains of Guiyang.

This was another excellent group. Nothing much seemed to faze them and they were willing to join in with the drinking and dancing. On our first day's hike with Fox to the Miao village, we had to follow the route of a new road that was under construction. This started off OK, but before long we had to walk along hillsides that dropped into sheer cuttings. Then the trail completely ran out and we had to follow the river. Then we had to cross the river. This hike was becoming more and more like an orienteering experience. For the first river crossing we managed to put some tree trunks across the stream. Our second and third crossings were more difficult and we had to enlist the help of a local who placed stones and logs across the river and waded in to help us cross from one man made islet to another. The four hour trek was turning into a six hour endurance test by the time it started raining. Somehow, Fox managed to find a mini-van in a hamlet called Gan Rong, and as it had all 'gone wrong' we paid to be transported to the village of Xi Jiang.

The Li Family homestay in Xi Jiang was even better than the last time. We were met with fire crackers, rice wine and singing and for the rest of the night I don't think our rice wine cups were empty for more than a minute. The local ladies sang, we drank, they sang again, we drank again. At some point in the evening, we went out to the village square to watch the cultural show. This was a bigger version of the singing and dancing that had been performed for us on out last visit. We were also very drunk at this point and for some reason, we performed the 'Macarena' as our "gift song and dance" for the whole village and on-looking Chinese tourists. Then we finished with a rendition of "New York New York" before heading back to the Li Family guesthouse and the last rounds of beer and rice wine.

The trek the day after was a killer and we arrived in the next village around mid afternoon. This was a new part of the trip as the groups had complained about the stay in Ao Chang because the hotel was so bad and the village had little to offer tourists. Oddly enough, this place was even more basic. There was a shop, a basketball hoop and a derelict school amongst the twenty or so wooden houses. Our homestays were two or three of these houses, a three room affair of kitchen, living room and a bedroom. There was no toilet; there wasn't even any running water in the village. Out at the back of the house was a midden heap and a pig. The pig watched as you performed your bodily functions and in so doing, provided the pig with his next meal. How the Norwegian girls screamed. Some of our group would be staying with other families around the village, in spare rooms with piles of grain in the corner. Our hosts cooked up dinner and out came a teapot containing rice wine. There was nothing else for it, alcohol has an amazing effect of making you forget your surroundings and before long we were toasting our hosts and the obligatory household picture of Chairman Mao before the singing started. Fox and our hosts were eager to entertain, which got us more involved, to the point that we were singing Bohemian Rhapsody to the complete astonishment of our Chinese hosts.

It was hard leaving Fox and the wonderful families that we'd met, but the next stop was Kunming. This is where Mike had to get a visa to travel into Vietnam. Alan had decided to stop overnight on the border at He Kou before re-joining the group once his visa became active. Zeb had had so many problems already that he never showed me his passport. Obviously, he had the correct visa, didn't he? Kunming was a well-deserved break. It was around about this time that I'd got another email from my friend in London Estelle. She'd been talking about travelling the world for the past year and had been trying to convince some of the rest of her gang to come too. This just hadn't materialised. But now, she'd been offered voluntary redundancy, with a cash pay off. She asked me about coming to China and I said it was a fantastic idea. I did a bit of an explanation as to what my trip schedule and she'd looked up the details and had decided that she wanted to come. My next trip was to be the Hanoi to Beijing active trip, climbing three mountains in three weeks among other things. Estelle hasn't really travelled and a visit to China would be both a culture shock and a physical challenge for a novice traveller. But she said she was up for it. I'd not had a new schedule from the office for over a month, so I thought I'd better get in touch with them to see if there had been any changes. I was really looking forward to doing the new trip, to leaving the Vietnam trips behind and getting back into China proper. It was after all, the reason why I'd applied for the job and I really needed to be able to practice my Mandarin and take some lessons up in Beijing.

In Kunming we tried the Half Past Eight nightclub. This was a little different than my other nightclub experience. It was more like an auditorium, with a stage. The host and hostess did their thing, like 1970's British T.V. or a night at the Butlins' Pig and Whistle. Then out came the performers. First of all there were acrobats. A slow start, but a quality performance. The next group was a Shaolin Monk performance, complete with stone slab breaking, bending spears with the point on a monks throat. There were tumbles and leaps and all choreographed with the precision of the best Beijing or Shanghai shows. Then came my favourite. A fifty-something year old rocker, with long shaggy permed hair and well-worn jeans took to the stage. There was no backing band, but he belted out a Chinese rock classic to the accompaniment of some piped music and the clapping of the "plastic hands" that we'd been given. Then came another song, in which there was an instrumental break. As the fake guitar solo took off, he got a bottle of Budwiser from someone in the crowd and downed it. The best bit about this was the way he held the bottle way above his head to let it pour like a waterfall into his mouth and down his throat. He drained the bottle and went straight into the next verse. Needless to say, we were all very impressed. The crowd clapped their plastic hands and shouted encouragement and there was an extended applause at the end. So then he launched into his third song and did the bottle draining trick again. Then did it again on his fourth and fifth songs. A true performer and even though the songs were predictably awful, he carried them all off and gave 100%. He left the stage pissed and was replaced by a Brazilian Carnival. All costumes and Chinese faces that didn't really go together, but they were having fun and they got the audience up on stage to dance with them. Our western group was never going to avoid the spotlight and before long we were up there dancing in-front of hundreds of Chinese in a nightclub in Kunming. What an excellent last night in China.

The next day should have been straight forward. An eleven hour bus journey to the border. Then I took Alan to the Ming Feng Hotel, which I had booked for him for the night. I gave him all the info about crossing the border the following morning and left him top it. Back with my group and a few westerners hanging on, I rang to get a bus to take us from the Vietnamese side of the border up to Sapa. This was all going to plan. Then Zeb got to the checkpoint. They wouldn't let him through. After all we had said, done and been through, he had never checked his visa dates. The Vietnam visa he had was not valid for entry for another four days. He looked like the world had just ended for him there and then. There was little that I could do. I told him to go and find Alan at the Ming Feng hotel and try and get a visa to enter the following day. I had met a guy on the border called Li from the Sunshine Hotel on my first trip, who said that he could get visas issued in a day. I had his phone number, I told Zeb to try and track him down. That was his only option. Otherwise he was staying in He kou for four days. The rest of us crossed and we all got my tour bus up to Sapa and the Mountain View Hotel where we were welcomed with smiles and some of the most elegantly decorated rooms on any trip, wooden four-poster beds and masses of netting. We went for pizza and wondered how the two boys were coping across the border.

The next day was a free day. Alan joined us at around 10am and said that Zeb would have a visa by 6pm. I got onto internet and found that my manager in Beijing Tracey had emailed me to say that because of the Chinese visa restrictions, with foreigners finding it increasingly difficult to get a visa, let alone a multi-entry; I would have to do another Hanoi to Hong Kong trip, starting in three days' time. This was a complete blow. Estelle was in the process of booking onto the trip that I was no longer doing. I was not going to have any time off, in fact, the next trip started on the same day that this one finished, giving me no rest or preparation time. Then I found out that the trip hadn't even been booked. That meant no hotels; no transport and I had a group of eight arriving in a couple of days' time. I rang the Victory hotel and explained my predicament. I couldn't even do a booking form because I need a computer with Excell and there aren't any in Sapa. I got in touch with the Beijing office and asked Tracey and Li for help. There wasn't anything else that I could do. I was pissed off, big time.

I was less than enthusiastic about the hike to the homestay the following day. Too much on my mind. We had a new guide 'Sho' a Black H'mong girl in traditional clothing, just as 'Doung' had been on the previous trip. Show was a far better guide though, lots of snippets of information and she genuinely seemed happy to be with us. It certainly helps when you have such a fun group. We didn't mind the mud or the slippery slopes. We got to the homestay and didn't complain that we would all be sleeping on the floor in one long line. Sho cooked a good dinner and out came the rice wine again and she taught us a new card game where the loser had the forfeit of drinking a shot of rice wine or singing a song. There was a lot of very drunk singing again that night. The following days hike back was a real struggle and the Norwegian girls opted to get a moto back up to the top of the hill. I wish I could have done the same. Then it was back to Sapa for a shower and some food before getting the overnight train back to Hanoi again.

My Tour Company have made things difficult here. Instead of us staying at the Victory hotel, which is a short walk from the train station, we now stay at the Sunflower, located a couple of K's away in the Old Quarter. We arrive at 5am and what little transport there is at that time is three times the price that it should be. I had a group of tired, frustrated people hanging around the train station car park, being hassled by all the locals whilst I went off in search of a mini bus. Splitting the group and getting three taxis to take us to the hotel would open up a whole new can of worms. I was not in the mood for protracted haggling and the group didn't want to listen to my negotiating skills, so we squeezed, somewhat uncomfortably into the only vehicle that would take us for a half reasonable price. The Sunflower hotel was in darkness when we arrived and I had to wake the door man who was sleeping in the lobby. This was to be expected, all hotels have the security guard asleep in the lobby, along with a couple of motorcycles. He didn't really understand what was going on, but I got enough rooms for all of us and we all got a couple more hours sleep. I arranged to meet the group at 11am. Before this I went in search of internet and spent a couple of hours getting my trip report out of the way. Then we did brunch and a walk around the Old Quarter. Most of the group wanted to go to Cat Ba Island after their trip had finished, so I phoned Mr Hai, who said he could meet everybody the following morning and take them over. Then, I spent a couple of hours on my accounts before we went out for Dinner. We went to beer hoi corner until it closed and rounded off the night in Hair of the Dog, in traditional style, singing and dancing through to 3am. I was woken at 8am by Mr Hai and I hurried the group out of bed and said goodbye to them. I would be seeing them again on Cat Ba when I took my next group over there in a couple of days. Rather than going back to bed, I got a moto over to the Victory and spent the following hours until I could check in doing my accounts. Whilst I was doing this, two gorgeous girls came up to me and asked if I was the Tour Leader for the Hanoi to Hong Kong trip? I said that I would be at 6pm. They said that they had a slight problem. They didn't have a visa for China. I hadn't even finished my last trip and I was having problems with my next one. The hotel said that they could sort out visas and send the passports on to Lang Son where I would collect them in three days time. At some point in the early afternoon I got a room and had a couple of hours sleep.

So my next group was an interesting mix of four Norwegian girls travelling in pairs. Pam, 43 from Australia (independant female traveller type). Alice from Liverpool (on the way to becomming an independant female traveller type) and Frances and Nigel, mother and son. Nigel was 18, had been studying Chinese and was over on the trip in order to practice. Luckily, Frances had travelled extensively in the past. The four girls were absolute stunners. With every move they seemed to burst further out of their bras and it was difficult for me to concentrate on the meeting as they started to chat and ask each other questions. Hannah and Corina travelled together, as did Carolina and Elsa. I don't think they were quite prepared for China, but that is the case for most groups and at least the weather had improved.

If anything, this was a straightforward trip. The pity was that at the beginning I was still so tired from the last one and not focused on this one at all. I still had bookings to confirm and guides to organise and I had done no preparation for the trip. I made my first mistake on the boat, not going through the safety drill or looking for the life vests. That night there was a storm that could have got much worse. The weather in Cat Ba hindered most of the activities, but the girls were on a budget anyway. We met my last group on Cat Ba and had a good night on the jugs of beer hoi. At Lang Son, Hannah and Corinas passports and visas were waiting, as the hotel had organised. We crossed the following morning and butterfly valley was the same beautiful slice of paradise as it always is, though still a little cold. Once back on the Chinese mobile phone network I contacted Farmer Tang and the other Chinese contacts to confirm bookings. Farmer Tang said that he couldn't guide me this time, but I tried Monkey Jane to see if she had any suggestions and she actually agreed to guide me herself. This could definately be fun. I also got a call from Amy. She was full of nerves about her "training week" in Beijing. It was the first time that she had visited the capital, or just about anywhere outside of Sichuan Province. She was asking me what would happen? Was her English good enough? What if she didn't pass? I had no worries about her at all. I knew that she was going to wow the trainers and I was only disappointed that I was going to be still in Southern China, instead of being involved in the training and all the fun and games that would be going on in Beijing. I had hoped that I might get someone to train too, it would add another aspect to the job and I had started to feel a bit isolated down on the Hanoi to Hong Kong loop. I wanted to get back to China and Beijing.

I had my second mistake when leaving Butterfly Valley. Grass had not come to collect the payment, so I paid the guest house directly. I arranged a bus for the morning and all was going well, but Grass wasn't at Nin Ming bus station, so I purchased the tickets to Nan Jing and sent everybody off to the supermarket with instructions to be back on the bus in 20 minutes. Then Grass' husband Mr Wu arrived. He wanted me to give him the payment that I'd already given to the guest house. There was a lot of confusion and a phone call to Grass. It was now time for the bus to set off and the assistant was pushing me on board. I finally sorted the payment problem and got on the bus. As I went to my seat the bus started moving off. Then Pam said that we were not all on the bus. Hannah and Corina were still out shopping somewhere. I did a quick explanation (my Mandarin improves rapidly when there is a possible disaster) but the bus driver was not letting me get off the bus to look for them.

Chinese busses go on time, and as the bus pulled away again we were very lucky that the girls were just around the corner and running towards us.

Liuzhou and Chen Yang were straight forward as was the bus to Long Ji. We arrived at 11am, but Monkey Jane had called to say she would be late and was bringing someone along with her. She arrived at 1pm with Heinz, who was an interesting bloke in his early 20's and added more than he took from the group. It got everybody talking and drinking again at Ping An and Jane proved that she was fun and an excellent guide. She is from a farming background and her local knowledge was every bit as good but completely different from Farmer Tangs.

A relative of Monkey Jane's had recently died, so when the girls saw the grave-stones in the hillsides, Jane became very articulate about the funeral ceremony. After someone was buried, you would wait for three years, then dig up the bones again, clean them and install them in the final resting place. This would often be the place with the best view over the valley. I had read articles recently that had talked of villages where there was an underhand dispute over who had the right to bury their ancestors in the best places. It seems that in one village, there had been a plague and mis-fortune on one of the families and the village elders had only got to the bottom of the problem when they discovered that one of their ancestors had been removed from his final resting place. Another family had done this, in order to give their ancestor a more privileged position in the afterlife. This is a heinous crime and no one would admit to it, or the whereabouts of the previous occupant of the best tomb in the village. Jane also said that if a son had died before his parents, he would not be able to be buried until his parents died. This is because a child would only die before a parent if an evil spirit had been at work. The coffin of the son would not be allowed to enter the house of his parents for the funeral ceremony in case the spirit decided to move into the hose and haunt the parents. I had seen another side to Jane. For all her westernisation and modern girl outlook, she was still very superstitious; she believed everything that she was telling us.

Yangshuo was its familiar self and I did the usual rounds. We had a good first night and got to a club on West Street, but that was the highlight, it was still cold and there were few people in town. Then it was Hong Kong. We didn't dine at Blues on the Bay. A couple of the girls said that their budget would not stretch to it, so I had three curry's in three days.

There had been a change with the apartment over the last four weeks. There had been a management decision. The Shekou apartment had gone and instead there was to be a new one located on Lantau Island in Hong Kong. Bruce was sorting this out. He was also in town and we arranged to meet up in Murphy's for Sunday lunch and go to the new apartment in Tung Chung. When we got there it was far from ready. We scouted the area to check out the facilities which we were pleasantly surprised with and stayed the night in the unfurnished apartment. In the morning I went back to The West. My tour company were going to pay for the next two nights there. Bruce did some sorting out and got back around 7pm when we met a contact of his who took us to dinner. This was another wonderful experience that I never would have had on my own. We went to a Taiwan noodle bar, then a place that specialises in deserts. Bruce left early the following morning with a request that I register at the apartment complex and get some keys cut. That gave me something useful to do in the day. I had also been told that Lyn was arriving from the States, so I was looking forward to a good night out.

When Lyn arrived, she said she'd been ill and wasn't going out. So we just did some catching up as I had dinner. She had spent much of the previous season doing the Hanoi to Hong Kong trips and was asking about the Wu family in Chenyang, she said it was her favourite place. Then asked about the Li's in Xi Jiang and Fox, who she thought had a thing for her. Then she recounted a story of her falling into a rice paddy. "I must be the most unlikely person for this job" she said. I have no sense of balance, so I'm always falling over when I am trekking. Luckily, I'm always at the back of the group, so no-body ever sees me, but this time I fell head first into a rice paddy and my group and Fox had to come back and rescue me." She continued "I have no sense of direction; I even got lost and drove up the wrong side of a free-way when I got home". On her trip back to the U.S. she had also forgotten about the International Date Line, so had arrived a day earlier than her mum had expected, so hadn't been met at the airport. I'm glad that she could tell me these stories and laugh at herself, just like I had so many stories of stupid situations and near scrapes to tell her too. The following day she decided to head off to Shenzhen and Beijing rather than have another night in Hong Kong. She said that she would not be able to enjoy herself, being prepared and professional for her next trip, so it was better to leave. A few hours later I got a phone call from her. She was at Shenzhen Airport but her company credit card had been suspended during her time off, which she knew nothing about and would not be accepted so she couldn't fly. Also, she couldn't get any cash out. She was stuck there. I was going to arrive at the airport following day, to fly to Guiyang with my new group and I was the only person who could lend her the money for her flight.

So I met my next group. A family of three with a fourteen year old daughter was the surprise package this time. The other surprise was that although all were on British passports, Liz (mum, married to Anthony, daughter Ann) was born in the US and my visible shock at her accent didn't go down well. There were two best friends in their late 20's, Mike and Tim, both up for the trip. I had three from the attached Roam China trip that had come from Beijing to Hong Kong with another Tour Leader. Alison and Eion were very much in the "Roam Trip" mould. One was on a gap year after school, the other one on a gap year after Uni'. Then there was Rita. Asian British and another nice surprize. I actually had five well-travelled, capable, educated and interested people in the group. Barristers Tim, Mike and Anthony talked about the law, and the cases that had recently been brought against the British government for the detention without trial of suspects in the wake of our "war on terror". Both could not believe how the British legal system was being manipulated by the politics of the day. I couldn't quite get them to admit that this was the law being used to defend the government, and the ruling classes, as it always had been. We covered a lot of interesting topics on our hikes across southern China.

Being my third trip from Hong Kong to Hanoi, there were no real issues. The weather was generally improving, so that meant we got a couple of excellent days in with the grey ones and the drizzle. The highlight of this trip was the homestay again. After the alcohol frenzy of my last group, I wasn't really expecting too much, but it just so happened to be the 'tomb cleaning ceremony'. This is an auspicious date in the Chinese calendar, calculated to fall on the 15th day after the Spring Equinox. This is when families will get together and pay their respects to their ancestors. This often takes the form of going out into the fields where the graves are situated and having a pick-nic. There they tend and decorate the grave stones with red lucky paper and fake paper money and burn yellow paper or more fake money. Some of this is fake dollar bills, or 100 dollar bills as the bigger the (fake) currency, the more prosperous a ceremony for the ancestor. There were other fake bills with what looked to be a Chinese Emperor on them, but he may also have been Lu, one of the three lucky gods found in Daoism that represents good fortune and which you see in many Chinese and all Vietnamese house altars. Though I couldn't get a satisfactory answer I'm not sure if the farmers knew who he was anyway. Once back home the party would get into full swing with neighbours visiting each other's houses and having a drink. The family next to our homestay were having guests around and we were invited. We were possibly the first westerners that they had seen up close and we were introduced to the whole family including Mr Yellow and Mr Flower (literal translations) who were brothers and their elderly father and mother along with various other relatives. A lot of rice wine was circulated and we all got quite tipsy again.

As the night went on, Grandpa asked how many chickens we had (a quite suitable question in a rural community) but was disappointed that Mike was the only person who replied and that he only had two chickens. We were obviously from very humble families. Other people came and went including a man from a nearby village who was extremely drunk. He got the full welcoming ceremony with the singing and rice wine and still pestered the hosts for more. We asked where he came from and found out that he was probably just doing the rounds in an attempt to get as much free alcohol as possible. As he staggered around, I was told that he came from 'Hong Sing', this took a little while for me to get the joke as they laughed at the drunk from the next village. They had just told me that he had come from Mars. As the night drew to a close, grandpa was refusing to call it a night as grandma looked on scornfully as I passed him another beer. She made it obvious that we had outstayed out welcome, so we departed.

The other highlight of the trip was in Sapa. We had a different guide once again. A Vietnamese lad called Ham, he made the joke "like ham sandwich". He was every bit as fun as Sho, my previous guide and got the group singing and playing games as the rice wine flowed again. This time we rounded off the night by singing karaoke. This was a very strange scene. At around 10pm, already drunk, we walked out of the homestay, through an unlit village to a small bamboo and wood hut. Inside were a couple of locals quietly drinking. The place just about fit us all in and one of the men began to plug in what was to be our karaoke machine and T.V. From behind a wall hanging, a snoozing old lady was woken by our noise and she grudgingly went to a fridge and supplied us with beer. Ham started with what I was now realising were the Vietnamese "favourites". There has been a bit of a time warp in the hit parade over here and "Whoa whoa, yeay yeay. I love you more than I can say" is possibly the most popular song over here. I remember it as a one hit wonder by someone from the sixties. There were some appallingly mushy ballads, such as "My heart will go on" and "Everything I do". At least I could mimic a Bryan Adams voice to that, but there wasn't much in the way of anything more modern, or any good music. I had to settle for "Hey Jude". Once again, the strangest of nights in the most improbable of surroundings amongst the best of new found friends.

As we waited around in Sapa for our bus to Lao Cai and the train to Hanoi, I hovered by the groups of H'mong girls that were playfully trying to sell their home-spun wares along with the manufactured clothes outside our hotel. Listening to them accost the other tourists, then get side tracked with chat about future boyfriends. Then I went to the local market, where no tourists go, among the butchered animal parts that sit on wooden stalls. Then I saw something that I didn't understand and had to go back to ask Ham what was going on. There was a lot of incense and paper burning next to a life size paper motorcycle. Ham told me that this was a funeral. In Vietnamese tradition, when somebody died, they would like to bring all the best things with them, for use in the afterlife. In the old days, there would be paper effigies of horses and water buffalo. These days, the paper representations were of motorcycles and mobile phones.

The trip came to a close in Hanoi again. There were problems with the notoriously bad Sunflower Hotel, meaning that I didn't get a room until mid day. This meant that I spent from 6am until 9am doing my trip report and accounts, so at least I was ahead with the paperwork. The two lads, Mike and Tim were up for a trip to Cat Ba and I had a few days off in between trip, so on the last night we all ended up saying goodbye to the rest of the group and readied ourselves for the next day. We had decided to book on a trip run by the Youth Hostel in Hanoi. The idea of doing the over-night boat with the backpackers from the hostel looked like a fun way to get to Cat Ba. As part of the trip, we went sea kayaking between the karst islands on Ha Long Bay. As one of the few singles on the trip I partnered a red wine drinking, already half plastered Italian semi-retired businessman. At first I thought this was going to be a lot of fun, but then it started to look like we might capsize and drown in

Ha Long Bay. We managed to alter some of the karst scenery by crashing into some of it in our kayak. We annoyed the other boats by crashing into them too. By the evening, we all knew each other pretty well. At least half of the group were up for a drink and a laugh and we ended up singing karaoke again and staying up until midnight, when we got the order from the boat captain "now you sleep". Once on Cat Ba, Mr Hai sorted out transport and accommodation and the rest was easy. The lads filled the next few days with rock-climbing and hiking. I managed to have dinner with Mr Hai, Mr Hai's friends, Mr Hai's family and all the rice wine and squid tentacles and fish heads that I could stomach. I was thankful when he was called away for business because my liver was crying out for a rest. The weather on my last day there had improved to a pleasant 25 degrees, which I soaked up on the beach and swimming in the sea.

I returned to Hanoi a couple of days before the trip started. I had been given a Chinese girl as a trainee called Cindy and wanted to meet up with her. She'd replied to an email but hadn't contacted me since. I checked into the Youth Hostel Dorm, It seemed like the best option at the time. I was just about to take up Jimmys offer (he's one of the staff there) of drinks in the terrace roof bar when Bruce from the office got in touch. He was in town with Cindy and he gave me the address of a restaurant. We all met up and did the introductions and she came across as somebody who I would enjoy the next couple of weeks with, although she had only recently had her first ever alcoholic drink and Bruce said that her limit was only to manage two Gin and Tonics. We'll, training involves everything I suppose and I have the experience of training over 1000 bar staff, so one Chinese girl would be easy. It took a while to find the restaurant that we were looking for. I'd been to Highway 4 once before, around about five years earlier and was happy to be heading off there again because it had a sort of traditional Vietnamese feel to it as you sat on the floor on cushions, even though it was a restaurant chain and you could buy their T-shirts. Admittedly, Hanoi Old Town is a complex network of streets, but when Bruce was going completely the wrong way, I had to point this out. I mentioned that we were in the vicinity of the Sunflower Hotel, the awful one that we now used at the end of the Hong Kong to Hanoi trips. The exact same hotel that Bruce had organised and which everyone was pissed off about because it was so far away from the train station. 'Well," said Bruce. "I've no idea where that is . . . I only went there once, with somebody from the Indo-China office, in a taxi". Another great quote from another great manager.

After dinner I headed back to the hostel and the roof top bar. There were over 30 residents and hangers on getting drunk at a Mexican themed night complete with chilli vodka that made you skull your next bottle of beer just to get rid of the taste. I was quite enjoying the atmosphere, so when Jimmy from reception asked me to help lead the group on to Dragonfly bar, I donned a Mexican hat and along with another hostel staff member headed into the old town. I did actually take a wrong turning and had a dozen people walking into someones living room at one point, but that was only a minor detour. Once at Dragonfly, the nightclub kicked in and the complementary drinks took effect and before I knew it, it was time to go home again. Tomorrow, I would be starting another trip and I would be back on the road.

Chapter 4.

THE PROCESSION OF THE OLYMPIC FLAME

"One's destination is never a place,
but a new way of seeing things."

Henry Miller.

Over the weeks leading up to this trip, I had seen some snippets of international news. I can't remember whether it was in Hong Kong or Hanoi, but certainly not in China. The BBC had shown footage of protests in some of the Tibetan towns across China and also of demonstrations outside Chinese Embassy's across Europe and the world. I'd got talking to some of the local guides in the towns that we visited about it, but they were largely unaware of what was going on. We picked up CCTV9 news in one place. It said that 18 people had been killed in the rioting across Tibet, including 1 policeman. It showed footage of monks smashing shop windows and people running along the streets and hurling stones and having scuffles with the military. My guide, "Fox" had said that there were some very bad people who wanted to cause trouble. That was as far as we got. Whilst in Hong Kong I saw the BBC coverage of the Olympic Torch Relay in London, and the attempted snatch. The China Daily the following day also reported the attempted snatch, but failed to mention what all the fuss was about. I think some Chinese readers actually believed that the Europeans had got so excited about the Beijing Olympic Torch passing through their country that they tried to steal the mighty emblem. There was footage of protestors outside some embassies, with the report that China was putting pressure in the countries in question to protect Chinese embassy employees abroad and to take full measures against those who would disturb their right to go about their lawful business. According to the news, the foreign powers had apologised and would be cracking down on the demonstrators. Elsewhere, there was a report on how much support had being gained from other countries concerning Chinas quelling of the protests in their own countries' Tibet province. A long list of nations, totalling over 100, headed by Russia and Pakistan had come out in support of China dealing with protests within its own boundaries. The Chinese government accused the "Dali Lama Separatist Clique" of stirring up all the trouble inside and outside the country and urged no-one to deal with the "international mischief maker".

I got to the Victory Hotel in Hanoi with the usual hangover from my night out with the hostel crowd. I got to work, printing off some info for the trip before Bruce and Cindy arrived, so at least it didn't look like I was too affected by my night out. Then we spent the next couple of hours producing mini booklets for the trip, full of photocopy maps and information to give to the passengers. Bruce told me that there were going to be proper Tour Company booklets produced for the Vietnam trips, they were supposed to have arrived already, had I not received them? As I'd been doing these trips without any real support for the last 5 months, with little to no information to draw on, it was a bit too little and too late. Cindy took to the prep work well, then before we knew it, it was group meeting time, with introductions and the usual information, but this time with one of my managers assessing me and a trainee monitoring my every move.

So I started off this trip, with the new group asking what was going on in China and me saying that the news on the T.V. that we'd just seen was as much as I could tell them. I might live in China, but that only means that you know less of what is going on in that country than the outside world does. My Chinese trainee Cindy could shed no light on the subject. She was from a farming background, had gone to University in Beijing and had just spent most of the last year back in her provincial capital city working as a translator in an agency. She knew nothing of politics, but thought it was all bad. She thought that people should be happy and whoever was causing all this trouble should stop. The majority of my group was in their 20's and agreed with her.

China has a pretty awful human rights record. Its treatment of Tibet and the Tibetans is also a contentious issue. It's difficult to give a thumbnail sketch of what it's all about. A lot of what has gone on in China gets lost in the detail. There is a lot of political point-scoring on the part of the west. It's difficult for me to have an unbiased view of what goes on here, but if anyone can shed a bit of light on the subject, well, I'll give it a try.

In the second century B.C. the first Tibetan king Nyatri Tsenpo, descended from the sky on a magic chord. In 640 AD, the 33rd king of Tibet, Songtsan Gampo, married a Chinese Princess called Wen Cheng (along with a Nepali princess) in order to placate his more powerful neighbours. The princesses converted the king and with him, the country to Buddhism. From that time onwards, all the kings of Tibet married a Chinese princess. During the Tang Dynasty, in the 8th Century it was acknowledged that the boundaries of China extended beyond modern day Tibet, until military defeat and a peace treaty defined the two countries borders in 821, or 822. The Tibetans see this treaty as underlining their "independence" from China. They also note that although Songsten Gampo married a Chinese princess, he not only had a Nepali wife, but other Tibetan wives and it was these who produced his heirs, not the foreign princesses. The Tibet Empire split into smaller autonomous states from 642, the religious sects became more powerful controlling more land than the old lords.

With the Incorporation of China into the empire of Genghis Khan in the 13th Century, The Tibetan states were also seen as part of this Greater China, and ruled over by the Yuan Dynasty from Beijing. Tibetan Buddhism was in vogue in the Chinese court and the Ming and Qing Dynasties adopted the Tibetan Buddhism tradition as the state religion. The Tibetans rejected the Ming dynasties clams as the rightful successors to the Yuan and therefor rulers of Tibet. They refused to pay tribute, however the Ming sent envoys and influenced the rulers of Tibet and gained what they saw as control over the Tibet region. The Dalai Lama came into being in 1569 when the head of the Gelugpa sect (yellow hats) was invited to the Mongol Empires court and declared the new emperor to be the re-incarnation of the great Khublai Khan, whilst he himself was the reincarnation of the Lama who had converted Kublai Khan to Buddhism. He was then known as the third re-incarnation of the Dalai Lama or "ocean of wisdom". The fourth re-incarnation of the Dalai Lama was the grandson of the Mongolian Emperor and in 1641, a Mongolian lord defeated the last Tibetan lord with claim to the Tibetan throne and made the 5th Dalai Lama the leader of Tibet.

In China the Qing armies of the 18th and 19th Centuries are documented as entering Tibet on a number of occasions in order to "protect" it and settle disputes. Once again the Chinese court took tribute from the Dalai Lamas and Panchen Lamas. A garrison was placed there and Ambassadors or "Ambams" controlled the court. A stone monument regarding the boundary between Tibet and neighbouring Chinese provinces, agreed upon by Lhasa and Beijing in 1726, was placed atop a mountain. Territory east of the boundary was governed by Tibetan chiefs who were answerable to China.

At the beginning of the twentieth century, Britain and Russia were in a power struggle for control in Central Asia. It was known as "The Great Game" or to the Russians "The Tournament of Shadows". All the western powers were similarly trying to get a piece of the action in China. In 1904 there was a treaty between Britain and Tibet after a British invasion had caused the then Dalai Lama to flee to China. Britain tried to make Tibet a "Protectorate" and traded with them through the East India Company in Calcutta, then in 1906 another treaty between China and Britain recognized Chinese suzerainty. In 1910 the Chinese invaded Tibet for the first time since 1792 and the Dalai Lama fled to India. The Tibetans declared independence in 1911 following the Chinese revolution as the Qing dynasty ended and the new republic was fighting battles with the resurgent monarchists and provincial warlords. Tibet once again asserted its autonomy and had tried to remain closed off from the international community and world affairs, but history was catching them up. To the Chinese it was a medi-evil theocracy that survived on complete submission to the religious overlords who ran the country. The Chinese troops "liberated" Tibet in 1950-1, bringing the "Tibetan brothers once again into a united motherland" (so said Chairman Mao) and with it ending both serfdom and freeing tens of thousands from slavery, bringing Tibet into the modern era and signing away the totalitarian rule of the temples. There was a 17 point agreement between the Dali Lama, who represented the Tibetans and the Chinese Government. Tibetan activists today say that this was signed under duress. What the Chinese people also don't know is that this cost 80,000 lives as the Tibetan people fought against the Chinese army. Whatever improvements there may have been in the early years for the semi nomadic and devoutly religious Tibetan population, they were short lived. Following an uprising in 1959, the young Dali Lama was smuggled out of the country, thinking that his life was at risk. During the years of the "Cultural Revolution 1966-78" there was a lot of oppression of everything that was not part of the plan of the Chinese Communist Party. The Tibetans and their religion suffered badly. In more recent times, China has developed Tibet's economy bringing transport, education, better housing and jobs. It has also taken the natural resources to pay for these and changed the traditional Tibetan culture and way of life.

In order to understand the Chinese position, the Chinese mind-set; you have to see where they are coming from. They believe that for over 4000 years, China was the most powerful and advanced country in the world. By the late 18th century, when Europe turned its eyes eastward, China accounted for over one quarter of the worlds' GDP. That's a similar amount to what the USA had at the end of the Second World War. China saw the other nations as backward and had no interest in trading with them. The other nations wanted a piece of China. Over the following two hundred years we invaded, drew up dubious contracts and drugged the population in order to get a foothold in China. Where the western powers were fighting each other across the globe, they banded together to take on China. This has been the history of the relationship between China and the west. In 1949, Chairman Mao closed the door on the west. They had had enough of us. This door has slowly been opening, on the terms of the Chinese, since the 1980's, but they are wary of dealing with us. As a result, they see every action of the west as trying to stop China from being a power again. Whether this is criticism of environmental pollution, human rights' issues, the governmental structures, the manufacturing process. This is why when it comes to Tibet, the Chinese have their version of events and we have ours and a mutual miss-trust exists with both parties.

In Hanoi, my first group meeting went well, but Candy hadn't arrived. She turned up at around 10pm. I soon found out that she was a vegetarian and also had a peanut allergy. This was going to be impossible. The food is difficult at the best of times, but it is nearly all cooked in peanut oil. I went off bed to ponder this one and Candy went out for a cigarette. In the morning, her room-mate Sarah told me that Candy hadn't returned all night. This could be a very big problem. The first thing I thought was that she'd eaten something and had a reaction. Was she in a gutter somewhere? I told Cindy who advised me that when she was in training one month earlier, she was told that people with peanut allergies would not be sold a trip in China. Well, we had one. I emailed the Melbourne Office about the peanut status. I got in touch with the Beijing office about the present situation. I was given the number of the Tour Companies' Indo-China office. They could help me phone hospitals and the police. Bearing in mind that this was 8:30am, I wasn't surprised that the only person in the Indo-China office was a girl who said that the manager was not in, but gave me his number anyway. They could not help. It was ten minutes to nine and I was having limited success with the hotel management who said that they would help as much as they could one I'd left. I had to leave at 9am. The trip has to continue for the other 11 passengers and if Candy didn't show up, all I could do was contact the Indo-China office again and hopefully set them to task. I looked out of the door, and there she was, having a cigarette. I don't think I'd ever felt quite so much relief at seeing a passenger. Cindy helped settle everyone down and got in touch with Beijing again to say that everything was now O.K. This was one instance when I was so relieved that there were two of us doing this and that she was turning out to be quite a capable girl.

So, panic over. We started getting everyone on the bus and I got a phone call from Ching in the Beijing Office. I'd emailed her the day before, questioning whether the boat to Cat Ba was booked, because I knew from talking to Mr Hai earlier in the week that we were changing boats. Ching told me that the old boat company had been cancelled. Unfortunately, no-one had booked Mr Hai's new boat company. "Could I possibly contact Mr Hai and ask him to sort us out with a boat?" O.K. so I'd lost and found a passenger, now I had to find a boat, and I only had three hours to do it in, whilst on the road to Ha Long Bay. Mr Hai was not impressed, but said he'd do his best. It also had me wondering that now, with so many new people with new positions in the office, why was it less organised than when there were fewer? This was easily the worst start to any trip I'd ever done. We all got on the bus to the coast. I explained to Cindy that one thing that you should always try to avoid was letting passengers know that there may be a problem. They panic and begin to judge your ability and question the trip and the Tour Company that they have booked with. Unfortunately, the damage was already done and my text messages kept being replied by phone calls from Ching and Mr Hai. We were, after all sorting out this mess through three people and three languages across two countries. Mr Hai came through, as I knew he somehow would and we had a boat upon arrival at Hai Phong. It was possibly the worst boat I've been on in Ha Long Bay, a bit dirty, needing a few repairs and my cabin was being slept in by the captain until late afternoon, but it was a boat, with lunch being prepared as we arrived. Apart from the relief off managing to pull this one off, another thing also brought a smile to my face. I showed Cindy around the boat, starting by going up on deck. Up there, she counted the sun loungers and only got to 7. There were 12 of us in total. She asked "where will the rest of us sleep?" she thought that we were to sleep up on deck. The idea that we would have our own cabins hadn't occurred to her. This was going to be a fast learning curve for me and the girl from the Chinese countryside.

This boat trip also gave me one of my best memories of China (even though we were in Vietnam) and Chinese people. Trip after trip I have brought groups outside the city wall in Xi'an to see the local people spontaneously dancing, or forming a choir and singing to the night air because this is what Chinese people are really about. Not a care in the world, no self-consciousness, no ego, no worry about where they are or that someone may poke fun at them at work the following day and also all done without alcohol (well, to the most part, anyway). We westerners have lost all this, as we worry about ourselves and what others must think of us and doing the right thing. We've lost our sense of fun for the sake of it. Cindy cannot swim. However, she wanted to get into the water at Ha Long Bay, so we donned her a life jacket (that was so big on her as to almost smother her) and a life-belt, and into the sea she went. She could hardly see over the top of the life jacket and she laughed constantly. Everybody looked on as this pathetic thing tried to swim, at the same time having the time of her life. Before long, everyone got involved and the group was all helping her and encouraging her on. That sense of enjoying yourself, no-matter who cares, instantly rubbed off on the rest of the group. I would never have managed to have that effect on them, whatever I had done.

I'd had a feeling that the amount of money that I was carrying was wrong. I usually count my money and that of the Tour Company every few days, make a note of it and calculate if it looks correct or not. I hadn't done this for a while. Not being on a trip meant only spending my own cash, so the last time I'd checked was on Cat Ba during my time off. Unfortunately, my worst fears were true. I knew instantly when I came to count my Hong Kong dollars that some were missing. Then I compared my US dollars and Chinese Yuan. All in all, around HKD2000, USD200 and CNY600 was missing. Someone had been cleaver enough to take some, but not enough out of each denomination for me to notice until now. Bastard. That was a hell of a lot of money over here. Bastard, the only places where it could have been taken were in Mr Hai's hotel (the only place I'd taken my money belt off in over a week) or in the dorm at the Hanoi Hostel whilst I was sleeping. Bastards. This had completely wiped out my earnings from the last trip and would take months to earn back and we weren't even going to be getting that much work over the coming months. Bastards.

It was also around this time that I got another bad email from Lindsay back in London. Over the last few months, Moo had either forgotten to or just plain hadn't been paying off any of the bills for the flat. Lindsay has found reminders, then had paid them off and Moo now owed her his share of the bills. Then came the big one. The Council Tax still hadn't been paid from last year. There had already been a letter in January to this effect and we'd all emailed each other and Moo had said it was sorted. Lindsay had been really pissed off about it that time and had threatened to move out of the flat. I'd given Moo the low down on this. If she moved out, I couldn't afford to cover the cost of the place, especially as he was behind with his rent. If she moved out, I'd need all his back-rent. I'd probably have to move back to London before the end of my time in China and then, immediately, have to find a well-paying job, otherwise we'd both be homeless. I'd got a pissed off email back from him. Unfortunately, pissed off, doesn't pay the bills. Lindsay had just opened a letter from the Bailiffs. The Council tax still hadn't been paid. She was panicking and said she would probably be moving out. The way things were looking, especially with the China visa problems, it looked like I may have to leave China early. This last year has been amazing. How it could all be fucked up by somebody back home was about as shit as it could get.

On Cat Ba Island, I introduced Cindy to Mr Hai and we did the usual dinner around at his house. She loved this, almost as much as I loathe it. I also let her into the secret that there is no way that I'd eat what was being put in front of me if I was back home, but as I'd already done the invite half a dozen times already, there was no way that I could now get out of it. Still, the hospitality was fantastic, with Mr Hai's older brother and his wife visiting, along with some friends, so the rice wine was a particularly knock out variety. Cindy said that it reminded her of home. The simple house, eating on the floor, the hot-pot and all the seafood, still struggling as it is boiled alive and pulled apart was just like it was with her family. She deftly split open the crab and along with the Vietnamese was sucking through the shell as I looked on all western and helpless. The alcohol was another story, but she got away with sips to each "mot, hai, ba, yow" so we were at about the same consistency when we left. She and Mr Hai got along great and she was soon showing him photos of Snow and Scott's wedding in Hong Kong. That was news to me too. We made a detour to the Koala bar on the way back to the hotel to check on the rest of the group. Most were in there playing pool, so I did my old bar manager trick and got Cindy to sniff the bottle caps of all the spirits to see what they would taste like, then tried out a Baileys. She was learning fast and enjoying every minute of it.

Compare this with what happened a few days later. As we crossed the border, I prompted the group, saying that usually, someone will be moved aside, passports would be inspected thoroughly, along the stitching and every visa stamp and if any official found a Lonely Planet, it would be confiscated. I wasn't quite prepared for what happened next. As we stood in line, we were all asked to open our bags for inspection. This became a long and arduous process for 12 of us, all with a lot of luggage and only three officials inspecting. One by one they went through us. They found my visa to Tibet from last year and it took a bit of explaining that I wouldn't be going to Tibet this year and neither would any of the group. They found my Lonely Planet, but whilst they were distracted with another bag, I wrapped it up in some dirty laundry and stuffed it back in my back-pack. This would have been the 4th guide book confiscated in the last couple of months. Then they started on the cameras, the memory cards the DVD's and the USB's. One by one they were taken away to be viewed and you can guess that with avid photographers in the group and round the world travellers, there was a lot to go through. The officials were pleasant enough and about as efficient as they could be, but it was a wholly un-necessary process. After an hour or so, we all got all of our belongings back. As we finally pass immigration, there was the machine on the counter with three buttons. Each button with a face, one smiling, one indifferent and one sad. We all pressed the smiling face. Every one of us had visions of a trap door opening up over a pit of doom for those who dared select any other option.

50. My Friend Mr Hai and his friends 17/04/08

Dinner in the front room of Mr Tho's
Surrounded by boxes of bottles of fish sauce
He decants his two litre plastic container of rice wine
Into a "Grants of St James" bottle that looks far more fine
And asks once again, in Vietnamese
And my friend replies once again that I'm British

A seafood hotpot and a silent wife
Fish heads stare and whole shrimps writhe
Tickled by squid tentacles
and unbuckling mussels
That reveal the rubbery inedible
Octopus sphincter or something more terrible
Until my friend says 'Chuck Mung'
And we down a glass of something strong
Which is instantly re-filled by Mr Tho
His rice wine, fish sauce face is beginning to glow
Eyes popping from his head like the boiled fish
that he is about to eat whole from his dish

The children at the dinner table
Watching cartoon, then the squabble
That the youngest, cutest daughter wins
To pluck the fish-eye from the head and fins

and hold it lick a pearl with her chopsticks
Opens her mouth, in it pops and the lips are licked

Then from house to house in the Tet celebrations
Invites and rice wine from friends and relations
Rooms where wives and children lie in a front room bed
Whilst the husband goes off with his friends instead
Hot pot and drinking in the cold days of Tet
Filling my head with things that I will drunkenly forget
Til I make slurred excuses about my obligations
And get an hours sleep before another invitation

Mr Hai's house, a single room
Where his son plays and watches a Russian cartoon
A cabinet, a large T.V. and a bed
His other suit hangs on the wall from a peg
And his cute younger sister
Obediently serves dinner
And we are joined by his friends
To fill the rice wine glass again

The fans are unplugged,
The light stops spinning
T.V. characters finish their dialogue before leaving
There is still a breeze, in the air
The afterglow of the magic spell that surrounds me when I'm
here.

51. Cat Ba Beach 1 18/04/08

Four o'clock ends the working day
Cat Ba goes down to the beach to play
The boys strip their shirts off chiselled bodies
The girls stay covered and surprisingly modest
But still wade into the waves
Screaming at every drenching they're gave
Holding onto an inner-tube tyre
The boys leap into the white foamers
Footballs bounce high, some kick, some catch

T-shirts for goalposts for a football match
Running in and out, waves in the waves all at play
Until the sun casts the shadows to end the day.

52. Cat Ba Beach 2 18/04/08

I'm standing on the shoreline
Looking out across the ocean
Thinking about how lucky I am
Back home, flatmates squabble
And governments around me struggle
To control and supress people
I think what tomorrow will bring
Then, when I think of everything
I must trust to fortune and count my blessings
I've made it this far down life's path
And for just a moment I can sit back and laugh
For every problem, there is always an aftermath.

53. On leaving Vietnam 17/04

News reel of kicking
The desperately clinging
Would be
Refugee
Out of the door
Of the helicopter
A final Action
On leaving Vietnam

Then all these movies
That tried to change what the truth is
Making heroes of losers
Editing out all the abuses
So that it is comfortable
To call it a tactical withdrawal
Where you win a propaganda war
And change the history books once more

I am no deer hunter
Or any war movie character
Or a veteran re-visitor
I have no agenda for being here
Save, that I am passing through
With a group of travellers with things to do
Seeing new places, making new friends
With the hope that this won't end.

As we travelled on over the next days, it came to light that China had closed the borders on westerners. Not entirely, but it was making it plain that it would make access a lot more difficult in the run up to the Olympics. In order to get a visa from now one, westerners would have to submit a travel itinerary, receipts for all accommodation and a return flight. The trouble surrounding the Torch and Tibet had not gone away and China was taking no chances with a load of westerners turning up on the eve of the Olympics, intent on disrupting their showpiece games. It became a topic of discussion for the group as we travelled into China. Most of the group knew nothing about the issues; Cindy could not give any more insight as to what was happening. She could not see why the westerners were having a problem with believing that Tibet was part of China, when it so obviously was. The lines on the map proved this. I tried to explain that it wasn't that the foreigners didn't know that Tibet was part of China; the discussion was that it should not be part of China, that the Tibetans wanted it to be a free country. A concept completely alien to any Chinese, proud that they were the Middle Kingdom; the Centre of the World and the greatest civilisation, now the worlds fastest growing economy.

I remember growing up in the 1980's that "Free Tibet" was one of the many issues of international politics, but hadn't really heard much about it in the following decades. Chinas human rights record is no worse than many of the other countries that we deal with. In fact, to take a look at what is happening in Guantanamo Bay, I can see little difference. I've said this many times before; China is a lot like Britain (or other western counties) was in the 1950's and 60's. Be it their drive to industrialise (remember the "white heat of technology" from the Wilson Government?), renew the old towns and give people a better life. We were also interfering in countries, our British, French, Dutch colonies or American wars in South East Asia. Also in our countries we had civil rights marches and peace rallies, as our nations industrialised, went to war, denied citizens abroad and at home their basic human rights, through to the early 1980's and even to the present day. In many ways, that is what China is experiencing now.

These changing circumstances, whatever happened were obviously going to affect my visa applications and any prospective tourists over the next few months. Cindy brought up the subject of Snow and Scott getting married and it got me thinking. Maybe I could marry a Chinese girl for a visa. For most of the last century, Chinese girls were trying all ways possible to get a new life in the west, now the shoe was on the other foot I wondered how this could all pan out. I had a couple of top candidates for a shot-gun marriage of convenience. I texted Amy, just to see how her first solo trip was going, we had been talking throughout her Beijing Training and Training Trip with Zef. Well, you never know, and it's always best to be prepared for all circumstances.

My conversations with Amy, along with a couple of other people brought something else to light. Cindy was not liked by any of the new leaders that she had trained with, and there were a number of reasons. Firstly, she was Bruces' girlfriend. The way that I was told the story was that Bruce had spotted Cindy at a party and more or less said that if she became his girlfriend, then he would get her a job working with the Tour Company. She already had a western boyfriend, an American English teacher from her University days, who she was visiting in Beijing. To those I talked to, the American had served his usefulness in getting her through Uni and now that she wanted a better job, Bruce was the answer. This didn't seem like the girl that I was getting to know, but once we had talked about my impending visa problems, then my lack of a girlfriend, she came clean and said that Bruce was her boyfriend.

Things got even more interesting. There had been at least one other girl in the Training in Beijing who had also been one of Bruce's girlfriends, who had a similar story about how she had been offered the job. However, in recent months, Bruce had been demoted from his lofty position as Acting General Manager and had moved to Yangshuo as the "South China Manager" with Tracey leapfrogging him for the Operations Manager position whilst the General Manager Max had been drafted in from outside. Then, Cindy had done her training trip with another Chinese leader, called Cherie. At some point on the trip, Cindy had reported back to Bruce that she had evidence of Cherie taking commission and Cherie had then been sacked. Unfortunately for new and naive recruit Cindy, doing her boyfriend's bidding, having no loyalty to the Tour Leaders, or her fellow countrywomen, along with her reputation just meant that they all turned on her. "Watch out for her" somebody had told me. "She got Cherie sacked". Now I knew the reason why she was the first Chinese Leader since Snow, two years earlier, to be doing these Hanoi to Hong Kong trips. It also had me wondering why I had been chosen by Bruce to be her trainer. Was there some other agenda here? Did he have it in for me too?

The trip continued into China and on Liuzhou. I'd been in contact with my friend Estelle from London, who had now finished her tour with Steven and was in Beijing. Both her and Steven had emailed me stories of her crashing a motorbike in Sapa, sleeping in the wrong hotel in Li Jiang and countless other drunken instalments for a piss up of a journal along the way. Estelle had been classed as officially bonkers and had jokingly been added into Stevens trip report as a possible complaint because she had said there was "not enough beer in China". In the light of my new discoveries about Cindy, I was wary about Estelle joining me on the trip. I'd previously contacted my new boss Tracey in Beijing about her joining my trip for some of the way and was told that she couldn't partake in the groups included activities, but otherwise, things would be pretty cool. However, if Bruce was out to get me, for whatever reason, I had to cover my arse for any eventuality. So I cobbled together an itinerary for Estelle where she'd meet me in Liuzhou. Then I would send her on to Yangshou to meet Snow and the gang. After a couple of days there, while I went to Chen Yang and did some activities with the group, I would organise her coming up to Long Ji with Farmer Tang. This wasn't what Estelle had planned and it took a bit of convincing, as she'd traversed China to join me, only for me to be telling her that she couldn't travel with my group. I got to Liuzhou with the group in the afternoon and then met Estelle in an internet cafe. It is odd meeting someone you know from somewhere else on the other side of the world. The strangest thing about it is that it is somehow completely normal when it shouldn't be. We chatted about stuff, just as if we'd both woken up on somebodies living room floor in London, with a hangover. That's about as normal as we ever get.

That evening, most of the group decided to go out. I'd been trying to get groups to go to a nightclub in Liuzhou for months and this was the only group who were up for it. I had to do a bit of an explanation (how drinks are served, what to expect etc.) and we also, temporarily lost four of them with a confused taxi driver en-route. By 10pm we were in Soho Nightclub, one of a chain of Soho clubs that are in almost every sizeable town across China. Some of us drank more than others. Candy and Keith (who I had nicknamed the cool kids) certainly enjoyed it all. Lots of dice games and "gan bei" with the locals. Then came the bar show, with a bit of a twist. Often enough the bar shows are just a bit of dancing behind the bar, or a mime to a song on a small stage in the seated area. This time, the bar staff had all been taught how to juggle, with fire. At one stage there was a dozen staff all behind the bar, flipping flaming bottles, jumping around and blowing fire. The best I could do in response was light a cigarette and pop it in my mouth. As the night went on

I got quite drunk and Estelle says that we had an argument, but I can't remember anything about it and she's usually more argumentative than I am anyway.

The following Morning I got Estelle on the Bus to Yangshou and called Monkey Jane, Snow and Farmer Tang to expect her. Then it was on with the trip to Cheng Yang. The highlight here was Sarahs 21st birthday, which degenerated into a game of "I have never" which is a game which I'd swore "I would never" play as it all turns into a who's who of shagging. Some things are better left alone. Especially when we found out that one of the girls had run away with her teacher at the age of 15 and we got a gasp of "you slag" from one of the other girls. Then it was Long Ji again and we were joined by Farmer Tang, with Estelle still recovering from a hangover after going on the piss for two days solid. She had been with some Irish boys who had party tricks that included rolling down hills, crossing borders without shoes and not knowing who people were until they found them in their photographs. I think she was enjoying China more than my group was. Whilst on the bus, I got a call from Tracey in Beijing. She asked me what my visa status was, as mine was going to run out in about three weeks' time making it impossible to do another trip on the one I had. She then asked me to get another visa on entering Hong Kong, as she was going to put me on a Silk Road Trip. If I was unable to get the visa I should tell her as soon as possible, but at the moment I was the only person who she would put on the Silk Road trip. This is the trip that everyone wants to do. I'd obviously risen up the pecking order to be allowed to do this trip. All I needed was the visa, just one more visa.

Then it was back to Yangshuo again. We had the usual merriment there. I had dinner with Bruce, his mum and some other currant and ex-leaders. I met Eric, a crazy Canadian who had been trained by Scott years earlier. They had stories of drunkenly scaling construction cranes in the days when it seemed "anything goes" was acceptable as long as you completed the trip. I danced on the bar top with Estelle at

Bar 98, only to look down and see Bruce looking up at me. Not the best move to make in-front of one of your managers. I lost Estelle for 24 hours, but she turned up after she'd met random people at Monkey Jane's and ended up spending the day with them. She had even driven a Jeep across a river, and she doesn't know how to drive. Needless to say, alcohol was involved again. I also got to see "the light show" for the first time.

The "Light Show" is actually "Impressions" by Zhang Yimou who was also going to be responsible for the opening ceremony of the Beijing Olympics. A part of the Li River has had an arena constructed on its riverbank and this is where there is a nightly, sometimes twice nightly performance and what a performance it is. Set with the backdrop of the river and the karsts, there is a cast of 600 who entertain with singing and dancing. The music is both traditional and modern, some by famous and popular Chinese composers. They are songs from the different minority groups that live locally, so lots of traditional costumes but it is all with a very modern twist. One of the segments of the show is based on a legend of Liu Sanjie from Zhuang minority group who had a beautiful voice at very early age. Her voice was so beautiful it even could raise the dead. In the legend a local gangster falls in love with Liu Sanjie and wished to make her his concubine. Liu Sanjie's boyfriend and his friends in the village free her and the couple escape turning themselves in a pair of larks. It is called "the light show" because that is what wows the audience the most as there are projections onto the surrounding karst mountains and others that turn the river into a flotilla of tiny boats, at other times a ballerina dances on a crescent moon, the shore is invaded by hundreds of tribes-people and there is the synchronicity of the performers turning on and off lights to some unfathomable sequence. I was impressed and what's more, Bruce had footed the bill. Maybe he wasn't as bad a bloke as what people had been making out either. I'd had dinners with him, I'd been invited to his house, met his mum and I'd just spent two weeks with his girlfriend. O.K. my experience of him as a manager wasn't good, but it wasn't as if anyone else had even wanted the job when he took it. He talked about the trips being "real life experiences" like having homestays and eating local foods. He had certainly immersed himself in the Chinese culture and the language to a greater extent than many of the other Tour Leaders.

We got to talking about what had happened to all the other Tour Leaders that had left. So many had said that they were signing up for another year, then at the last minute had quit. He talked about Janet, how her last couple of trips had proved that she was just not interested in Leading. She had wanted to manage her own travel company in Shanghai and had only joined up as a Leader to gain some experience. He mentioned "last trip syndrome" with leaders just not caring anymore. He mentioned Jay moving on, as he just wanted more money and to run his own trips. Then we got on to a story that I had heard before concerning Ting Ting. I had heard that she had got in trouble for bringing her boyfriend on a trip, but this was only the tip of the ice berg. She had spent all her time with him, completely neglecting her group until her mum also joined her trip for a few days. By this time, Bruce had been called by the group members. At the end of the trip, he had a meeting with Ting Ting and her group saying how unacceptable her conduct was and apologising on behalf of the company. This was what the group had requested and should have been the end of the story, but Ting Ting cried. Before he knew it, Bruce was being lambasted by the group for being so hard on Ting Ting. "What was I supposed to do?" he asked me. Now there were Leaders moving over to join GAP, they were offering what looked like a good package to experienced Leaders, opportunities to join an expanding company, trips Leading in far and away places and he felt let down by them leaving. He had spent the winter off season working out contracts for better hotels, better trips, just to have the new managers go back to the same old operators as before. He was a bit dismayed with what had happened. Was he such a bad bloke? Or was it just the boss bating that you get in any company?

I got talking to Snow about her marriage, but it wasn't all good news. Over the previous year, they had tried to get married, but to do this; Scott needs documentation to say that he is not already married. This takes time and by the time everything had been processed in her native Mongolia Province, his six month time window had expired. Next, they decided to go to Hong Kong to get married and had done this two weeks earlier with Bruce and Cindy acting as witnesses in the hastily arranged affair. However, China does not acknowledge a Hong Kong marriage certificate if one of the partners is Chinese and the other a foreigner. The old paranoia about people getting married to escape the country. There was the lawyer in Hong Kong who could get the translations done and hopefully register the marriage in China for them, so she gave me the address and some photographs for me to pass on to him when I got there.

Then it was the train to Hong Kong again. Cindy left us at Guangzhou to fly back to Vietnam to start another trip. She had been given the job of immediately training another new Chinese Tour Leader called Qing, from Xi'an. I wished her luck. I was sad to see her go, we both learned a lot from each other and I knew that I now had another good friend in China.

It looked like I was going to be in Hong Kong for a while. I'd been given a trip starting in two weeks time with enough breathing space to get a new visa for China. This was possibly going to be my last trip as the news on the street was that there would be no visas issued before the Olympics. It was the trip I'd also been looking forward to the most. I'd decided on having one last blow out night with Estelle and whoever else wanted to come along, then concentrate on Visas and possible flights out of Hong Kong to somewhere warmer and cheaper until my next trip started. I knew Amy was in town, she was in between trips and she asked to share my hotel room the night before her trip started. I was hardly going to turn down the girl who, if circumstances regarding visas came to a head would be my number one choice as a prospective Chinese wife. I joked about it to her and my visa situation. It was not the way that she saw it, saying "you should not say that" but I thought to myself "there is time, and I can be charming, when I'm not too drunk and maybe, just maybe, fate is playing some game and the time has come around for me to settle down". That's when Lyn arrived. She was on her way to Pingyao and Datong, for a little exploratory trip. She had never been to these two places and had to lead her next group there. She had booked on a 36 hour train journey. I convinced her that this was a bad idea and she should come out and get drunk with us and fly the following day. It then took her four hours and two border crossings to trade in her ticket, but yes, she'd do that for a good night out. It actually wasn't one of the best, but the four, Me, Estelle, Amy and Lyn, put back an excessive amount of alcohol and Lyn threw up out of the taxi door on the way back to the hotel. She shared the room with Estelle, who was so suitably impressed with the way that Lyn woke up with vomit all over her hair, that they immediately began planning Estelle's trip back into China with Lyn They both caught the plane to Pingyao that evening.

The next day I said goodbye to Amy, put in a visa application, and moved into the new Hong Kong Apartment. Big Chris was there. I'd met him once before and I'd got to like the man through reading his funny and hard hitting trip reports. We went out for a couple of pints and I got the low down on the Tour Leading and Tour Company world as he saw it. Chris has been around for about four years. He loves the work, loves the company, but has a healthy disrespect for the management. He firstly pointed out that the apartment only had one registered key (mine) and the computer still didn't work (they were the same ones that hadn't worked in the old apartment and had just been moved over) and the place only had two beds. This was going to make it difficult sleeping the four leaders that would arrive in the next couple of days, because, as I've already mentioned, Big Chris, is Big. Not the sort of person you would want to share a bed with. He chatted about the sacking of one of the leaders, Cherie, who was one of Chris's friends. She had been a very experienced Tour Leader as far as everyone was concerned. It seems that her downfall was in taking a back hander when it's pretty impossible for the Chinese leaders not to take the odd back-hander. If they refuse them, it can cause a lot of offence. Chris thought that she was doing no different than a lot of the other leaders, but there was another agenda.

As stories about Bruce's mis-conduct and general bad management came to light, it was looking like even his reduced roll was under threat. It looked like he needed to do something to keep his position. Cherie was also a bit of a spokeswoman for the Chinese leaders and didn't take any shit from Bruce, she knew all the bad stuff about him, and more; she was a thorn in his side. She had been around for a couple of years, longer than most Tour Leaders, or any of the management and didn't mind telling them (especially some people in management) how crap they were. Also, her western Tour Leader boyfriend had recently left our Travel Company to join our main competitor, GAP Adventures. For Bruce's sake, it was better to find evidence against her (as you could with just about anybody) and get rid of her. It would be a feather in his cap, and he was telling his new managers that he had been watching a few leaders for some time. Chris found it unsurprising that the people who were giving her back-handers were still working with the company and the evidence had been gathered, somewhat underhandedly, by Bruce. He was not Chris's favourite person. Chris made a comparison between the two of them. He said that whilst he loved the Tour Leading job and China, Bruce's sole interest in the place was to stick his dick in as many of the girls as possible. He had a point. I had to laugh.

So the next few days, we made the most of a frustrating time off. Travelled around a bit, I picked up my Visa and booked my flights to Beijing for the following week and looked at plans of going to Thailand, Laos, Cambodia, all of which were far too expensive, so just got as far as the outlying islands of Hong Kong. Bruce arrived with his mum, spent a couple of hours trying to fix the broken computer, took us all out to dinner, then left. Chris and I bought two new beds from IKEA on a mammoth shopping trip, but the computers were never fixed. I really liked Chris. He was only a couple of years younger than me, had given up a conventional life as a Food and Beverage Manger to travel and experience life in other countries. He liked Heavy metal, he liked a beer, in fact a few beers and he would just burst into song as he walked around the apartment. He filled the place in every sense of the word, from his six feet six frame and his massive personality through to the sound of him singing along to some half-forgotten rock track. He had an enthusiasm for what he was doing that was enviable and he talked about the background issues of working in China, what we were doing as a tour company, what moral obligation we had as we worked and lived in a foreign country. Chris had been at the training in Beijing. As one of our most experienced leaders it was obvious that he would be involved and he had trained Ting Ting and Ada in my year. Whilst there he had also met a girl that he liked called Mei Mei. They were now emailing each other and I quizzed him about it. "I haven't had a girlfriend for four years" he told me. On a couple of occasions he thought he had come close, but the job always gets in the way. A couple of days a month you might be in a city, then you're off again. With the state of the new Chinese visa regulations, he didn't know what trip he would be running in a months' time, if any. There was a lot of uncertainty around. Chris knew of other Leaders leaving, simply because there was no guarantee of work. Some were getting trips in South East Asia, but the company was changing its policies on recruiting westerners in some of these countries as the individual governments tightened up on the legislation on "working as a Tour Guide without a license". There was similar legislation being rolled out in China and we were being told by the management that this could be the last year that foreigners "without a guiding license" could work as Tour Leaders with our Tour Company. So Chris had got himself in a strange and new dilemma. He had found a girl that he liked, but at the same time had asked an old Tour Manager friend in Malaysia if she had any work for him, and she had said yes. "I've got to go where the work is" he told me. Four years of Tour Leading hadn't given him any savings at all. "It's probably not going to work out with Mei Mei, she is so far away now, we will always be on trips, I've seen it happen with so many Tour Leaders before, I'm not expecting anything". And it was true. Very few Tour Leaders manage relationships; sooner or later they split up, or have to stop Tour Leading.

A couple of new Chinese leaders came and went in a day, all new to everything and not understanding quite what we were doing there or even what the Tour Leading job that they had been hired to do was all about. They were Local Guides in every sense and couldn't see the bigger picture of our international Tour Company with philosophies such as responsible travel, or environmental ethics, or any political discussion. All asked how much we were getting paid and when we told them, all complained that they were being paid less than the foreigners. None could be convinced that there were three levels of pay and that I was being paid more because I had been working for over one year, continuously. Chris was being paid more than me and so were the Chinese Leaders who had been working for one year longer than I had. There seemed to be a definite change in the reason why the new Chinese Leaders had applied to work for us.

One girl who stayed a bit longer was Z from Chengdu. She was quite enthusiastic and was just starting the Vietnam trips, so we had a bit to talk about and she would also drink beer with us. Chris, Z and I all went over to one of the islands to watch the "Bun" festival, in one of the fishing towns where 50ft high towers of buns are erected for locals to scamper up. There were parades through the tight streets that included a Bagpipe Band, Chinese opera and "floating children". For some reason, children, dressed up as painted mannequins holding a pose would be placed on top of a long pole as if to look like they were floating and paraded through the town. Whilst we were there Chris got a text from Cherie saying that there had been an earthquake in Chengdu and that she had been trapped in a lift. Chris said that everything for Cherie was a drama and especially now, she was also one of Z's friends as they came from the same city. We didn't think that much more of it until that evening.

As I watched CCTV9, it became apparent that something big had happened. The news wasn't saying too much, the same real was playing over and over and the first estimate was that over 1000 people had died. I got in touch with Amy as I knew she was supposed to be in Chengdu. She said that she was at Chongqing railway station when it happened and the ceiling collapsed. That was about 300 miles from the epicentre. We had been on a boat at the time, we hadn't felt anything. Z tried to get in touch with her family, but the phones were down. It was impossible for me to get in touch with any of the other people we knew from Sichuan either. Not Chicory in Chengdu or Patrick in Emei Shan. The Chinese news was not helping much, so we got onto the BBC with Chris's laptop. That padded things out a bit, but there were still only fragmented reports and pictures, but the death toll had already reached 10,000. My heart went out to Z and all the people we knew. We stayed up late into the night, waiting for news.

Z got in touch with a relative the following morning who said that everybody was O.K. Our Tour Company office in Beijing passed on the message that all out contacts in the area were fine. For those of us working through the province, this created yet another problem as trips now had to be re-routed again and there was another flood of holiday cancellations. Hardly a priority under the present circumstances, but it all adds up into a complicated work schedule. We watched the Chinese media propaganda machine slowly gear itself up. Mr Wen, the Prime Minister, was constantly on T.V. shaking a lot of hands and giving heart rending speeches. To be quite honest, he did an excellent job for a politician on the scene and worked tirelessly, it just became overkill very quickly. Very little actual news was coming out of the disaster area, but the body count was steadily growing, as was the numbers of people missing as were the new destinations that the army had only just reached. There were pictures of the heroic "People's Army" as it cleared landslides, dug under collapsed buildings, pulled out survivors. There were now rousing sound tracks put to these videos, each with slogans that flashed on the screen praising the soldiers and emergency workers efforts. At least in a country like China, there is the political will to throw whatever resources they have at a problem. It was always just going to be too little too late. Then somebody noted that Premier Hu Jin Tao had been conspicuous by his absence. Then we saw footage of him, interjected with the old reports. Then I got the western press propaganda, emailed to me by Kim Looi back home in London. Somebody had said that the earthquake was payback for the treatment of the Tibetans. When the area most effected was a Tibetan area. Another questioned why so many schools collapsed when other government buildings remained standing, without mentioning the literacy campaign in the 1970's and 80's that built the schools where before there weren't any. Yes, there was corruption, but no more than in other countries. The School I went to in Darwen was constructed from asbestos in the form of "temporary" pre-fabricated porta-cabins that were still being used 20 years later than they should have been. They leaked in bad weather, so god knows what would have happened if a real natural disaster had occurred.

Chris and Z left and Qing arrived; he had just finished his Hanoi to Hong Kong training trip with Cindy. He didn't have any complaints about her, so at least I felt that she had one more friend. I felt sorry for her, that maybe the other Tour Leaders had got it wrong and Cindy was a pawn in Bruce's survival game.

The apartment in Tung Chung was situated on a new build around the Metro station. There were fantastic views over to the airport and then beyond it to other islands. It quickly became one of my favourite views as I watched boats cross the straights, cities of skyscrapers on other islands lighting up in the evening, the freeways carrying the cars next to the metro line carrying the trains. From my twentieth floor vantage point it all looked like a model railway city, my Town Planning daydreams from childhood coming to life. What's more, all this was happening in one picture and an artist could not have conceived a better composition. At the foot of our building was an amenity area, supermarket and other shops and some cafes and bars all surrounding a square with a fountain. The metro station was on one side, the bus station on the other. And at the bus station were the Falun Gong people. I didn't know too much about Falun Gong, there was a bit in the Lonely Planet and Rough Guides about them that said they were a spiritual sect, of which ten thousand of their elderly members sat cross legged in front of the communist Party head quarters in Beijing in 1999. This protest has been enough to bring them humiliation and suppression ever since. Most of the rest of the info that I'd acquired about them was from the Australian tourists who said that they had a high presence in Sydney and Melbourne. I decided to get their newspaper. There was a lot of information about people being tortured in Chinese jails, even having their organs removed. They proclaimed to be a peaceful Buddhist organisation that was being victimised by the Chinese government, so they had changed tactics and were now openly protesting against the Chinese. This to me was a bit of a "chicken and egg" scenario, did the protesting lead to the unwanted attention of the Chinese government, or vice versa? I asked one of the Chinese Tour Leaders what he thought about Falun Gong. "They are crazy people" he said. I then expected the usual pro government rant about people trying to de-stabilise the country, or having political agendas, but was surprised how he continued. "These people think that there is a wheel inside of them" I knew what he was talking about, a sort of Buddhist prayer wheel, or Kalachakra or what Falun Gong call the "Law Wheel" that was a representation of a "soul" that was supposed to be spinning inside you. "And they cut themselves open in order to see it" as a sort of proof that they were spiritually blessed I concluded. Where these the "organ removal" scars? Whatever the agenda of Falun Gong, I've never been one to listen to religious groups of any sort and even though I was very sceptical about my Chinese Tour Leader friend's story of self-mutilation, though he qualified this with "they recruit uneducated peasants from the villages" I decided that I had heard enough.

Pierre arrived a day later and we had a good catch up about his latest adventures and schemes. He had run his own side trip in the off season. He had applied to "The Venetian Casino" in Macao in an attempt to get involved there, but had been surprised that there was a waiting list and a training programme. He couldn't wait for that and didn't want to be "trained" on shit wages and doing what other people wanted him to do. He was ready for the "big time" it was just that the big time was not ready for him. He was thinking of opening a Paint-ball park in Yangshuo with Tour Leader Jane. He had talked to the authorities about it, but there was a problem in getting the land, the paint-ball guns imported, raising the capital, and signing all the paperwork. We took it pretty easy, unlike the Pierre I was used to, he said that he was tired and needed to ease off the drink and late nights.

I geared myself up for the return of Estelle. I'd booked us into the Garden Hostel Dorm, because at only $60 it was better to stay there rather than get a taxi back to the apartment. I had plans of going out in Hong Kong's Lan Kwai Fong and Wan Chai areas. Estelle hadn't read her instructions for meeting me, so that took a while, but soon we were off on another night out. Lan Kwai Fong was a bit boring, so by midnight we'd moved on and found a bar that played live music and the beer was as cheap as you're going to get on Hong Kong Island. By 2am we were in Dusk 'til Dawn, a well-known hang out, and we were singing and dancing. We made it back to the Mirador Mansions at around 5am. The next day was very painful. Whilst in the internet cafe, Estelle looked at me and said "I'm going to throw up". I hastily got the bin liner from out of the waste-paper basket and she crawled outside, to throw up in a bag in the middle of Chunking Mansions. A helpful fellow came over to her and offered her a black plastic bag, to put her transparent, vomit filled bag in, so that she could throw it away easier. Considerate people these Hong Kongese. Our plan of saving money on budget accommodation went straight out of the window as Estelle said that there was no way she could take the Metro back to the apartment, so she paid for a taxi. Once there, she didn't move off the couch for six hours. We tried Pizza Hut, but that ended in a run outside to vomit before we'd even ordered. Then it was goodbye, with a broken Estelle waving from the airport bus window as she left. Who said that there was not enough beer in China? She just hadn't been drinking with me.

I managed to run into Cindy again before I was flying off out of Hong Kong myself and back to Beijing. We walked and talked as we wandered around Tsim Sha Tsui looking for a camera for me. I had decided to replace the one that had disappeared six months earlier as I was going to do the "Silk Road" trip, full of places that would stretch my imagination and I had decided that a camera was necessary to record my adventure. We went in and out of a few shops, but the sales staff were trying to rip me off, I knew nothing about cameras. Cindy was also surprised that I knew nothing about cameras, or didn't carry a lap top, or didn't seem interested in any of the things that you "must have". Everybody she knew wanted the latest of any kind of gadget as did she, so she was just saying that I should go ahead and buy one. After one, three way exchange between the shop assistant, Cindy and me, I once again said that I didn't want to buy and was walking out. The angry shop assistant saw me as a rich westerner with a "Mainland Chinese" girlfriend, and started to insult her. The Hong Kong people class the Chinese as uncouth peasants and at the same time it looked like Cindy was trying to be a social climber. I distinctly heard him call her a "fried banana", and that I wasn't really rich so she was wasting her time.

It was my first visit to Beijing in six months and I was really looking forward to spending some time there and then the trip. Nothing ever goes as planned, so I lost my bag at the airport. I thought, my first trip back to Beijing will be a shopping expedition to replace all my lost clothes. Not really what I'd intended and I had a lot of preparation to do for this blind Silk Road trip. The bag eventually turned up, but by this time I had run into Steven and on my first night there we went drinking, so that wiped out another morning. I went to the new offices, met my new bosses Max and Tracey along with Li, Suzy, Ching and all the new staff with a hangover. Start as you mean to go on, is one phrase I was thinking along with "you only have one chance to make a first impression". Well, what was done was done. I was still leading the Silk Road trip and I reckoned that I could pull this off and prove myself as an excellent leader. I had already done quite a lot of preparation and now I had chance to talk to Zef, Rockhard and Tina about the Silk Road trip as they'd done it before. This was the trip I'd been waiting for.

I arranged to meet up with Eugenie and Amy who were in town. Eugenie and I had not seen each other for months and there had been big changes for her. She had decided to stop Tour Leading. She had applied for a job at the Beijing Olympics, taking western corporate clients around. After this, she wanted to study in England and was asking me about the merits of each University and the cost of living in London versus Birmingham. She wanted to get a Master's degree in Business and Tourism from a western University as it would enhance whatever future career she decided upon.

I got on to talking to Eugenie about pets as I had noticed that there wasn't the same attitude towards keeping them as there was in England or the west. I could see that they were a bit of a luxury, especially in a developing country with not enough space, but I'd also seen the recent trend of keeping small dogs. In Beijing, they were copying the eccentricities of the Japanese or Korean fashion fads and even dyeing dogs different colours. There was a famous celebrity who always wore pink and had died her Chihuahua's the same colour. There would been an outcry in England from the animal rights people, here it was seen as very fashionable and cute. So I asked Eugenie about why the Chinese didn't keep cats or dogs as pets. This was Eugenie's cat story: "Many years ago there was a beautiful queen of China, who everybody loved, but the Emperor had many concubines and they were jealous of the new queen. One of his favourite concubines concocted a plan to kill the queen and become queen herself, so gave the queen a gift, it was a cat. The cat stayed with the queen everywhere and would even stay overnight in her bedchamber. One night, the cat went onto the bed whilst the queen was sleeping, the cat sat on her chest and breathed on the queen, this sucked all the good breath out of the queen and replaced it with bad breath and the queen died in her sleep. Since then, Chinese people have never trusted the cat. Some say that the cat was sly and did the bidding of the evil concubine; some say that the concubine had found a magic potion and had changed herself into the cat". So I asked about dogs, hoping to get a similar story. "The dog bites you, it guards the chickens, don't you know anything?" was her reply.

I also met up with Amy. Her first couple of trips had gone OK, but she was concerned about a lot of things that had gone on. She had rung me a few days earlier, asking if she should buy her group presents, because something had not gone to their liking. She was not at fault, it was just that some food, or some arrangement was just a bit too foreign for them and she hadn't prepared them for it. She had been doing the "basic" style trips and was confused as to why the people in the groups didn't know anything about China, or even seem to want to know anything about China. They just complained that everything was "disgusting" then talked about home, then talked about visiting the beaches in Thailand and Australia. They couldn't wait for the China part of their trips to be over. It seemed as though S.T.A. travel in the U.K. was promoting the Roam China trip as part of a gap-year, round the world ticket. I asked about her feedback. She was getting excellent feedback, and tips? She was getting excellent tips, more than I was getting. So I told her not to worry about it. We touched on the subject of her ex-boyfriend. She had broken off the relationship months earlier, before she had become a Tour Leader but hadn't said anything more than that. Now she told me it was because it was going no-where and she felt that she was doing everything for him, whilst he was incapable. His mother solved all his problems, typical of the younger Chinese generation and a result of the one child policy where sons are particularly doted upon. She felt that if the relationship had gone any further, she would be spending the rest of her life looking after this spoiled, useless boy. He had been upset about the break up. In China, once you say that you are boyfriend and girlfriend, it more or less means that you are engaged and soon to be married. "He said that we couldn't break up because I had met his parents" Amy told me. "He told me all sorts of things, but now he has found another girlfriend, already. Was he lying to me?" I couldn't answer this, but I knew that he would have to "move on" as soon as possible, in order to "save face" after being dumped. "He told me that he loved me so much, that I thought I might go back to him. Now he has another girlfriend. He still rings me up, but I don't want to talk to him anymore." Amy's breaking off the relationship at any stage was a bit scandalous. Now, her ex-boyfriend had gone from wanting to marry her, to being with someone else and about to be engaged far too quickly for Amy to get used to. However, this was the Chinese way as well. You have the pressure to get married and this seems to be more important than who you marry. Moving on, meeting someone new, getting engaged as quickly as possible saved face, it meant that you were following the prescribed plan, it was the correct thing to do. Amy knew this only too well, no-matter how much it hurt. As we walked around the mini-market, sharing in each other's lives, I popped some pot noodles and some western style snacks in the basket. Amy dropped in some vacuumed packed chicken feet. That sort of summed it up. A most comfortable and natural past time for two close friends followed by the reminder; the obvious difference that we from completely different cultures.

In Beijing I caught a lot of the spirit of the Olympics and the national outpouring of sorrow for the victims of the Sichuan Earthquake. Everywhere we went there were shops opening up dedicated to Olympic merchandise and there were life size dummies of The Five Friendlies or "Fuwa"; the Official Mascots of Beijing 2008 Olympic Games. They are animations designed to represent each of the five Olympic rings and embody the natural characteristics of four of China's most popular animals, plus the Olympic flame. Beibei is the Fish, Jingjing is the Panda, Huanhuan is the Olympic Flame, Yingying is the Tibetan Antelope and Nini is the Swallow. When you put their names together "Bei Jing Huan Ying Ni" it translates as "Welcome to Beijing," Everywhere you go, on every T.V. channel, there is the official Olympic anthem, also called "Bei Jing Huan Ying Ni". Each Fuwa also excels at a certain discipline, water sports, athletics, ball games, track and field or gymnastics and Fuwa also represent the five elements of nature; the sea, forest, fire, earth and sky and these are stylised on their headpieces. I found all this to be ridiculously clever, a far better approach to promoting the spirit of the Olympics and China than anything that had gone previously and the Fuwa also had their own cartoon T.V. series where they were off saving the world. Then a sixth character started to appear along-side them. This was a blue rectangle with arms, legs and a face. This was going to be the mascot of the Shanghai Expo in 2010 and looked very amateur by comparison. The rivalry between the two cities was legendary, each trying to trump each other over the last centuries regarding which was the most important. This time it was obvious that Beijing had won. Whilst visiting the office on 19th May, one month after the disaster, there was a three minute silence. We all stood still, at 2:28 pm, the exact time that the earthquake struck one month earlier, Chinese and westerners together. Out of the 6th floor window, all the traffic on Zhang Zi Zhong Lu and everywhere else in China had ground to a halt. All the traffic lights on red, all the pedestrians on the pavement, nothing moved but the wind. The car horns sounded, all of them, an air-raid siren like noise as if the country was being threatened by a hostile air attack, but nobody moved. As it ended, with the collective sigh of a nation of over 1 billion people I saw Xiou Feng out of the corner of my eye. She is the Local Tour Operator who allocates my train tickets and she was weeping. There were others in the office also dabbing their eyes and looking away.

In the aftermath of the earthquake, the government subdued the celebrations surrounding the procession of the Olympic Torch relay around the country. In more recent weeks, they had turned the relay into something more (and this is where the goose-bumps start—thanks Lyn). Everywhere that the torch goes to, there will be a one minute silence for the victims of the earthquake. Money will be raised for the survivors and their families and the torch will be a rallying point for the reconstruction and the future for those people in Sichuan.

Chapter 5.

BEYOND THE GREAT WALL

"There are no foreign lands.
It is the traveller only who is foreign."

Robert Louis Stevenson

I had a 'Silk Road' trip. The sort of "Jewel in the Crown" of leading in China. I'd got as much info as I could off other leaders, Tina, Zef, Jane, and 'Rockhard', whose trip I had adopted. He had quit to start up a business with his Chinese girlfriend Stephanie. They were renting a space in the City Central Youth Hostel and selling T shirts and items for travellers. Rockhard really wanted to run a bar, but that would take a bit more time, money and organising. Zef had also set up a bar which he was running with his girlfriend Li Mei. They were on the up and coming tourist street of Nan Luo Gu Xiang and Zef was splitting his time between his day shift as Operations Manager (north) and running the bar in the evenings. Jane was actually on a trip elsewhere but had called about where to go in the new cities that I would be visiting, so this was all good stuff and much appreciated, but essentially, it was still going to be over two weeks of leading a group to places I'd only ever heard about.

The Silk Road is a historical network of interlinking trade routes across Asia linking it with the Mediterranean and Europe. Extending 4,000 miles, the Silk Road gets its European name from the Chinese silk obtained along it, but there were many other goods traded along it and for the Asian traders, silk was not so significant an item. Some of the other goods traded included luxuries such as silk, satin, hemp and other fine fabrics, musk, other perfumes, spices, medicines, jewels, glassware, and slaves. China traded silk, teas, and porcelain; while India traded spices, ivory, textiles, precious stones, and pepper; and the Roman Empire exported gold, silver, fine glassware, wine, carpets, and jewels. The trade on the Silk Road was a significant factor in the development of the great civilizations of China, India, Ancient Egypt, Persia, Arabia, and Ancient Rome. Silk was first traded from China during the Han Dynasty (206 BC-220 AD) as well as other goods, various technologies, religions and philosophies and even the bubonic plague travelled along the Silk Roads. What's more, very few who travelled the route traversed it from end to end; for the most part, goods were transported by a series of agents on varying routes and were traded in the bustling markets of the oasis towns. The first traders were the Indian and Bactrian traders, then from the 5th to the 8th century the Sogdian traders, then afterward the Arabs and Persians.

There was a fall in trade along the Silk Road from the 9th century when the Muslim Caliphate gained control but in the 13th Century the entire route came under the empire of the Mongols after Chengis and Kublai Khan. This allowed one Marco Polo to become its most famous traveller in the late 13th century, but with the disintegration of the Mongol Empire that kept the route safe for merchants and the re-emergence of warring states, the Silk Road finally fell into decline as a trade route and Europeans looked towards the sea for trade with the east.

There was more than one Silk Road. The northern route started at the Chinese capital of Chang'an; modern day Xi'an, travelled northwest through the Chinese province of Gansu, and split into three further routes, two of them following the mountain ranges to the north and south of the Taklamakan Desert to re-join at Kashgar. The other going north of the Tian Shan Mountains through Turpan, Talgar and Almaty in what is now Kazakhstan. This would be as far as I would travel. The northern route continues through Kokand in Uzbekistan and then west across the Karakum Desert. A southern branch heads towards Uzbekistan and Afghanistan. Both routes joined the main southern route before reaching Turkmenistan. The southern route was mainly a single route running from China, through the Karakoram, connecting Pakistan and China as the modern day Karakoram Highway. It then set off westwards crossing the high mountains, it passed through northern Pakistan, over the Hindu Kush Mountains, and into Afghanistan, re-joining the northern route near Merv. From there, it followed a nearly straight line west through mountainous northern Iran, Mesopotamia and the northern tip of the Syrian Desert to the Levant, where Mediterranean trading ships plied regular routes to Italy,

I had a group of 12. Two older Australian couples, Then a bunch of late twenty-somethings. A Canadian couple and Kiwi couple, both with the female part being of Chinese descent. Two Kiwi girls travelling together, another Aussie girl on her 8th organised trip and a 22 year old British girl on her first trip ever. A whole range of expectations and experiance. A whole lot of work for me. This started at the group meeting where I had to ask the group about flights back from Kashgar (where we end the trip) to Beijing or Shenzhen. Then organising this over the internet and paying for it when I already had enough paperwork to do and we were off to The Wall the following day. In the end I left somewhere in the region of $3,000 with the reception of the Harmony Hotel, hoping that I'd get plane tickets from a courier whilst I was on The Wall. Any mistakes, and it would be my fault and too late to do anything else.

My problems would not end with the trip. I would have about 6 days in which to leave China once the trip finished as that would be when my visa expired. I would then have to spend a few days somewhere (somewhere being the major sticking point) before re-entering China, to reactivate my visa and give me enough time to do the next trip before that visa ran out. Confused? How do you think I felt? Especially as the options on leaving China were pretty limited. Financially, flying from Kashgar (where I would finish the trip, look on a map, it's practically in the Middle East) to anywhere, was going to be very daunting, not to mention expensive. The nearest countries to Kashgar are (in no particular order, so as not to offend them—they are mainly in border disputes with each other) India, Pakistan, Kyrgyzstan and Kazakhstan. Other options, included flying to Russia, Mongolia (both with protracted visa issues for me) or further afield, South Korea, or back to Hong Kong. I'd spent enough time on email whilst in Hong Kong to figure out what my best options were and at the moment it looked like a trip to Kazakhstan was in the offing. All I knew about Kazakhstan was that it was an ex-Soviet satellite country and the home of "Borat". It was bound to be a laugh. My friend Lyn was also in need of a visa run out of China and was considering joining me on this dash to Kazakhstan, so at least I'd have company. But all this would have to wait; I had a trip to run.

So, I went to the Great Wall for the first time in six months. It was as magnificent as it always was, though just as much of a surprise to those in the group who were not expecting it to be straddling a range of mountains. Some did the hike from Jin Shan Ling to Si Ma Tai with me, some chose the bus. On the way back to the city, I had been requested by some in the group if we could stop at The Olympic Village to take some pictures of the "Birds Nest" which was now near completion. I was interested in this too, as when I had last come this way, the site was surrounded by hoardings and if I could get the bus driver to stop for us, all we could do was try to strain our necks to view the building site from our vantage point on the expressway flyover. No one had achieved anything like a good picture of the stadiums. Now, our opportunity to stop and take photos would cost the group an extra 200 Yuan, there would have to be a compromise with a the Canadian couple (with the Chinese girlfriend) who had already travelled to see the Olympic village having to go along with the rest of us.

The bus driver pulled up alongside the near complete Birds Nest, which is an impressive site even standing in its barren surroundings of a construction site. Over the last months the amount of information and propaganda about the Beijing Olympics and its stadiums has been at overload level on CCTV. Anything and everything had a connection to the Olympics and there were programmes being aired about the great achievements that were being made. Beijing's new subway system was to grow from only three lines to eight in the space of a year. The design of the Birds Nest and Water Cube were also the subject of much air time. The Chinese were glorifying their achievements and rightly so, whilst we westerners were only finding faults in building that would never have been conceived for an Olympics in another country. There was some chit-chat amongst the group that it would only last for twenty years, that beyond that time the design would be unstable and it would have to be demolished.

The Birds Nest Stadium is actually two independent structures, standing 50 feet apart; a red concrete seating bowl and the outer steel frame around it that was originally designed to hide the support columns for a retractable roof. The inspiration for this design was actually from Chinese ceramics and nothing to do with a birds nest at all, but as the Swiss architects later went on to say "a building can be perceived in many ways". The roof was dropped from the scheme but the steel supports for the fixed roof remained. This construction needed an entirely new process of steelmaking to be developed in order to attain the strength needed in the supporting beams. The Water Cube is no less an impressive structure and is covered in segments that look like bubbles, there are 4000 of these and they are made of "EFTE". Compared to glass, ETFE film is 1% the weight, transmits more light and costs 24% to 70% less to install. It is also resilient; able to bear 400 times its own weight, self-cleaning due to its non-stick surface and recyclable. It is true, these building were remarkable structures in every way and the pride in the achievements of the Chinese designers and engineers in constructing these stadiums was justly deserved. London 2012 would not and should not even attempt to compete with what the Chinese were doing.

For our tour of the Forbidden City the following morning, I had Kevin. With all the changes that had happened with the company since my last times in Beijing I was now seen as one of the experienced Leaders and it was easier for me to book the best Local Guides. The Canadian and Chinese couple didn't want to come. They had already been there and wanted me to give them their money back, as they were not going to use the tickets that they had paid for as part of the trip package. I could see that they were going to be trouble. On talking to Kevin, asking how he liked the changes with our company, he told me that a lot of the new Chinese Leaders were not booking a local guide. Instead they were taking the money and doing the job themselves, no matter where in the country they had come from. Many had never been to Beijing before their one week of "Training". Kevin was an excellent guide again. He pointed out the security guards that were listening to him speaking in Tian An Men Square and told us what he could not tell us about, all very tongue in cheek. Once in The Forbidden City he was pointing out the architecture and it significances. The animals carved on the elongated eves of all the buildings, the relative heights of the male wing, to the east, where the sun rises, compared to the lower female courtyards in the west. As we descended from the Palace of Supreme harmony he pointed out the great stone frieze at the centre of the ramps leading up to the terraces. It featured an elaborate and symbolic bas-relief carving of a dragon from a single piece of stone 16.57 metres long, 3.00 metres wide, and 1.7 metres thick. It weighs some 200 tonnes and had been transported from the mountains 70km away, possibly by putting ice on the road in wintertime. He also pointed out to me that the "Starbucks Coffee", much to my amusement had been removed. "There had been a petition" said Kevin, "so the authorities had to do something". He told me that Starbucks had been told that if they took down their signs and livery, then they would be able to continue selling their merchandise. By his account, Starbucks had said "no", so the Forbidden City Museum had decided that Starbucks would have to go. In its place was still a refreshment kiosk in the converted palace courtyard building, still selling coffee, snacks and souvenirs, but with no big "Starbucks" sign, or any other advertising for that matter. A small, very small victory I thought to myself.

Kevin then took us to Emperor Dowager Cixi royal chambers and told us the story of the "Dragon Lady" who was "the power behind the throne" during the last years of the Qing Dynasty. He reminded us of the opening scenes of the film "The Last Emperor" where a pearl was put in the mouth of the dead Empress as she lay in state, then talked about her life.

Cixi had come to court as a concubine of the Emperor in 1851 aged 16 and gave birth to Emperor Xiangfengs only son in 1857. Upon Xiangfengs death, her son became regent while she and the late emperors queen, named Ci'an became

Dowagers, both overseeing the young Emperor and the court officials appointed to rule for him. However, young Emperor Tongzhi was an inept ruler and only held power between 1873 and 1875 when he died, possibly of syphilis, or smallpox. The two Emperess Dowagers named Cixi's four year old nephew Guangxu as the new Regent, allowing the women to continue to control the true power in the land. In 1881 Ci'an died, in mysterious circumstances leaving Cixi in sole control of the heir to the throne until Guangxus ascent in 1894 at the late age of 19. However in 1898, after suffering military defeats and being accused of having too much foreign influence, the Emperor was deemed "not fit to rule". He was placed under house arrest until his untimely death ten years later and Cixi once again held the reigns of power. In 1900 she backed the Boxer Rebellion, which wanted an end to western influence and then had to flee the western powers to Xi'an. On her return, the court had to pay reparation to the foreign armies. She died in 1908, only a day after Guangxu, still under house arrest, died, from poisoning. Her last political move was to install Henry Pu Yi, a younger half brother to Guangxu on the throne at the tender age of two years and ten months.

Her rooms were one of the best preserved areas of the palace and although I had visited here before, with the stories that Kevin had given us, it was now one of my new highlights. As we exited the Palace, Kevin had one more story to tell us, concerning the "Dominating hill", what is now Jing Shan Park to the north of the Palace. It used to be a private garden to the Emperors and is where the last of the Ming emperors hung himself. Once again, this is a story of corruption and palace intrigue.

In its final years the Ming Dynasty was weakened by corruption, power-hungry eunuchs and political trouble on its borders. The decline was accelerated after a costly war against Japan over Korea. There was a peasant rebellion launched in the Shaanxi province after a devastating famine there and an invasion of Manchus from the north. Unpaid and unfed, the army was defeated by peasant leader Li Zicheng and deserted the capital without much of a fight. On May 26, 1644, Beijing fell to the rebel army when the city gates were treacherously opened from within. The last Ming emperor Chongzhen killed himself by hanging himself from a tree in the northern edge of the Forbidden City rather than being captured. There were rumours that the Emperor had been having an affair with one concubine of his general Wu Sangui, she was called Chen Yuan Yuan. She is renowned as one of the eight great beauties of China and the Emperor had sent Wu Sangui to the frontier to get him away from court and his desire for Chen Yuan Yuan. Some say that Wu Sangui opened the gates on the border to the Manchus out of hatred for the Emperor and wishing his defeat. Others say Wu was about to join the rebel forces of Li, who had already sacked the Ming capital Beijing, when he heard that his concubine Chen Yuan Yuan had been taken into custody by Li. Enraged, Wu contacted and negotiated with the Qing leader which resulted in the opening of the gates of the Great Wall. Wu also had desires on the title of Emperor himself and may have thought that the Qing would aid him in his ambition, but the Qing forces swept through the gates and on to Beijing.

Our Silk Road trip took us on to Xi'an for three days, the real start, or end of the ancient Silk Road, depending which point of view you are coming from. I did the regular visits to the Terracotta Warriors, the Muslim Quarter, Big Goose Pagoda, Shaan Xi Museum, and contemplated trips to Hua Shan and the local Pandas who were reportedly housed in some shambolic conditions in a private zoo. These were new suggestions now on the possible itinerary of all our trips as the area around Sichuan was not allowing tourism or panda visits because of the earthquake devastation. Over the last six months, the hostels had got their act together a lot more, in preparation for the Olympics. They had English speaking staff, had organised tours on the "East line" and "West line" taking in different sights around Xi'an. There were new hostels, all advertising western menus and bars. They were assuming that the Olympics would have a spin-off of tourists to Xi'an. The hostels in Xi'an now advertised trips further afield to Chengdu, the Yangtze River, Yuunan and there were flyers from hostels that had sprung up in these places too. In only six months, the whole concept of tourism in China was changing.

I'd decided to try and find the Silk Road Statues whilst here. I thought that it would be a good place to take the group, but as it happened, they were not where our tour guiding information booklet said they would be. This became a familiar recurring theme for the trip. These booklets contains information and maps on many of the places we visit and this particular version covers the Silk Road and on into Central Asia and Russia. Or rather, it is supposed to. After the best part of two afternoons walking around Xi'an, I finally got to the Silk Road Statues, my feet as blistered as one of its legendary travellers. It was not in the most romantic of settings, in the middle of a dual carriageway. So much for taking the group around here for a dinner of inspiration. I took a couple of photos and got the bus back to the hotel. Then, from here on in, everything was new to me.

We arrived at Jiayuguan, the city around the legendary last fort on the Great Wall. The translation of this place is "barrier to the pleasant valley", that valley being China and beyond it was the hostile barbarian world. A pre-arranged bus picked us up and we were to have this luxury of private transport for the next five days. Being my first time through here, it was a godsend. My first challenge was to have a walk around town with the group and find somewhere to eat. For all trips we run off the notes of previous leaders, as well referring to the booklet, however, the previous Silk Road trip had been nine months earlier and the trip notes were not good. I'd also printed off copies of the previous trip notes from 10 months and a year ago in an attempt to get a feel for the trip. Chinese Leader John He hadn't written much, but had incorporated photographs. I was having to delve back over a year to get any good information which in reality may or may not have been any good, because, once again, the booklet wasn't much help either. Unfortunately, I didn't know any of this, until I actually tried to use the information and found out that it was incorrect. So once we'd checked in at Jiayuguan I just picked what seemed to be the most likely route into town. As I headed to where I believed the recommended restaurant was, I got a call from Jane. Fantastic timing. She proceeds to tell me that there is a night market, close by to the hotel. This isn't marked on any of the Tour Leading info, or the Lonely Planet, or Rough Guide. Half of me didn't believe Jane but she was quite correct and we found a night-market for later. We continued on to the restaurant, then some of us walked on to the other night-market that was on the map. Here we found a wonderful array of possibly 100 stalls, all selling food ranging from noodles to barbeque. This was a real find, but unfortunately a good 45 min walk from the hotel. Taxis would be in order for the following day, which obviously meant me working on a written translation of where and what the night-market was into Chinese characters, not one of my strong points.

We visited Jaiyuguan Fort the following morning. The wall had a Middle Eastern feel to it with the turrets shaped in an Arabic fashion and being built from rammed earth, mud brick and some sort of sandstone. In places, some sections of the wall was under renovation, some of it looking a bit too new, whilst other sections may not have been touched since its construction during the Ming dynasty. The fort is trapezoid-shaped with a perimeter wall of 733 meters at a height of 11 meters. There are two gates: one on the east side of the pass, and the other on the west side. On each gate there is a turret. We climbed up and around, overlooking the spaces in between the three defence walls. There were small groups of Chinese tourists there too, all getting involved in the opportunities to try archery, or dress up as a Ming Dynasty soldier. Housed in the wall there was an information centre with maps showing the locations of the outlying forts in the "He Xi" corridor and into "Xin Jiang" or the New Frontier province where we would be heading.

The Chinese history of this region starts with the Han Dynasty and the sending of military general Zhang Qian to appease the five barbarian tribes which would periodically raid China from North West. This man is a hero in China and his story is amazing. He was sent to form alliances, but was captured by the Xiongnu tribe and held for 10 years. He escaped and was on his way back to China, documenting the peoples of the region as he went for a year, then was captured by the Xiongnu again and imprisoned for another two years. When he escaped again and finally reached the Chinese Emperor, he had reports on all the tribes to the west and the greater civilisations of Persia and India with whom the Chinese could establish trade with. It took another generation of battles to defeat the Xiongnu tribe. What we call the Silk Road, because we in the west could get silk from China, is where the Chinese first traded for many other goods including the large and powerful horses of the Eurasian steppe. These animals were sought after by the military and it is somewhat ironic that it was these animals from the west, which helped the Chinese to conquer the Xiongnu and the western territories.

The existing fort which we were visiting had been built to improve inferior Han Dynasty fortification in 1539 as a response to the constant incursions from the nomads from the north and west. The building of the wall had come at a great expense and had taken many requests in order to gain the funding from the Ming court in Beijing. The architect had been asked to calculate exactly how many bricks it would take to construct the fort. He had come up with the figure of 999,999 bricks. Upon completion, there was one brick left over and a government official chastised him for his wastefulness. The architect replied that the last brick was to go above the portal and would act as a good luck talisman for all who passed beneath it.

The fort was the final part of the Great wall, but there were more forts further west, into and through the He Xi corridor. As part of the Northern Silk Road running northwest from the bank of the Yellow River, it was the most important route from

North China to the Tarim Basin and Central Asia for traders and the military. The corridor is basically a string of oases along the northern edge of the Tibetan Plateau. To the south is the high and desolate Tibetan Plateau and to the north, the Gobi Desert and the grasslands of Outer Mongolia. At the west end the route splits in three, going either north of the Tian Shan or south on either side of the Tarim Basin.

From our vantage point up on the wall you could look over the desert. This gave a real sense of isolation. Being posted here 400 years ago would really have seemed like the back of beyond. There was nothing out there apart from hostile wasteland. It really was the end of China and the civilised world. Then, take a look in the opposite direction, towards the town of Jaiyuguan. Framed by the turrets of the ancient frontier wall, the frontier town had grown in typical Chinese style. Smoke stacks and tower-blocks, like a mixture of pre-war and post-war industrial England, but placed here, as a new town on the flat desert plane.

Our next stop was the 'overhanging wall' a bit of an anti-climax after a steep walk to a tower. Once again, there was the vast wasteland, but the 'overhang' didn't live up to the billing. Here, on the barren hillside, locals had written messages with stones, much like carving names in the sand of a beach. There were messages in Chinese and English, love-hearts and what really caught my eye was a large penis and balls, half way up the hill-side, displayed proudly for all to see. Even out here in this desolate no-mans land, there was space for a sense of humour. Our last trip around the wall took us to the First Beacon Fire Tower. At first glance, this looked even more depressing and desolate than the last two places, but the show stopper was the view, where the wall ended abruptly over a river gorge. This really was the end of the Great Wall, the end of China, beyond which was a vast wasteland, hostile, forbidding. An image was conjured up in my mind. This wall was as much a defence against the elements and a statement of what was being protected as a human domain as much as it was an actual defence against a living army. Around this place, the Chinese had constructed an underground museum. The reasons for this was to protect the wall and also to protect us from the heat. But there was more. You could stand on a viewing platform over the gorge, or even take a zip line across it. Further along the cliff, a film company had built a set for some period drama. Even this final frontier was in the process of being brought into the fold as just another theme-park and with it, destroying its fundamental reason d'etre.

The next day we travelled the five hours by our private bus to Dunhuang. This was an oasis where in imperial times, had been an outpost for disgraced officials to be sent. My contact here was Marco. He'd spent time in Rome and spoke Italian. I never found out exactly what he'd done for CITS to send him here, but I had been told by the other leaders that he was obviously a dodgy bloke and enduring a modern day exile. He seemed to be doing quite well for himself anyway, having tour groups, hotels and contacts throughout the town. My first impressions of Dunhuang were good. Restaurants and tourist information in English made my job all the more easier. Johns, Charlies' and Shirly's cafes all vied for my business in western looking lunches, tours, internet and bicycle hire. The town was easy to get around, clean and modern. After a day of this though, it was obviously a too modern tourist town. Large sections of what would have been the traditional city had been pedestrianized with the vendors selling handicrafts from fake wooden carts. There were opportunities to have your photograph taken next to a life size stuffed toy of a camel. Tourism was big in Dunhuang but it had that fake and Disney feel about it, the real ancient oasis of Dunhuang was either hidden from me, or completely redeveloped. There was one oddity, an entire street of garment makers who specialised in PVC. Was Dunhuang the centre of Chinas underground fetish scene?

The following morning we set off at 5am for the sand dunes on the edge of town. We had to wake the gate keeper. It was a massive wooden gate, like you would only see defending a giant's castle. We entered, like thieves in the night, like in the Arabian Nights. Under the starlit sky and the cool night air we walked across the sand. We traipsed to the nearest sandy mound that would give us a vantage point, then in silence and awe watched the sun rise from the nearest dune, bringing light over the desert. This was definitely one highlight of the trip. At around 6:45 we were mounting camels for a ride out into the dunes. I've been on camels a few times now, so no bother at all and the group looked good, casting long shadows of themselves in the camel train, across the sides of the dunes. We stopped at a particularly large dune. Here, a stall was set up and a cross between a plank pathway and a ladder that ran up to the top of the dune. If you wanted to pay Y20, you could walk the plank to the top of the dune, where you had a choice of getting back down on either a wooden sledge or toboggan, or a large tyre inner-tube. Some of the group went for this. I just took a walk up the dune and marvelled at the way it extended across like a sandy mountain range. Its high ridge towered over the valley below, containing the suburbs of the town of Dunhuang. It all looked so precarious, like the sand could collapse at any moment, sending waves of the stuff to engulf the town, completely drowning it like some burst dam or tsunami. Another 20 minutes took us to Crescent Moon Lake. At first, this was a disappointment. A concreted in pool, with broken concrete seating and tables. It was only after a wander around that we discovered that the real Crescent Moon Lake was beyond another dune, another plank pathway, toboggan slide and archery shoot. The real Crescent Moon Lake's setting was pleasant enough, complete with wooden temple on the shore of this real oasis in the sand but I was beginning to realise where I really was. As we rode back to the starting point of our morning excursion, we saw hundreds, if not thousands of tourists. They were getting ready, mounting their camels then filing across the desert to where we'd just gone. We were lucky; we had had a unique experience being alone for the sunrise on the dunes before setting off on our own. We had been the first of very many. As I looked on, yellow buggies and golf carts came into view and a micro-light aircraft took off. The noise was rising to a crescendo. I'm glad we were leaving before the experience was completely ruined.

We took a side trip to the White Horse Pagoda on the way back. This is where (in legend and in 'Monkey Magic') the monk "Tripitaka's" white horse died as they brought back the Buddhist scriptures from India. These scriptures were housed in the Big Goose Pagoda in Xi'an, bringing legend and fairy-tale together again in that city which is always part myth and modern day reality. The Horse was actually The Dragon of the East Sea, sent to aid the monk and the monkey but we don't want to complicate things, so I won't elaborate. That night the passengers went to the night market to eat and I dined with Marco. The night market was a more modern affair, newly built, with permanent built stalls and areas with comfortable chairs. The group got ripped off, the first time they'd had to find their own food. The girl who could speak Chinese and her boyfriend had eaten elsewhere and spent more and more time away from the rest of the group.

Our last day in Dunhuang, we went to the Magoa caves. This is a UNESCO World heritage site about 25Km from town in the surrounding desert. As we approached, we saw the ancient caves cut row upon row in the mountain side, small niches dug into the sandy coloured rock and all looking like a real adventure of ancient archaeology. There must have been hundreds of them. I thought that we would be scrambling over the rocky desert hillsides, ready to unearth some long forgotten fragment of a mosaic but wasteland soon gave way to a more modern setting. The Magoa Caves are now safely in an open air park, behind a wall with ticket booth information centre and souvenir shop. The caves had all been repaired, or renovated. For fear of collapse, a 'pebble-dash' style of facade had been pasted over the front of all the caves. There had then been uniform wooden doors added to each cave, some of which remained closed and a number was on each door to each cave. To finish off the job, a few concrete walkways had been added, just so that you could get access to the higher level, or would that be second and third stories of the caves. It looked just like a North of England Council estate from the 1950's. The caves themselves were spectacular. There are over 500 in total, just over half of which are open to the public, as long as you take a guide. All of them are (or at least, were) finely decorated. Giant Buddha's over 25m tall. Paintings from different styles and influences spanning 1500 years. With each influx of Indian, Mongolian, Tibetan or other culture, the statues and styles of the Buddha painting changed, he grew more "Asian" and less "Indo-European" over time, and the scenes depicted around him took on the interpretation of the Tibetans and Mongolians rather than the Indians who first came there. Artists had been hired to paint the cave interiors with often wildly colourful scenes from the Jataka Tales (the life of the Buddha), Buddhist mythology and illustrations of the Buddhist sutras (scriptures), as well as scenes of court life with musicians, dancers, and courtiers. Statues of Buddha, Bodhisattvas, kings and demons often carved directly out of out of the walls. Dunhuang supported a community of monks and over time it became a centre for meditation, burial, worship and for the storage of documents and artefacts. Documents in Chinese, Uighur, Tibetan, Mongolian, Syriac, Sanskrit and Brahmi have been found.

We saw where 'archaeologists' from the west had removed paintings and sculptures. The British archaeologist and explorer Marc Aurel Stein learned of the Library Cave, as it was first known and befriended the monk "Wang" who was its custodian. Over time, he was able not only to gain access to the cave, but to take away tens of thousands of manuscripts in exchange for a small amount of cash. Most of them are now to be found in the British Museum. Later the French Sinologist, Paul Pelliot, would remove more of its treasures, to be followed by others. We went on to the museum which was more like an anti-museum, where it catalogued the 40,000 or so artefacts that had been taken from the Magoa caves and now sat in collections in the

British Museum, France, the Hermitage and other places dotted around the globe. A real lesson in grave robbing.

Our next overnight train took us to Turpan. This is another desert oasis on the Silk Road. It is the hottest place in China, with temperatures reaching a staggering 46 degrees. It is also the second lowest place in the world with over 140 sq Km lying at below sea level. The two guides listed for in the tour notes had not answered any of my text's or calls over the last week and I'd had to ask Rockhard once again for his advice. There was also confusion as to what was "included" as part of the tour and what was going to be an "optional" excursion and no one in the office could help, so between Stephen, myself and my new contact, a local guide called Momin John we worked out an itinerary and some process. For the next two days, he was to show us the wonders of living around this spectacular oasis.

We were now in Xin Jiang Province or Chinas 'New Frontier'. According to the history books, this area had first come under Chinese domination with the Han incursions nearly 2000 years ago. The Tang Dynasty claimed all of these lands as part of their Empire over 1000 years ago, but the "New Frontier" really only earned its name in the 1700's under the Qing Dynasty. This was also Uyghur country (say 'wee gur'). They are a Central Asian people, not very Chinese at all. They were one of the Turkic tribes that flourished before the Tang claimed these lands, but were then brought under the Empire of the Mongols as one of their "Hoards". Ming expansionism saw them come within the Chinese Empire. They don't look like the Chinese, they could easily be mistaken for their Persian and Turkish cousins and they practice the Muslim religion. They speak their own Uyghur language, which is a Turkic language and is written in Arabic script. There are over 6 million Uyghurs in Xin Jiang province and you can draw many parallels with them and their neighbours the Tibetans to the south. Relations with the ruling Han Chinese are not the best.

Turpan looked like it was under construction, or at least the roads were. We were in a big hotel that was used to catering for tourists and once again had the feeling that you were not really in the China of the isolated and inward looking Chinese, but a region that was definitely part of a wider world. It felt like the Chinese were the tourists here just as much as we were. However, as we walked around the town, it was definitely the Chinese that were turning the town into a modern city. Along with the new roads were the new buildings, shopping mall and stores and a new central square complete with "musical fountain". There were a couple of what looked like traditional covered roads. What I mean by this was that the paved walkways were lined by pillars or columns and above them was formed a sort of canopy from what looked like grape vines. It had a sort of "Roman Villa" feel to it, columns and creeping vines with an imperial opulence. Though I suppose anywhere in the ancient Middle East would have been proud to have city that looked and felt like Turpan did.

Turpan was an originally an oasis camp in what was the kingdom of Gushi, that was conquered by the Chinese Han Dynasty in 107 BC. The city was occupied at times by the Xiongnu, then the Gokturks and had periods of independence before returning to China in the Tang Dynasty. For much of this time, the capital city of the region was Jiaohe, a city that was on our itinerary to visit. As the Tang dynasty waned, the Uighur tribe took control of the area. Then during the Yuan Dynasty it administered the region as a vassal state. The Moghuls invaded in 1389 and the people were converted to Islam over the following century. At the same time the Ming Dynasty re-exerted their claim to the land and by the early 16th Century there began the "Ming-Turpan border wars" concerned with "tribute" and by 1528 the whole area was annexed again by China. With the fall of the Ming Dynasty, the Moghuls gained their independence again until 1755 when the Qing conquered all the territories now known as Xinjiang Province. However, since the nineteenth century, the whole area became part of the "Great Game" of the western powers, mainly Russia and Britain, who were vying for influence in the area at the expense of the Chinese. Western backed independence movements around the notion of a "Turkistan" began to evolve. We heard modern day echoes of this unrest as we travelled through the country.

Most of us took a trip out to the Flaming Mountains, Tuyoq village and on the way there, Momin John talked about the Uyghur people, the local produce of grapes, raisins, sultanas, wine, pomegranates, watermelon and other crops. Statistics he came up with showed this 'desert' region to be a very productive land. Across what looked to be an arid country, were fields of crops and dotted amongst them were clusters of brick buildings that could have been dwellings, however, the brick walls were constructed so that there were spaces in between all of the bricks. Momin John told us that these were the drying houses for the sultanas. Then somebody asked "what is the difference between a raisin and a sultana?" We got the answer that the raisins were dried directly in the sun, whilst the sultana was dried in the houses that we saw, making them more succulent. It didn't matter what type of grape was used, it was all in the drying process. Then he showed us the oil wells and explained about the vast natural resources under the ground. He called Xin Jiang 'the pocket of China', with the hand of the Han Chinese, taking out all of the wealth. On the way to past the Flaming Mountains (so called, not only because they are in the hottest part of China, but because, in a certain light, the red mountains can shimmer in the haze and look like flame) we passed the biggest thermometer in Asia. This is at a photo stop for the flaming mountains and will now cost money if you want to take a picture there. The Chinese, as ever, 'erected' the thermometer in true 'Chinese Tourism Theme-park style'. The thing actually looks like a large cigarette sticking out of a metal ash-try. By the way, the temperature was 43 degrees.

On to Tuyoq village. An ancient mud brick village, still inhabited by locals, living a traditional lifestyle. As ever, there is a story or two. I'd been warned by other leaders that the place had gone touristy and the locals were not happy about it. The full story is this. As the village attracted a trickle of visitors (we were the only ones when we visited) a branch of the CITS in Urumqi decided to set up a ticket office at the gate to the town and charge people for entering. This pissed the locals off, and they started to hassle the visitors for money too. More recently, the local government got involved. It took over the ticket office, but regulated the tourism and now gives a percentage of the entrance fee to the villagers. Happy faces all round, apart from two of my passengers who didn't see why they had to pay at all. Inside the village, Momin John explained why the village was so well preserved, as the locals gathered around in a scene reminiscent of a Cecil B Demille film of the early Chiristians telling a parable to the villagers. This was ironically a Muslim holy place. To cut a long story short, some Muslim princes had escaped attack and slept in a cave here, which was a magical cave for 309 years. This story was also in the Koran, placing the cave at Tuyoq village. A temple had been constructed and further along, there were caves with paintings. The whole village was in the process of preserving itself, in its original state. Only the re-built mosque was a modern building, but in a traditional style. A strange idea occurred to me that the preserved village was a little like how the cave preserved the princes. Back in Turpan, to round off our day, we went to a show, put on by a local troupe. The music was obviously Middle Eastern and Arabic, dancing rhythms and melodies. We all took donkey carts back to the hotel, a fabulous day.

Our second day in Turpan was no less spectacular. First stop was the Emin Mosque and Minaret. This is the only Arabic style minaret in China. A brick construction, the bricks laid to form patterns as they ascend the tower. It is not an entirely straight tower, more 'gherkin' shaped for those familiar with the new skyscraper in the City of London. It's one of the must have photographs of a journey to these parts. Next we went on to Jiaohe ancient city. This is around 2,800 years old and was abandoned at the start of the last millennium. It is truly what the Silk Road is all about. Lost cities in the desert, once thriving civilisations, then covered in the shifting sands of time.

If it wasn't for the 45 degree heat, I could have wandered around there for hours between the archaeological remains of the sand coloured walls that were abandoned palaces, temples, gate houses, all now weathered crumbling walls, returning once again to the desert. Our last stop was the Karez museum. This is straight out of one of my school geography textbooks. I'd learned about this years' ago, but never thought I'd see it in action. The locals have ingeniously designed a well and underground channel system that brings water from the high land, to the low. Wells are dug to the water table on the hillside, then channelled through tunnels to the villages in the valley. Here it is filtered through open channels to fields and orchards and through the town as drinking and washing water. There are over 5000km of these and many date back 2000 years. This is the reason why the land is so fertile and explains the diverse and plentiful supply of crops. The Karez museum had a cut away section that showed exactly how it all worked and Momin Johns information only added to the excursion, he said it was the eighth wonder of the ancient world and even through his local pride, I could see that he had a pretty good claim. We also had a dinner here at a local house, sitting on mats around a low table and served local kebabs and long noodles. It was another fabulous day out.

That night, most of us ended up in the night market. This was on a central square, in between the hotels and new roads and building developments, close by the musical fountain, but in an area still not "developed" Chinese style. Here you wander through the stalls with entire animals on sale in different states of being cooked and eaten. You can buy the most succulent roasted lamb at Y50/Kg chickens for slightly less, kebabs on swords for three Yuan and local long noodle dishes along with cheap beer and rice wine. We got quite merry that night and the locals joined us, filling our glasses over and over again. I left quite late. As I entered the hotel, I couldn't help but notice a beautiful girl, dressed in a red ball gown, coming down the stairs. As we passed, she looked at me, 'massage?' she said. The illusion was shattered, but a massage in a ball gown?

The next morning we set off in our tour bus with Mr Wu the driver to Heavenly Lake. Here we were going to stay in a Kazak (minority people) family nomadic yurts, in the hills around Heavenly lake. We headed there via Urumqi. This is a big modern city and the only reason why we were going there was because we had to pass through it in order to get to where we were going. I decided that we could do a side trip after lunch and go to the museum. Some of the group had also been reading up on the Urumqi museum as they have some quite extraordinary exhibits. There are 2800 year old mummies preserved there along with a worthwhile exhibition of the local minority cultures in Xin Jiang. It took a bit of negotiating to get in because we were supposed to book group tours in advance. The museum was well worth it and the exhibits and information were second to none.

It was a modern museum and everything that you would expect it to be, well lit and organised with a multitude of exhibits from around the region, but we wanted the main attraction. Wang Binghua, a local archaeologist had discovered the first of the mummies in 1978, before then, little was known of the pre-historic settlements in the area. There, under glass, lay the corpses of a family; a man, a woman, and a child of two or three. Each wore, dark purple woollen garments and felt boots. The information said they were 3,000 years old, yet the bodies looked as if they were buried yesterday. It was thought that they were preserved merely by being buried in the parched, stony desert, where daytime temperatures often soar over 100 degrees. In the heat the bodies were quickly dried, with facial hair, skin, and other tissues remaining largely intact. What was most interesting was something that I had recently read about them and had to see for myself. These corpses had obvious Caucasian, or European, features, reddish blond hair, long noses, deep-set eyes, and long skulls. The question was, "where had they come from and what were they doing in this part of Asia so long ago?"

Our next venture was not so successful. The driver took us to a place for lunch, which was a sort of Middle Eastern style restaurant. There was a central "courtyard" with seating on two floors overlooking this and it was all decorated in an Arabic style. There were musicians playing and the place was obviously one of the places to go to for lunch, but we just couldn't figure out what to do. There was a canteen style service counter, but we were shown to tables. No waitress could communicate with us and in the end we just went to the counter and pointed at what we thought we might like to eat. In the confusion, the Canadians left, thinking that they could do better on their own and they were followed by a couple of the girls. The rest of us got tickets, waited, were ushered back to the tables, and waited some more until the food started to arrive.

Heavenly lake was a little less inspiring than the name suggests. On my research of this part of the trip I'd been warned about basic facilities, but a fantastic, out of the way, local experience. John He, in his own impressive style had attached a photograph of "Rasheets Yurts" covered in snow, exactly one year earlier. I was bracing myself for this. We arrived, passing campsites of plastic yurts in neat white rows along with pre-fabricated kiosks on our way up the mountainside. There were Chinese "Four by four" cars parked, gleaming in the sun, next to the yurts and the reception and restaurant building. A new road was being put in and the campsites of tourist yurts were evidently branching out along the highway. I hoped that this wasn't where we were staying. Rasheet met us; he was the Kazak "nomad" who had the yurt where we were staying. This man was a complete surprize to me, thick set, speaking flawless English, even joking with me and exuding a confidence that I believed was gained from a life of being self-reliant in the hostile Kazak mountains. We had to get out of our bus at a terminus; we got a tourist bus past the cable car, up to the car park with the souvenir shops. Then we walked for 20 mins along a concrete path by the lake, which had the fake wooden handrails that I'd seen before at Emei Shan. My memory went back to my conversations with Jane about this part of the trip. She had groups of girls who had refused to walk around the lake and I had pictured some sort of complete wilderness where you had a test of strength and character. Jane had told me that you could hire ponies for the trek around the lake, but that was just "selling out". This was literally, a lot more like a "walk in the park" than I had been lead to believe. We had even passed electric buggies to take the tourists from the car park to the hotel. Then we spotted a statue, just on the other side of a fake wooden bridge. The statue was of a woman, carved in white stone, looking out to the lake. I asked our host, Rasheet what it was all about. He said he didn't know, it had been built last year, imported from Guangzhou and it was crap. Rasheet and his family had a business organising accommodation in his families Yurts. However, what must have been a fantastic out of the way experience, only a few years ago, was now well within the grasp of Chinese Tourism. My "nomad" was not a nomad, he was a confident businessman.

I'd slept in yurts, or gers before and these are just traditional round tents, made from a wooden frame and covered with animal skins. Traditionally, the nomads would assemble and dissemble these in a couple of hours and move with them on their bi-annual move between the low and high pastures. In Mongolia, there were furniture pieces or Buddhist shrines in the gers. Each family member would have their own space in the ger, parents to one side, children to the other and the Shrine on its own. There was no furniture in these yurts, possibly because they only functioned as tourist accommodation, but we all bedded down on the floor around a central metal stove with a chimney through a small opening in the canopy. Just like how I remembered.

The highlight of my stay at heavenly lake was going horse-riding. There were not enough guides, so off we went, climbing up the hillside, slowly through the forest and on to the high pasture where we could see the snow-capped mountains in the distance. This was the world of the Tour Leader that I had dreamed of, especially the bit where I rode myself back to the encampment, like a returning hero. The food we ate was also better than I had been led to believe. There were two options, "noodles" or "kill a goat". Both Rockhard and Jane had told me of the times when they had to kill the goat. The local custom is that as a "leader" (of your people) you must feed them and it is your duty to kill the goat for food. Jane had told me that she had kissed the restrained goat just as she slit its throat. I wasn't looking forward to this, but was making myself feel better about it because I knew that the Kazaks in the yurts would be able to use every part of the animal and both it and the money we spent to purchase it would be very welcome and not wasted. In the end, not enough of the group wanted to purchase the whole goat; at a cost of 500 Yuan, it needed all of us to agree to the sale. So, in the end, it was noodles. The downside of staying there was toilets, with no water. I get the basic nomadic way of life thing, but considering we were more or less in a country park, the lack of water just didn't wash, literally.

The next couple of days of the trip were the most difficult. We were traversing the fringes of the Taklimakan Desert before crossing it to our destination of Hotan, which meant a couple of nights in a couple of random towns with no other reason for us to stop there apart from the fact that we needed to break up the journey. Once again, we were arriving in towns where I'd never been before, there would be no guides to help me, no-one spoke English and the Tour Information booklet had been completely inaccurate about every single place we had visited so far. We were staying in new hotels, which were not listed in my information and left me wondering where I actually was every time we checked into a hotel. This would be followed by me trying to get information out of the receptionists as to where we could eat, find supplies for the following day, or what we could do in town for the evening when non spoke any English at all. On arrival at each hotel, after getting the most basic information from whoever would try to communicate with me, I would spend an hour walking around the vicinity of the hotel, or in some direction that I had just been pointed in, with the hope that it might lead me somewhere. Back at the hotel, usually with the group waiting, I would then lead them to whatever I had just found. Somehow I pulled it all off. We ate, found internet and found our way around town on my hastily drawn re-maps.

One thing about these towns and these hotels is that they are havens of prostitution. In most hotels there will be a phone call from a girl every hour asking if you want a massage, in many of them, the girls will be loitering around the hotel lobby. This usually attracts some unsavoury characters, prospective clients and pimps, but they are usually quite harmless. However, there is always the possibility that something might happen, and this it did in Kurla. One of the girls went down to the lobby to make a phone call, but before long was being directed to the massage parlour (most hotels have these, or karaoke rooms that act as cover for the working girls) by one of the prospective clients. She left, but was followed up to her room by the bloke, who then knocked on her door. It was all over in a matter of minutes as she screamed at him, and quite terrifying for the girl. On a lighter note, in the hotel in Ming Feng, along with the usual can of coke, pot noodle, condoms and "after sex wash for man", "after sex wash for woman" on offer in the room, was a space helmet and a length of rope. One can only guess what they were supposed to be used for.

The big adventure in this part of the trip is going across the Taklimakan Desert. Hemmed in by jagged black mountains and what once would have been impenetrable passes that still took us a day to cross. We stopped at one point to watch a dust devil rise out of the sand, it spiralled into the sky, growing like a Genie from a bottle and moved slowly towards us. It grew to a height of maybe 100 feet, picking up debris and swirling it around, trapping it in its vortex. Then moved on again, towards a series of low buildings and completely engulfed them, sucking the debris from around the small houses and trapping it in its power. It was time for us to move on. This is the second largest sand desert in the world (after the Sahara) and is straight out of Lawrence of Arabia. Rolling sand dunes, vast empty spaces.

For some reason I kept getting 'Frankie Goes to Hollywood's The Power of Love' going through my head with the video of the 3 kings in camel caravan crossing the desert. This was the Silk Road in all its glory. It made me wonder what actually possessed the first people to think that they could cross it. It truly looked like it should be the end of the Earth. We rolled into it. A barrier was erected across the road with a number of warning signs. It may as well have said 'abandon all hope, ye who enter here'; it may as well have been hell. We journeyed for hours, the wind rising into a sand storm, sending dust devils at us across the highway. Snakes of sand would run across the highway, trying to form into something more sinister before we punched through them, leaving them behind before they could form into real dust devils, or demons. This was an inhospitable environment. Over 40 degree heat. The wind lashing us with sand, cutting visibility down to only a few meters in places. We would slowly rise and fall with the road over the dunes, occasionally seeing another vehicle. Then disaster struck.

We hit a bump in the road. The driver knew what had happened immediately. He quickly stopped the bus and inspected it. We had no breaks. We were in the middle of the desert, in a sandstorm, with no hope of repair or rescue. Our mobile phones were out of range. We had to carry on. We gingerly headed back out onto the abandoned highway. Luckily, there were no other vehicles to contend with and a desert is relatively flat. This still didn't stop a couple of my passengers repeatedly saying "we're going to die! we're going to die!" The driver kept a steady 40km, peering our way through the sandstorm. At each sand dune that the road crossed he would slow on the up side and cut the engine at the top of every rise. Then we would free-wheel like a go cart down the other side of the dunes, hoping that the drop would not be too long, or have traffic or blind curves up ahead on the sand-blind road. Yes, it was terrifying, and it did cross my mind that we were going to die.

It was very late when we made it out of the desert and to the next town. We had a late start the next day as the bus got repaired. There was an almighty cheer as we stopped, without any problem, at the first set of traffic lights out of town. Then it was another 6 hours on to Hotan. Hotan looked like yet another identikit Chinese town as we drove to our hotel just off from the main town square, It was built in 2004, after they tore down much of the old centre and most of the remaining old city wall. Remnants of the wall can be seen west of the square, I was told a similar fate was about to befall our final destination city of Kashgar, all in the name of progress and modernisation. It was also whispered that it was a way of controlling the traditional Uyghur communities that would on occasion riot against the Chinese government from these fertile grounds for East Turkistan nationalism. The centrepiece of the town square is a statue of Chairman Mao with a local man, I knew there would have to be some story to do with this.

Hotan had been another planning nightmare for me. The highlight of our trip to Hotan, was to be a trip to the outlying villages. Here, a charity that we sponsor called Silk Road Tapestries helped local women earn an income from making embroidered cloths that could be turned into everything from wall hangings, to bags, to mobile phone holders and in turn they would be sold on to tourists. The woman who set up the scheme was not in the country and out of the local people only one woman spoke Mandarin called Aysham. There was no way that I could organise this without help, so once again, with the aid of Rockhard and emails from the organiser; I enlisted the guiding services of Helil. The deal was that he would translate for our tour in the morning. Then in the afternoon he would take the group on, around the local villages, for a price. I was becoming a bit of a wheeler-dealer. I reckoned most of the group would be up for the trip. We had a look around the modern centre of Hotan, in the blistering heat and that evening ate at the night-market in the town square. Lots of local food, kebabs and noodles again. Elsewhere in the square, game stalls had been set up. In the ornamental pools, some enterprising individuals had placed what looked like a cross between a large inflated condom and a mouse wheel. I will explain. These large floating, multi-coloured tubes worked as some sort of fairground ride, where you would climb inside, and run, spinning the tube around, until you inevitably fell over and got churned around, washing machine style. Great fun for the locals and for us. All this was presided over by the benevolent statue of Mao and a local farmer, watching his people running like mice in a wheel/condom.

The next morning we met Helil and our local charity worker Aysham. We headed off to a village. This was all mud brick alleyways and courtyard houses. At the first house, we entered to see chickens and goats in a pen. On the other side of the courtyard was a large, subterranean 'tandoor' oven, used for baking bread. It was market day and the oven was just being fired up. We were soon eating freshly baked 'bagel' style bread, washed down with a local tea. Our transport around the village was to be on donkey carts, it was just how it should have been, every moment surpassing the last one. Our next stop was a "tapestry family". The charity works to support women who otherwise have no other source of independent income. This is a traditional Muslim society where women are not allowed to go out of the house to work, I'd originally thought that this was a charity supporting destitute or abandoned women, but instead these are what is considered to be normal families in these parts. If anything the charity is challenging the norms and traditions of society and doing its part in emancipating women. Amongst the goods on display was one of a mountain scene and a lake. On closer inspection, this rural idyll of trees, horsemen and grazing had a red Ferrari in the back-ground. Well, everything has to move with the times. We also visited the wooden bowl makers who carve bowls, spoons and other things from one piece of wood.

We had lunch in the village after which Helils' trip got all but three of my group interested, the Canadian/Chinese couple not wanting to be involved again. We visited a water powered flour mill, one of the few left operating, then went on to what was possibly the best market that I've ever seen. As it was Friday and the beginning of the Muslim weekend there was the bazaar and it was an open air bazaar in every sense of the word. Our bread baking family had been baking just for this Friday bazaar. Local people were buying and selling everything that you could think of. Uyghur knives, clothes, food, a cattle market, pots and pans and everything else that you could think of for daily life on wooden stalls under a cloth awning and on the cleared dirt ground. All the trappings of the traditional nomadic life were there, bridles and bits, tassels, ropes, belts and camel nose-pegs. Elsewhere makeshift canvas-roofed food stands under which huge cauldrons of steaming noodles bubbled away, and clay ovens produce piping-hot dumplings and flat-loaf bread. We caused quite a stir being the only outsiders there. This was what these tours are really all about and it's a pity that there are now fewer and fewer places where you can see the real village life as it has been for hundreds of years. We took a look at the local silk workshop as a last visit, with information on the production and dyeing process before seeing a selection of the finished garments for sale, so the girls bought their silk scarves. One of the group was a textiles graduate and said that it really brought the whole thing to life for her. That evening, we were entertained by a local 'Bandola' player, a sort of guitar, with all the Middle Eastern rhythms and soaring melodies. Then it was a return to the night market in the square for another barbecue and noodle feast for dinner.

Helil told us the story of the statue of Mao and the farmer. It is of local farmer Kurban Tulum (whom the Chinese call Uncle Kurban). When the Communist party came to power, a lot of local people in Xin Jiang thought that the land reforms were a good thing, taking away the feudal landlords and making the peasant better off. Kurban decided to go to Beijing to see Mr Mao, to thank him, and bring him some fruit. So he began a three month journey with his donkey cart to meet Mao, which he did, and the story is now depicted in statue form. Another slight change to this story is told as a local joke. Once the farmer returned to Hotan, the other farmers asked what had happened to him in Beijing. The farmer then re-counts his days there, where he stood in Tian An Men Square with thousands of other people listening to Mao. The farmer could not understand Mandarin Chinese, coming from distant Xin Jian Province, so instead interpreted what was happening. He told of the many people in the square and Mr Mao standing in front of them, high on a platform. Mao raised his hat to the crowd. According to the story, the Farmer interpreted Mr Mao as asking "whose hat is this?" Then the crowd replied in unison "it's mine, it's mine". The point of this story was a little lost on me, but it's obviously a top joke in Xin Jiang and somewhat reminded me of the Monty Python sketch "the funniest joke in the world" with Hitler at a rally telling the "My dog has no nose . . ." joke.

So we had to leave Hotan and journey on to our final destination, the ancient oasis and Silk Road trading hub of Kashgar. Kashgar market is intertwined with the history of the Silk Road. Tales of caravan crossing from Europe and buying silks and spices from China. This city had a feeling of self-importance, was once the self-styled capital of Eastern Turkistan in the early 1900's and even had Embassy Consulates from the U.K. and Russia. Once again, the historical significance of the "Great Game" of the last two centuries which encouraged Uyghur and East Turkistan Nationalism. From our hotel, we walked through part of the old city, its Middle Eastern streets spilling stalls and children into the winding streets. We saw the remnants of the old city wall, soon to be completely demolished along with the old mud brick houses and the community that we had walked through. Then we came to the Grand Square and the Id Kah Mosque. It could have been an Arabic capital city, apart from the Chinese billboards and neon on some of the larger buildings. A large, open square with massive mosque, in decorative coloured tiles and twisting architecture along with the towering minarets, stark against the purple of the evening sky. It is the largest mosque in China, the 11th largest in the world and built in 1442 incorporating older structures dating back to 996. It covers 16,800 square meters. Every Friday, 10,000 Muslims prey there but the building can hold up to 20,000. We managed ice cream on the walk back home, we smelt the roasting lamb from the open air barbecues standing outside the restaurants. Arabic script and Uyghur language coming from the dark skinned, round eyed people. We felt so far away from China.

The earliest mention of Kashgar occurs when the Chinese Han Dynasty envoy travelled the Northern Silk Road to explore lands to the west. Another early mention of Kashgar is in 76 BC when the Chinese conquered the Xiongnu tribe in this region. The states of Yutian (Khotan), Sulei (Kashgar), and others in the Tarim basin succumbed to Chinese rule. Xuan Zang, better known as Tripitaka in the T.V. series "Monkey" passed through Kashgar in 644 on the return leg of his "Journey to the West" to India. The Buddhist religion was active in Kashgar and there were hundreds of monasteries with more than 10,000 followers. In a series of campaigns between 652 and 658, with the help of the Uyghur's, the Chinese finally defeated the Western Turk tribes and took control of all their domains, including the Tarim Basin kingdoms. In the 8th century came the Arab rule from the west and the Muslim religion acquired a steadily growing influence but it was not until the 10th century that Islam was established at Kashgar. All this changed again with the invasion of the Mongols and Chingis Khan in 1219. Marco Polo visited the city around 1274. As the Mongol Empire collapsed, Kashgar became the prize for warring tribes that would hold the city, then lose it over numerous battles until the Chinese once again invaded in 1759. There was a Muslim rebellion in 1865 and the leader Yaqub Beg entered into relations and signed treaties with the Russian Empire and Great Britain, but when he tried to get their support against China, he failed. From 1890 there were British and Russian Consulates, the British George and Lady Mc Cartney in residence for 28 years. Chinese control Xin Jiang collapsed with the Qing Empire in 1911 as war-lords vied for power. By the 1930's whilst China was in Civil war between the Communists and Kou Min Tang, with the Japanese controlling much of the North East of the country that the state of East Turkistan was again proclaimed and recognised by the British and Russians, eager to see the power of the Chinese on the wane. The Russians ended any claim or influence over the area and stopped encouraging the East Turkistan Nationalism when their Communist brothers gained control of China in 1949.

In the morning we got taxi's to the Sunday Bazaar otherwise known as Yengi Bazaar. Somewhat predictably two of the taxis ended up in the wrong location so even this last excursion of the trip had me running around and phoning the group members. To be honest, the Bazaar is a bit of a let-down as it has moved with the times and is now housed in a purpose built market, with wide clean aisles and all remnants of the traditional market stall, piled high with colourful goods and smells had been removed years earlier. There is more household items on sale than the silks and spices of old. However, it was not difficult to find the shops selling musical instruments, knifes, fruits and vegetables, butchers, carpets, wall hangings, silks and spices amongst the more mundane clothing stalls and kitchen utensils. There was a stall selling plumbing equipment, one selling T.V.'s and video recorders from the 1990's and so many selling pots and pans. At the back of the covered market there were stalls selling local foods, and what was the remains of the old open air livestock market which is still a most disorderly, messy, smelly, chaotic fair and what we had really come to Kashgar to see. I decided to walk back with a couple of the girls and we made a far more authentic discovery. Just following our map, we stumbled upon a street market that ran for over a mile, through the twisting streets, with only the local people there. Here were more stalls selling all the wares of the Bazaar, a horse trading section, on the road in between the houses. All this with the added bonus of the amount of curiosity we were attracting from being the only strangers. Mosques were tucked into the buildings that lined the streets, people cooked food in front of their doorways and the life and vitality of the place was real.

For the last night dinner, I decided upon Altazar. This is a traditional restaurant in what looks like a palace. It took me two attempts to go through the menu in the afternoon and there was no alcohol, but my group were blown away with the decor and the musicians playing. We had a couple of beers in the Old Russian Consulate afterwards and the last four of us found a late bar. It was a last departure in many ways. I didn't know what was going to happen with me leaving and re-entering China. I had just had one of my most fantastic adventures on the Silk Road, and now it was over. The last of the group said their goodbyes, leaving me to finish my beer and watch the last dancers leave the dance floor.

54. A Picture Window 05/04/08 (Xin Jiang)

A composition of the most incredible picture
Looking out over Hong Kong Harbour
Beyond any artist, or critics ability
Art could only imitate reality

55. The end of the Great Wall 27/05/08 (Xin Jiang)

A picture,

From the fort wall in Jiayuguan
A vast desert in one direction
The ancient turret as a picture frame
The smoke-stacks and tower-blocks of a frontier town

A picture

The known world ends in a vast empty plain
The horizon pinched in by a high mountain chain
The feeling that you really are out on a limb
Where even the Great Wall ends in an ancient ruin

That last crumbling tower stands
Decaying back into the sands
I look around over these no-mans lands
And dream of my desert caravan

The silk road west, the silk road home
A land far beyond the setting sun
Following the star that guides me on
To cross the desert, to be the one

Towns that are places in ancient stories
A mark in an atlas, a page in History
My schoolboy imagination only dreamed of this
These ancient explorers on their fantastic voyages

My part in a film, the sweeping orchestra
Over the sand dunes and across the sky
Soaring with all the imagination that I can hold on to
Forging the white hot dream into a solid reality

To touch all four elements with each of 5 senses
To be part of living history and history in the making
To dream the impossible then run with it in your hands
To try to grasp that tip of the ice-berg of understanding

I went to see the Silk Road Statues in Xi'an
Walked for two days, searching their mythical location
But my blistered feet were insignificant in comparison
To stone figures rising from the sand in a desert caravan

56. On the Silk Road West 03/06 (Xin Jiang)

On the silk road west
Winding between dune and black mountain crest
Where the grasses blow
Following the line where the stream once flowed
From the towering sand hills
Sand devils run whipping their snaking tails
Across the crest
Ten join together to become some daemon of dust

We pass quickly through
Before the daemon takes form
To bring the mountains of sand
To flood the valley floor

And it makes me wonder who
Would want to enter this land
That is surely the end of the earth
That is nothing but mountains and sand

The opening scene, the sweeping tune
I am riding over the sand dunes
The travellers, I have come from afar
With stories to trade, I follow a star

I have been beyond my imagination
The clear skies and stars beyond the horizon
And now my thoughts turn to home
I must return to the land that I call my own

From the rising sun, to a green and pleasant land
From the Middle Kingdom, to that jewel of an island
From this place of wonder, to where I'll wonder where I'll be
Plucked back into the real world from this fantasy

57. Untitled 06/06/08 (Xin Jiang)

Leaving everything to chance
And flying by the seat of my pants
Sand blows across the desert highway
Rippling running serpents al play
We cut a path through the devilish spell
Before the sand can take the form of evil
Trusting to prayer in this god-forsaken country
And maybe praying to the wrong diety
As we ride the crest of the wave of sand and over
That dispel the road with a dust-blind-curve
Over the hills without breaks on a wing and a prayer
For the gleaming minaret of the oasis to be there

58. Departure Cities 09/06/2008 (Kashgar)

There's a feeling that it's over
When people walk away
Lights flashing in the night-club
Like the memories of today
I wish that it could carry on
I wish that they could stay

There's a line in every song
About what we could say

There's dice games, games of chance
Hanging on six's like a possible romance
But it's over now
Over now

Many times I've been here before
An envelope of messages and so much more
I'll take another beer to the close of another door
There's no-one left on the dance-floor

There's a song that's playing
Like the song I used to sing
Don't know where I'm going
Or what tomorrow will bring

The lights in the night-club
Like an embarrassment of riches
And a many jewelled sky
Where my home is

I look up at the crescent moon
And that minaret, and desert dune
And I think it's all over now
It's all over now

Departure cities
So much more than they could ever be
Until it becomes only the end of the illusion
And if I died today, in all this random confusion
I wouldn't have my life flash before me in speed scenes
I would be smiling at the most wonderful of dreams

Even if it was all over now
All over now.

Lyn arrived two days later. I met her at the airport and went through what I had planned as an itinerary. She'd only just got to grips with where Xin Jiang was in relation to the surrounding countries, but was up for travelling to Kazakhstan via Urumqi, where we would have to get our visas. The trip was always going to be mad. Vast distances and getting our exit and re-entry dates to co-inside with my China visa expiring and also giving me enough time on my next visa to complete my next trip. We stayed at the Seamen hotel, part of the Russian Consulate complex and I took her into the city and the Id Kah Mosque on the first evening, which suitably wow'd her as she took photograph after photograph of the square, the children, the minarets. She has a much better eye for photography than I have. We also ate at Altazar and she couldn't get over the kebabs on real swords, or the decoration, or the musicians. At any other time, this sort of stuff would have been a guaranteed knickers dropper, but as it happens, Lyn has a boyfriend back in the states, which is probably the best thing in the long run for both of us.

The next day we went to the ancient Abu Mosque. This building on the edge of the city is a 1000 year old complex. An impressive colourful minaret towered at one end of the prayer hall and I took a photo of it as the sun shone like a halo around its onion shaped top. Along with the other buildings, much of it was covered in a green glaze brick, not unlike the toilets of a few Edwardian era pubs that I had visited across Britain in my time. There is a significant tomb, where local princes and caliphs are buried. The most notable of these are Mohammad Yusuf, in the original tomb of 1640. In another tomb is Apak Khoja who gained power just before his death in 1694 and whose descendants handed the kingdom over to the Qing Dynasty so is seen as a traitor. Lastly there is the tomb of 'fragrant concubine'. The story goes, that she was said to have a beautiful natural body odour, as well as being a real beauty of her time, another one of the great 8 Chinese beauties; so when she was sent to the palace in Beijing, the Emperor was besotted. However, she pined for her native land until a native

Ju Ju tree was planted in the Imperial Palace and so the story goes, the Emperor won her heart and she became the number one concubine. The Uyghur version is a little different. They say she was captured and taken to Beijing where she hid daggers up her sleeves ready to kill the Emperor if he ever came near her. He was besotted however (on this they all agree) and in the end the dowager empress fearing what would happen to her son, had her killed by palace eunuchs.

On the way back into the city, we stopped at the bazaar, which impressed Lyn more than it did my passengers and we ate from the local street stalls. I walked her back the way I'd gone a few days before. The market wasn't there, but the life of the old city was no more diminished with the hidden mosques, the street cooking and a small local market. We had decided to head off towards Urumqi as early as possible, in order to give us maximum time to get Kazak visas and leave China before my visa deadline. We rushed to get to the bus station, then found out that we were two hours early. China is a very large country and normally you would expect it to comprise of a number of Time zones, as you have in the U.S. or even Europe. However, the Chinese paranoia about everything and anything that isn't "One China" has meant that in the west of the country thousands of miles away from Beijing, they still work on Beijing time. There is an unofficial time difference in Xin Jiang only observed by the locals. It is two hours behind Beijing time. This means that people can go to work at a reasonable time in the morning when the sun is already up and are coming home in the evening before it gets dark. But don't tell the bureaucrats in Beijing. We took an overnight sleeper bus, a first for both of us. Three rows of bunk-beds along the length of the bus. It was definitely not designed for westerners, so it was a bit of a squeeze, but it was comfortable enough once we were in. The bus arrived at our first destination, Kuqi, at around 7am the following day. We only used this as a short stop over and were on another bus within a few hours

This was a trip that I would have struggled to undertake on my own, having Lyn around, with her tour leading experience and better Mandarin than mine, made things run a lot smoother. We had decided to just give ourselves the day in Kuqi. According to the Lonely Planet, it was where "strip malls met donkey carts" and there were a couple of sites near the town, including an ancient village. It didn't take long for us to be approached by people trying to get us into hotels, or asking where we wanted to go, so we quickly sorted out a bus ticket on to Urumqi for that evening and stored our bags at the bus station. Then we went exploring. This was all pot luck, because there was no map and the info in the L.P. was a bit random. Between the two of us, we speak enough Chinese to find our way around; after all, this is what we do as a job, with paying customers. The town was another new development, still being built. There was a pretty series of squares, with shops and cafe and then we continued off along the road out of town to where the old town was. This had a lot more character. We crossed a bridge with people doing their laundry in the river. There was an Arabic arch as we crossed into the old town and a town square, a market and a mosque. Here we met Muhammad, who spoke a little English and said that he'd show us to the old town wall and the great mosque, so we agreed. On route, he gave us an insight into living in Xin Jiang. He was afraid of the government and the police. He said the information boards on the old town wall were incorrect and had made it look like the Han Chinese were responsible for the building of the town, whereas it was the Uyghur people who first settled there, hundreds of years earlier. At the mosque, he explained that people could not be seen praying openly, except on Fridays. By now, it was mid-afternoon, so we accepted Muhammad's hospitality and joined him for a meal of kebabs from a local cafe. He was a local celebrity, to have two westerners with him, we were a curiosity and the locals didn't know whether to avoid us in fear of offending us, or fall over themselves in an attempt to serve us. As Lyn said, we'd done our intrepid thing, going somewhere off the map, meeting local people, learning new things. Then we were on our way again, on another sleeper bus to Urumqi. There was a strange video playing, which was supposed to be some sort of comedy about a man who was down on his luck, and his misadventures. He would get robbed, teased by children and the girl he wanted went off with another man, but no worries, it all came good in the end as he beat up the girl that was teasing him until she was unconscious. The bus roared with laughter as we lay, transfixed in disbelief. We needed a welcome break which by chance had the most wonderful of roadside stops where everybody was eating, shouting, running around with food on plates and kebabs on swords. More to our taste of real local life.

Our plan for Urumqi was ambitious. We had given ourselves three days, just in case anything went wrong, but our intention was to get our Kazakhstan visas and an overnight bus again. We arrived at 6am, got a taxi to a hostel and booked dorm places, with the main intention of just having a shower before heading off to sort things out. First of all, Lyn needed photographs for her visa. You would think it pretty unlikely to just stumble upon a Kodak shop, but, with Lyn's luck, she wished for one and one appeared, just opposite the KFC where we had breakfast, waiting for them to develop. Then along came the taxi that she wished for to take us to the Kazak Consulate. However, that was three wishes used up and the Consulate did not look promising.

There were two knots of people outside. One at a kiosk, one at the main gate. We couldn't make out where we should be; whether we should already have documentation or what we should do. The crowds were pre-occupied with getting their own stuff done, pushing as close as they could to the gate and the kiosk, some clutching pieces of paper, others yelling out. Once again, I asked someone what I should do and surprisingly, he asked where I was from, in English. It turns out that he had some documentation to get some people visas and was also trying to get into the Consulate. With us in tow, he saw it as an opportunity to jump the queue, so we followed as he pushed his way to the front with our passports, squeezed passed the annoyed mob and through the gate into the compound. He did an explanation for the staff and we were soon filling out our visa application forms. By this time it was 11am and the Consulate closed at 11:30. It looked like we'd done it. As we handed everything in, the woman behind the desk said that we needed copies of our passports for her to keep. We didn't have these. "OK, we'd nearly succeeded" I said out loud. It was a tall order to expect to negotiate getting visas in just one try and we had really been cutting it fine. It looked like we'd have to try again later. Then I thought, "No, I've got to at least try". As Lyn watched, baffled at what I was about to attempt, I picked up our passports and went to the gate.

Getting out was going to be just as difficult as getting in and I'm sure I hurt people as I crushed them against the iron gate when I pushed it against them to get out. I ran up the road and into the first hotel. Yes, they had a photocopier behind the reception. I explained, they understood, but it wasn't a usual practice, but they took money off me and copied our passports. I shouted through the crowd to Lyn, I passed her the passports through the railings of the compound, then began the task of getting back in again. We had 10 minutes to spare and the office had accepted our application. Next we moved into an adjacent room for payment and receipts. The man behind the desk indicated that we return in two days time until Lyn asked if they could be done the same day. I don't know what charm she used, but we were told that we could get them back at 4pm. I was amazed.

After all that excitement, we began a walk into the city, by way of slowly calming down. Then we got taxi's to the bus station and got tickets for the sleeper bus that night to the border. This would be our third consecutive night on sleeper busses. The pace was already beginning to show. I actually slept for a while in the park that afternoon. When we got back to the Kazakhstan Embassy, we were surprised to see that it was closed. There were also some other puzzled looking people milling around and the place didn't look like it was going to do any business for the rest of that day. We were outside, our passports were inside and we'd just bought tickets to travel. There was an old man who could possibly have been the gardener who was wandering around inside the compound. I called him over, tried to explain what we wanted and showed him the receipt for our passports. He took the ticket and walked off. Now, this may have been the most stupid of moves as we watched the gardener walk away. Now, we had no evidence that our passports were even inside the building. I'm not sure if the gardener had any wits about him, he may be just wandering off with the paper from the foreigners but he may have just out-witted us and be off to sell our passports to the highest bidder. Not sure how many people looked like me or Lyn though in Urumqi. Five minutes later, he returned with our passports, each with a new Kazakhstan visa inside. We were going to Kazakhstan. "Land of Borat".

Back to the hostel and we booked plane flights back from Urumqi for four days' time, only to get a phone call saying that our credit cards could not be accepted and could we pay by cash, by leaving money at the hostel reception and the tickets would arrive the following day. This is exactly the situation I had at the start of the Silk Road trip where I had left thousands of Yuan in the hands of the Harmony Hotel on the promise that they would hand it over for the tickets. This is a stupid system, just asking for someone to steal all your money and here at the hostel in Urumqi it was a non-starter. The receptionist knew someone. This became another mad dash as we ran back and forth between the hostel and the air ticket booking office, withdrawing cash and moving our luggage around and then got taxis to the bus station, getting there with only five minutes to spare again. We'd chanced our luck more than enough that day.

We arrived at the border town of Khorgas at 8am. The bus station was pretty deserted. Lyn remarked that there was a sign on a building that said "PECTOPAH" I said that was 'restaurant' in Russian. I haven't studied Russian for about 7 years, I was in for a tough few days, but I would take that over having to learn Kazak from scratch. We got to the border and it was closed. A man told us that it was closed all day. He was lying, but we didn't know that at the time and just decided to have a wander around for a while as it was early and we were guessing that the border would open around nine. We returned after an hour or so in a deserted, almost completed shopping mall. This border town had ambition, but it was going to be a long time before it would be fulfilled. There was now a queue, or rather a small gathering of people expecting to cross the border. Some people looked very Russian others were middle eastern, others Chinese; it was a real melting pot. Most were transporting boxes or cartons. The border would open when the guards were ready to open it. This is how things are done around here. At around 11am we crossed to the other side. Lyn was stopped. The inspector on the Kazak side thought she had a dodgy passport where the U.S. Embassy has added extra pages. By this time I'd already gone through and I couldn't go back, so she was quite rightly shitting herself, in no-man's land, without a passport. These things always work themselves out, but our ordeal wasn't over.

We still had to get to Almaty, the old Capital of Kazakhstan. We were told there was no $3.5 bus to the local town (as our 4 year old L.P. has described) and instead we were offered transport to Almaty for around $120. That was far in excess of what we'd budgeted for. Another bloke made a better deal. He bragged that he had an Audi and Lyn's eyes lit up. He said that if he filled it with 4 people, he would charge us $25 each. Two Chinese ladies completed our foursome and we got into a bus that took us through some gates and border fences to where the Audi was waiting and we started to load up. This is where it all went a little bit wrong again. The bus driver demanded 400 Tenyi (the local currency, around $3) of each of us for the journey. We all refused. Then he got arsey and pulled Lyn's bag out of the Audi, so we snatched it back and put it back in the car. He was causing a real scene and the other two women settled on giving him 300 Tenyi each. We had to do the same otherwise he wouldn't let our driver leave. We handed over the money. Then one of those things happened that although I was watching it, I just couldn't quite believe it. Lyn handed the money over, then in some sort of weird slow motion, bent over and did her best to spit on the ground in front of the man. Lyn is obviously not a champion spitter. For the amount of effort, she produced very little. However, it was enough. I was sort of spell bound as she walked back to the car and sat inside. The man reacted first. He went over to her and was close to punching her before I got there to pull him off. The driver was still shouting and demonstrating, our driver made out that we should all get in the car and be on our way. Lyn was more upset and shaken about what had happened. She was also very lucky, the man had just brushed her cheek as he had tried to strike her and when you tackle this sort of person, things could have been far worse. To round off our day of travelling, we were squeezed into a 1990's Audi, not what Lyn was hoping for. It was 40 degree heat and our trip to Almaty took five hours.

On reaching the city, out first destination suggested by the Lonely Planet was a hotel in the train station. This turned out to be very basic, with no toilet or washing facility (well, there was the station next door) for around $12. We moved on, but everything else was far more expensive. It turns out that Kazakhstan is now an oil rich country. Almaty, the old Soviet capital, planned with its wide boulevards, with all the signage in Russian, European style government buildings and parks has become a rich and somewhat expensive city to live in. The population that we met walking along the stone pavement block streets, bounded by walled gardens was generally Russian, well dressed and affluent. Lyn calculated that our Lonely Planet was out by 800% inflation in four years. Things must have changed a lot. Hotels were no longer where they should have been, others were definitely not looking like a budget option as described. Bars and cafes had been converted or no-longer existed. In the first two days, the only places that we found on the map were the American Burger Bar (not my idea) and the Irish pub, where we met a Nigerian football player, who had been brought to the town with the oil money, but now hadn't made the team and was working in the bar.

Almaty has an interesting history and I knew some of it from my days as a young neo-Communist reading about Leon Trotsky and more generally from the Russian literature that I had read in my twenties. First of all, it is known as "rich with apple", or mis-translated by the Russians as "grandfather apple" as apples were originally from this area and the main produce for centuries. The Kazaks had occupied this land as nomads for over two thousand years. The most famous archaeological finds is the Golden man, from around 2000 years ago who is covered in ornate armour showing a rich civilisation flourished here. In the 10th to 15th Centuries settlements situated on the territory of the so called "Big Almaty", more of a permanent encampment than a fixed city, became part of the trade routes of the Silk Road. At that time, "Big Almaty" was one of the trade, craft and agricultural centres on the Silk Road and possessed a mint. After the Mongolian Empire collapsed, the Kazaks and the Uzbeks to the south took over the forests and the planes as their own. The Kazak nation was formed through battles in the 17th and 18th Centuries with the Dzungars; then the Russians came. The city was founded in 1854 as a Russian frontier post, and the Russians traded with the local tribes and expanded their influence over surrounding countries. The Tsars had used Almaty as a place of exile to political dissidents and when Stalin began to tighten his grip on power in the old Soviet Union of the 1920's he did the same, exiling his main communist critique Leon Trotsky there in 1928 until his final expulsion from the Soviet Union in 1929. In more modern times, Russians had come of their own accord, following the oil and setting up business, now making Almaty a rich, Russified city in Central Asia.

The hotel in the train station got too much for us. Not washing was one thing, the windows not opening properly and the small single fan on the wall being insufficient for twin beds was another. But the deciding factor was that when the trains arrived, or left, at whatever hour of the day or night, we were subject to loud speaker public announcements, bright lights and crowds of people. Simply impossible. Luckily, I spotted a "Gostinitsa" on our wanderings around the city and it was only marginally more expensive. It was at this point that I found out that Lyn sleep walks. In the early hours of one morning, I was woken with her kneeling at my bedside saying "It's OK, the money thing will work out". She went back to bed in her own time, in her own world. We had plans of visiting the surrounding mountains whilst in Kazakhstan. Everything tourism wise pointed them out to be some of the most pristine alpine settings and trekking routs in the world, we could even see the closest ones from the city itself. I would have liked to have gone, even if just to say that I saw something more of Kazakhstan than the old capital, there must be more to a country of this size, the sixth largest in the world, than this very Russian city. But the journeying just to get across Xin Jiang province, the border crossing, then the hassles of Kazakhstan had put Lyn off. The prices of everything were a bit of a shock and there was nothing actually set up for tourists like us. Yes, there were a couple of places that ran excursions, but it was all in Russian and aimed at the affluent oil baron on vacation, not us backpackers. Our days walking around the town took us to the Central Mosque, the park and the Russian Orthadox Cathedral. Zenkov Cathedral built in the 19th Century in Panfilov Park, is the second tallest wooden building in the world and quite a sight. At night there were street cafes and bars set up and it looked like the locals took advantage of the summer months to get out, day or night, but it was not what we were hoping for.

Almaty is one place I will not go back to in a hurry. It was a bit of a disappointment. We ate well, the Russian city was a pleasant enough place, but it wasn't what we wanted and the expense was a deterrent. We got the overnight sleeper bus back to Urumqi and it was a "luxury" bus with far bigger beds than usual. This only had the effect of us having to hold on as we were bounced around in a sort of "It's a Knockout" style game where someone is trying to dump you from your bed and onto the floor. The border was a strange crossing, with the locals getting very excited as we passed through their lines on the Chinese side and one boy even 'tagged' me. We passed the stunning scenery of the Yurts in the mountains on the way into Xin Jiang province again. A real pity we never got out to them. Once again, we didn't stay in Urumqi, but on arrival, went on to the other bus station across town by way of negotiating a taxi, then waited for the public bus and set out for Turpan. Lyn wanted to see it, it was a highlight of the Silk Road and after Almaty I wanted to get back there too.

We were followed by a boy 'Murdan' at the station. He got us a reduced rate at the Hotel which I had stayed at with my group, but this time accommodation was in a building in the courtyard. We agreed for him to guide us. I'd texted Momin John, but he hadn't replied. First, I took Lyn to see the Emin Mosque, walking along the backstreets of the old town. Then we went to the Bazaar. We went looking for a big mosque that Lyn wanted to see, walking for miles until we realised that we had passed it along with three or four other large-ish and supposedly significant buildings. It was all starting to look the same, we were getting tired, we were missing things, we couldn't see the wood for the trees as it were, but the Lonely Planet descriptions are always a bit over-board and on the superlative side of description. That night we ate in the night-market and the chef from the stall where I was drinking with my group the previous month spotted me and I couldn't remember getting home.

Our tour day started at 9am. 45 degrees in the back of a taxi. First stop was the 1000 Buddha caves. To me the untrained scholar, they were like a smaller version of the ones at Dunhuang, but without the awful restoration job and something completely new to Lyn. Bizalkik Thousand Buddha Caves stand high on the cliffs of west Mutou Valley under the Flaming Mountain and 57 out of the original 83 remain intact. As with the grottos at Dunhuang, the caves are often rectangular rooms with a round arch ceiling. This ceiling is divided into quadratic fields, each of them containing the picture of a Buddha. So the whole ceiling contains virtually hundreds of Buddha's. Some larger fields contain a big Buddha, surrounded by other figures and scenes. Other murals show people of the area, including Indians, Persians and Caucasians. Also, as with the Magoa Caves; many have either been destroyed by local Muslims or by foreign adventurer-explorers. We went to the Astana tombs. These were burial mounds on the edge of the desert which served as graveyard of the citizens of the ancient Silk Road city of Gaochang from 273AD to 778AD. Over 500 have been excavated but now only held a few precious relics and mummified corpses. Most of the artefacts were in the Urumqi museum. Lyn visited Tuyoq village and we by-passed the flaming mountains. I also just had to go back to Jioa He, the ancient Silk Road city and Lyn loved the atmosphere just as much as I had done.

At one point, Murdan asked if Lyn wanted to drive the taxi. She said yes, so off she went. I was quick to notice that she was only holding the steering wheel with one hand, whilst the other rested on the gear stick. For most Americans 'driving by stick' is a novelty. I pointed out to Lyn that she should have two hands on the wheel. She didn't react very well to this. Soon, she was turning around to tell me to shut up, whilst driving single handed on a bumpy Xin Jiang road. That only made me point out the absurdity of what she was doing all the more and hinted that we might all die. I took photographs to prove my point. Finally, she relented and got back in the passenger seat. The one unfortunate thing about our day out was that Murdan and his father insisted that we eat in a restaurant of their choice. We sort of knew what was coming, but went along with it anyway and got a bill for Y232 for very average food. He knew that we knew that we had been ripped off and it was a very sour end to our great day out.

We moved back to Urumqi the following day and back to the hostel where we had stored our bags. We had left ourselves just enough time for preparation for our trips that would start for me in Beijing the following day and for Lyn, in Shanghai the day after. She showed me how to put the photographs that I had taken up on computer, the technophobe that I am. It was also the first time that I learned what the "tab" button on the top left of the keyboard did. Then we were on our way again, flying back across China from our adventures beyond the Great Wall.

Chapter 6.

THERE AND BACK AGAIN

"Two roads diverged in a wood and I—
I took the one less travelled by."

Robert Frost

So, another trip. Without any real chance to recover or prepare after the last one I was back in the City Central Youth Hostel. Steven was around, so it was good to catch up with him. Rockhard was doing a visa run to Hong Kong. This didn't go well as he only got a 15 day visa. This didn't bode well for the rest of us. Manager Tracey had said that there were no more visas being issued after the 1st July and probably for the following two months. The Chinese were taking any possible protest at the Olympics very seriously. I was in the office with Li and Ching introducing me to the new staff again. Suzy had moved on to work on the Olympics with corporate guests. It seemed as though the new management structure and new positions had squeezed out her role, so she had decided it was time to move on. I chatted to Tracey as she was busily working at her desk. She had sent out for "lunch" and it was sitting there, a pathetic half eaten sandwich. With all the problems after the earthquake and now the Olympics; meaning the closure of Tibet and trips not being allowed to stay in Beijing she had been working around the clock. All the leaders seemed to appreciate what she was doing and we could see some general improvements to our work. Emails were answered, trip notes updated, all a far cry from the old management team. Then I said to her "You may as well be back in London, working through lunch, no time to go out. What is the point of being in a foreign country if you can't appreciate it?" I found a letter addressed to me. It was from my dad and had the Christmas card he'd sent. It was now late June, the letter, card and clippings from the Lancashire Evening Telegraph were all dated some-time in November. It is at times like this that you start to think that you are quite a long way from home. My concern was that Dad is a worrier. Not that he actually gets around to doing much to stop him worrying, but I now felt that I had to contact him. Over the last months there had been earthquakes and uprisings and the last time I'd contacted him I was in Vietnam, not China at all. Dad had sent updates on how the Rovers were doing and the football season had been won and lost months earlier. He hoped I was well and that I was not drinking too much, especially in the high altitudes of Tibet. That was a story that would run and run.

My next trip was a back to Back, Beijing to Kunming and Tiger Leaping Gorge. I'd done the trip once before, the previous September and it had been one of the best. This group would have a lot to live up to but they started well. Kim, a Phd Laser physicist from Milton Keynes and Jo a larger than life American were sharing and they were out for a beer on the first night. Kim had just finished a trip with Wing, a girl I only knew from reputation. She was supposed to meet up with the girls and go out for a drink, but it seemed that she had found a 19 year old boy to play with instead. On the way to the Wall on the first day, I got to know Gordon a little better. He is a therapist, in his late 50's, from Australia, travelling with his wife Gen. Rather than sleeping, like everybody else does, he wanted to ask a lot of questions. Firstly, he and his wife had expected that all the 'optional activities' were included. Also, when it stated that "1 lunch and 1 dinner" were included, they took it to mean every day. This had seriously compromised their budget. They were a couple of hippies really and very much in their own world. Gordon started by asking me what the growing season of the Lychee was in China. So I had to make something up that sounded reasonable. He also had an interest in Bamboo; actually no. He was the worlds' number one authority on bamboo. I learned a lot about bamboo on this trip. Gordon also wanted to go to places where he could see bamboo. There is a lot of it in China, but I've never taken much notice of it in the past, but I reckoned that Chicory in Chengdu would be able to provide me with some answers. It turns out there is a bamboo park in the city. There is also a bamboo park in Kunming too. He was going to get his bamboo fix.

Our first overnight train took us to Zhongwei. We had a different guide than last time, Lionel, who confessed to liking Lionel Richie. His had only been in the job for 6 weeks and wasn't used to westerners and our peculiar ways. He tried his best, but was at a complete loss when nobody decided to opt for the Goat Skin Rafting down the Yellow River. At Y200 it was seen as being too expensive. Lionel fumbled around for a few minutes before asking me, "so what will they do?" My reply to the whole group and the guide was, "you have free time". This was a concept that was lost on all of them, either believing that I had an alternative itinerary hidden somewhere, or thinking that Lionel could drop the rafting price. Lionel asked if he could go home. I said "yes" and walked the group around town and left them at the temple. That evening I took them to the night-market, where they quickly started adapting and all managed to eat. I had dinner with Billy, the local operator and Yue, who was also running a re-routed trip through Zhongwei. I always like meeting Yue as she is a lot of fun and her background is as an artist. She has exhibited her work around Beijing. She's also been to Germany, so quite an interesting girl. She was late for dinner and had a good reason. Her group of three girls was completely useless. They had phoned her as she was leaving the hotel because they didn't know how to choose a restaurant or order food, so they'd asked Yue to go back and do it for them. I know that this is difficult in a foreign country, but if you can't at least attempt the basics, then you are on the wrong trip. Yue said that this happens a lot and she spent a lot of time with useless passengers when she'd much sooner eat local food at a third of the cost rather than going to restaurants and acting as a waitress.

The group had a spectacular time out in the desert on the camels. Lionel's English was not so good and there were a few comical turns. When we were asking if the camels were 'friends', he thought we said 'French', so we went into a conversation about how they were from Paris. He didn't have a clue. Back in Zhongwei, the Olympic Torch was in town. We tried to get back in time to see it, but somehow missed it. Only weeks later did I realise how this had happened, we were not supposed to see it. Gen got lost and ended up sitting on the Bell tower in the centre of town for an hour until she saw someone else from the group. Of course, she didn't know what the hotel was called, where it was and nobody spoke English anyway.

Then we were on to Xi'an again for three days. I was looking forward to this because Amy and Lyn would both be in town with groups at the same time. It didn't take long for us all to meet up and I chatted to Amy as Lyn got her and my group doing tequila slammers whilst teaching them the dice game in Music Man Bar. Lyn had just done another trip to the musical fountain and with all the traffic problems and the group not being on time had missed it for the third time this year; it was not a place I ever bothered to take my groups. Amy had had a similar problem to Yue, in that the group would always ask where they would eat for dinner, then end up at a restaurant where Amy did the waitressing whilst the group talked about British Soap Operas or Aussie Rules Football, which left her just eating by herself. This is a common problem for the Chinese and there is no quick fix solution. She'd left them to their own devices that evening and saw them as they returned, from Pizza Hut, complaining that they couldn't find anything else to eat. We got enough drink in us to drown her sorrow, then checked out the Karaoke in the next bar. This wasn't so good, so we all went on to Halo Laidi which is a chain of Karaoke bars that you can find right across China. Amy has a membership card. There is a supermarket at the entrance, where you can stock up on booze and fags, then we were in our booth. Amy left at around 12:30 am, it had got to a point where it was all English Language songs and I think she'd had enough of westerners and being asked to do the karaoke machine controls. The rest of us stayed until around 3 am. There is one particular photo doing the rounds of me in front of the TV, dancing, as "Spice up your life" is written across the screen. There are also a few of Lyn, passed out in the bar, sucking her thumb in her sleep.

Then Chengdu. Jo had made it a mission to get a "panda hat". She'd seen a picture of Chinese children all wearing these and wanted one for her and her friends back home. It's a panda head that you strap onto your own head like a bonnet. She also wanted her picture taken with the pandas in the breeding centre. After the panda ordeal and hot pot, I suggested the Irish Bar for drinks. This started out very well apart from the free massage that I was offered when I went to use the toilet. I have heard that this is becoming more common in Asia, where the toilet attendant will work on your shoulders and back whilst you stand there urinating. Maybe this will take on, but I was completely unsuspecting of what was happening as the attendant came up behind me and started a massage, I turned around sharp splashing pee across the bathroom and nearly hit the bloke one urinal to my left. Once I realised what was happening there was no way that I was getting involved in anything like this. I was also a bit suspicious about the dress sense of the "attendant". The 1970's disco gear including fluorescent flares was in keeping with the Irish pubs theme night, but it had such a compromising feel to it. We ended up at a nightclub night out until about four in the morning again. Lots more pictures and lots more embarrassment. I was five minutes late for the bus in the morning, I've never been late in this job for anything before, the nights out were starting to catch up. This part of the trip finished in Kunming. I had a day of office type work, then we met the new group for the second half of the trip through Yunnan Province. Jo was the only one not continuing on the second part of the trip and she wanted a big farewell. In some ways, I was thankful that my work kept me away until nearly 11pm. I joined the group after that for drinks and I was sober when we got home. Well, somebody had to be. This had become a much better trip than I was expecting after the first few days.

I had six new passengers including two American girls, one of which had allergies to Chicken, some fruit, cheese, some nuts and 12 different medicines. She was also working for NASA. She was going to be tough. I hadn't had too much time with them the previous night, so the first impressions were when we met in the morning to go to Lijiang. I've done this run many times before. On this occasion, my experience counted. At 7:45, Kim had still not appeared. I phoned the room and Jo answered with 'oh fuck'. That meant putting plan B into action. I left the bus ticket for Kim at the front desk and walked the group across the street to where the shuttle bus would pick up and transfer to the Bus Station (of which there are many in every Chinese City). I showed the driver the tickets, I put them and the luggage on the bus and decided to run back for Kim, just in case. She was just leaving the hotel, but had no idea where she was going. She'd got my room deposit back, which was good, but hadn't picked up the bus ticket. That evidently had gone somewhere into Jo's massive purse and was lost forever. OK, we were going to have to chance it. Whatever happened, I was getting on the bus to Lijiang, even if Kim wasn't. I got us back to the bus stop and the bus had gone. I wasn't really counting on this, as I still held all of the tickets and I'd banked on the group telling the driver to wait for me. It's not as if they can get anywhere far without me. I flagged down a taxi and we were off, me trying to explain which bus station we wanted, no, not the one by the train station, not the main one, but the other one. Somehow we got there. One of the group was waiting outside. He told me that once they'd arrived, the driver pointed out the bus to Lijiang so everyone put their bags on. The new people in the group were panicking as to where I was, but the old group knew everything would be OK. Wow, I was so thankful that the old group had been well travelled enough and calm enough just to get on with it. Double wow, they had the confidence in me to believe everything was going to work out fine. On the bus, I talked to the conductress, I explained that I had a group of 13 westerners; it was running close to departure time, she checked the list of 13 tickets sold via the Camella Hotel to Foreigners and we were on our way. How lucky was Kim? By rights she should have been left in Kunming. Furthermore, I then had to endure her being sick on the bus for most of the next 7 hours. I took the piss out of her. I explained that although time may be relative in physics world, the bus had to leave on Earth time and without the aid of a Tardis, we had to take a taxi, to get to the bus station in order to make our connection. I passed her a bucket to vomit in as she apologised.

We stayed in a new guest house in Li Jiang and I still think the town is pretty, even though it is now largely "fake". I also love the nightlife, well, watching it anyway, I didn't really get involved in the drinking and dancing this time around, remembering what happened on my last trip, through here when the local guides cancelled on me, last minute. Luckily, Margo, for all her eccentricities is reliable. She is also an exceptional guide and kept the group entertained with anecdotes and information that you just wouldn't get from anybody else. It was also good for us to talk about visas and the way the company and the country are dealing with these issues. "Himalaya" had been on TV earlier in the year and everyone had an opinion about Tiger Leaping Gorge. They took what Michael Palin had said as gospel truth and all wanted to see the "toilet" with the best view in the world". I'd been there (literally) the year before and although the whole area is full of spectacular scenery, I would not have singled out this particular toilet as being the best view in the world. The group also remembered snippets of the programme, which they mixed up with other programmes and then started to tell each other about misinformed aspects of Himalayan life, as if they knew what they were talking about. Experts after watching a 10 minute segment on a travel programme. Margo knew what she was talking about, and had no qualms about telling them as much. We scaled the side of the gorge with its silver looking mud, watched the miners in the quarry sorting through rocks and wondered at the chocolate coloured river far below us. Margo said that there was a plan to dam this for hydroelectricity, we thought it unthinkable, but the plan may well go ahead in a power hungry China. We left Margo the following day and got a bus that also doubled up as the local transportation for a clay pot manufacturer. The local people all sitting on the up-turned pots in the aisle. In Zhongdian, I found out that the Tibetan Training School that I had visited last time was closed for the summer. Considering that I'd been talking to the group about getting out into the villages, I decided to try and organise a trip of my own, through contacting some local guides. The Raven pub had contacts and I also had Kevin Trekkers as an option. Looking back, I suppose this is the point that I really did become an experienced leader. I asked around, got info and prices and settled on a guide and an itinerary to a local village and temple. Most of the group came along and I kept the price low at around $10pp. The guides weren't up to much, I filled in a lot of the blanks about Tibetan Buddhism, but what we saw was the real thing. An ancient village full of wandering water-buffalo and chickens. Old people sitting, working, pointing inquisitively at us. A temple that had been destroyed during the Cultural Revolution and the smashed pieces of the building, with all the decorative inscriptions, murals, carvings was piled up around a stupa. From this emanated the most prayer flags that I have ever seen. They were in all directions and over the hillside, towards the other ruined buildings and the sacrificial altar and incense jugs. A vibrancy of colours and life from the broken ruins. We had lunch at a local house. I'd never been in one so ornate. Murals in all of the panels on the walls. The family cooked on the range in the main room, smoke billowing out, the meat hung to dry above it as in so many other farmhouses. We ate Yak, of course, in a sort of burger, along with tsampa, washed down with Yak butter tea. Totally Tibetan and authentic. Then, just to end it all with a Chinese twist, we visited the new hotel complex that had just been built. The guide was more proud of this than the village house and couldn't see why we weren't impressed with us all commenting. "Yes, it is very nice, modern standards, everything, but it isn't real, it is not what we came here for".

I should also tell about a peculiar incident that happened whilst we were staying in the Zhongdian guest house. "The incident of the cat in the night-time". As I went to bed, I could hear a cat meowing. I was tired and thought nothing more of it, but in the morning, the cat was still making a noise. It sounded like it was coming from behind my bathroom wall. I got a knock on my door, some other passengers could also hear the cat and it was definitely coming from behind the bathroom wall. Here we had a situation. A trapped kitten, girls at their wit's end as to how we could save it and there we were in rural China, where the treatment of animals is about as basic as you get. I explained the problem as best I could to the girl on the desk, who spoke some English and the hotel owner, who spoke none. The girl thought the situation hilarious, whilst the manager offered me a change of room. I had to press the point home a little. The westerners wanted to save the kitten. They were even willing to pay money to remove the wall to get the cat out. I rang Bruce in the office, (now in charge of trips in Southern China, where I was) who was as useful as ever, telling me he'd just had a heavy night and only three hours sleep. He told me to ring the Operations General Emergency line for someone to help me out. I did this and Bruce answered again, "oh, it must be me in charge today" he said and suggested I ring someone else in the Beijing office for help. I got through to Ching and it took me a while to get her to understand the problem, her being Chinese. Then, she rang back the hotel, in an official capacity of a manager from Beijing and had to give an explanation of why the westerners were upset about the cat and that we would pay to get the stray out. I didn't hold out much hope. I reckoned that somehow they'd kill the cat to quieten it, but no, to my surprise, the hotel owner and some friends removed part of the wall and rescued the cat, returning it to its mother. Even more surprising, was that he wouldn't accept money for this. Chinese 'Pet Rescue'.

Our penultimate stop was Dali. I'd contacted George and River on the way there so they were ready for our arrival. The group got involved and explored around the town and onto the lake and most did Rivers' day excursion. Some didn't have the best of experiences with the Cormorant Fishing, but then again, I never encourage it. They had read about it and figured it out themselves, heading off to the lake and hiring a man in a boat with a cormorant. One vegetarian in the group was horrified when, first of all the boatman threw his oar after the birds when they wouldn't dive. Then, once he'd retrieved his oar and caught the birds, he smashed their heads against the side of the boat. I've no idea what that was supposed to achieve apart from upsetting the westerners. That evening was my birthday. I hadn't let on, but George knew. I was having a meal with him and his family, then a few drinks afterwards, when the rest of the group turned up. There was a cake too. So we had a party, though I ended up covering a large part of the drinks bill, they were a tight group at heart. It turns out that there was another party in town that night too. A "white party" of all things. The Americans in the group were very disturbed about the Klu-klux-klan outfits worn by a few if the local ex-pats, but it definitely was a party. It was the sort of thing you see on the beach in Thailand. Fire jugglers, hippies playing bongos incessantly, lots of stoned people. There was a rave going on in one of the rooms. We had a fantastic night and a real birthday party for me. A good job I arranged for the bus departure to be at 10am the following day. Then we were back in Kunming and a last night dinner that included bamboo shoots, just for Gordon. Our departure day was one of the most awkward ones that I've had to date. People that had all become friends, not wanting the four week trip to end. We went for drinks and ended up in my bedroom until 3am. They just didn't want it all to be over.

But over, it was. I got a plane flight to Shenzhen in the morning. As I was boarding, Tracey, the manager phoned me. "Could I possibly do an Essence of China trip, starting in Beijing in five days time?" I said I'd have to get another visa as soon as I got into HK, but would let her know asap. I had been in contact with Bataar and Bolo in Mongolia and had an invitation letter waiting for me to go for a visit. Steve, Jane and Lyn had all got trips there around the same time, so we'd been looking at having a big re-union. Well, that was now cancelled. The cost of flying there from HK was quite prohibitive anyway and I can't afford to turn down work. So I had a crazy run around again. I got the visa within a couple of days. Met up with a few of the passengers from the trip who had also gone to HK before flying home. I met up with a few other leaders as they entered and left the apartment. I was happy to see Z again and we chatted until the early hours. I met Henry, who talked about girls, cars, gambling and setting up property deals. I'd seen him once before when he started his training trip with Tang and all he'd done then is talk about girls. I just thought he was harmless with his head in the clouds. He told me he was in love with a girl from his last trip and wanted to get drunk to forget about her, I didn't want to join him, it reminded me too much of working at the Students' Union. He also told me that Tracey was quitting her job, but I didn't believe him until I read the email the next day. I met Qing again who was desperate to leave the Vietnam trips as he was covered in mosquito bites.

Li the admin assistant from the office arrived, she was in Hong Kong with her boyfriend and considering a change of jobs "don't tell anyone" she asked me. She had been the one constant source of help in the office over the previous year and the changes seemed to be making her less and less necessary to the operation. She was the one who had texted me the Chinese characters with which to buy more credit for my mobile phone in the first weeks of me being in China, had always been on hand to help out with and over the first year had held the office operation together in spite of the appalling management of Cathy and Bruce. But now there was a bigger office and all the roles that she used to play were now given to people with experience in them. There were three managers dealing with all things to do with the tour leaders, two accountants checking our payment. Ching had gone from tour leader to purchasing manager, with no experience and was now dealing with hotels and contracts. There was even an office manager brought in above Li to manage the office. She was left with little more responsibility than reading trip reports and making the tea. She had no experience when she first took on the office assistant role and it seemed that the new management thought little of her ability and promoted everyone else above her. No wonder she felt disheartened. She also had a western boyfriend and was hoping for marriage and maybe a move to England where she said she would study, probably English, though her English seemed pretty good to me. After a couple of years together, marriage had to be on the cards, it was unthinkable for it not to be for a Chinese girl. As Li had just left Beijing office, it meant that we got all the office gossip, especially about Tracey leaving. It seems that all the work had got too much for her. She had no life outside of the office and I think that those words that I had said to her in the office one month earlier had really hit home. So that was where she was going, "home".

Qing was a bit of a character. As he and Li chatted about life, I found out that he was divorced. This is a bit of a shock, as he was in his mid-twenties. He explained that he and his wife had married without ever really knowing each other, under pressure from their families and "convention". He still wanted to see the world and live a little, whist she was very traditional and immediately wanted to settle down, have children and work on the business they had together. This essentially has been Qing's tour agency business before they were married and this is where he had got the inspiration to be a Tour Leader. He had broken convention and with it, his marriage. His wife said that she needed a husband who was around her whilst he wanted to wander, so in the end, the families came to agreement (always the families getting involved, in courtship, marriage, business, divorce). Qing gave his wife the business as part of the settlement. He started the Tour Leading job, but on his visits to Xi'an he was finding out that his ex-wife was now seeing somebody else, so he had asked to transfer elsewhere, meaning the Hanoi to Hong Kong trips.

Once I'd got my China Visa (double entry 30 days again, for a whopping HKD 1600), I bought a train ticket to Guilin. I'd decided to spend a two days in Yangshuo before flying up to Beijing. The HK apartment still didn't have air conditioning, computers, washing machine or a TV that worked and in my short time there I'd paid the water bill in order to avoid disconnection and re-stocked all the basic supplies. Yangshuo seemed a much better option and I'd checked the schedule, so I knew that Amy was going to be there too.

There is some relevance to me singling out Henry earlier. I got a call from Cindy, she wanted some advice. She'd agreed to share a room with Henry while she was in Xi'an, but things had taken a bad turn. He'd got into bed with her and tried to have sex with her. I don't know any more details, but she was OK. She was confused as to what she should do about this, if anything. In China, al lot of this sort of stuff will be swept under the carpet, but we work for a western company and should be open. I said that it should be reported, as even though she was OK, it's just unacceptable for this sort of stuff to happen. Henry is working with many other girls, he has a bit of a reputation and this sort of stuff should be nipped in the bud. She didn't want him to get sacked, and I told her that this was definitely a sack-able offence.

I hadn't seen Amy in nearly three weeks again, so had the usual catching up to do. She was still lacking confidence about her trips, although to me, she was doing an excellent job, far better than many of the new Chinese Leaders who were not copings with the demands of the job or the expectations of the western travellers who just didn't know what to expect from China. She had rung me quite regularly over the last months, sometimes about a particular problem, sometimes just to chat. She had called me at the end of her first trip, as she was worried that her group were not happy and she had wanted to buy them a bottle of wine or some present. I'd told her, "these are not your friends" and that if they weren't happy, it was often because their expectations were not quite the reality of travelling in China. It's difficult to get somebody who has never been to another country to know how different China really is from the rest of the world. I told her not to be concerned that the passengers didn't like the food or all the hustle and bustle. It was all part of the experience. She told of passengers complaining because they fell off bicycles during the ride through the paddy fields around Yangshuo and it was her fault because she had not told them how bumpy the path was. Others who asked what the names of all the skyscrapers were during the lightshow in Hong Kong, others who just kept complaining, saying "it's all rubbish" whilst they were laughing and telling each other funny stories, to which I tried to explain sarcasm and irony, that it didn't mean "rubbish was bad" at all. She was still a class above the new leaders who had never really met westerners before starting the job. We talked about home life, her apartment which her mother was now also putting money towards and every now and then they would go to the bank and pay off another lump sum. Amy said, "you know what my mum said, that my apartment has everything apart from a school close by, I didn't know what she meant, then I realised, she was talking about me getting married again." Amy was still getting the treatment, another birthday had gone by and she seemed even less likely than ever to provide her mum with grandchildren whilst she was working as a tour leader.

For me, two days in Yangshuo was probably as much as my liver could take. I tried to be good, going for Sichuan hot Pot with Amy and taking a Mandarin class, but once the sun went down it was crazy crazy nights again. Snow and Scott were not in town as they were off trying to organise their marriage certificates again. The first one had not been recognised in China, even though they married in Hong Kong. Other leaders in town included Yolanda and Tracy, both Chinese who surprised me by staying for drinks at bar 98. Their passengers came and went and we got on the cocktails. I remember having one long conversation with them about leading, covering all sorts of aspects. Tracey had lived in Australia whilst studying and was quite westernised, but there were so many things that they were unsure of. When we got around to the subject of tipping, they were all surprised when I told them that only the U.S. and Canada are tipping cultures, the rest of us don't really do it. We may round up a bill at a restaurant, but we didn't really understand tipping ourselves, not like the Americans did. Whilst the beer flowed, one of Tracy's passengers proved that his camera was waterproof by throwing it in the well next to the bar then went in fully clothed to fish it out, it was that kind of night and in the end we all went out dancing in the Kingfisher Bar on West Street. One of Amy's friends from home was also there. He and his wife had just got divorced and he had decided on a break in Yangshuo, to get away from it all. He'd been in the Army and he and his wife, also one of Amy's closest friends had drifted apart. Most Chinese would marry young, with their first boyfriend or girlfriend and with the liberalisation of the society, these young couples were now finding that marriage was not everything and divorce was becoming more common. Amy had held off on the marriage thing, but mum was putting a lot of pressure on. She had been so disappointed when Amy had broken up with her last boyfriend, it just wasn't the done thing. I really liked Amy, we enjoyed spending time together and I was liking her more and more.

A day later, I was in Beijing again and getting ready to start another trip. My first Essence of China in nine months, it seemed strange, it felt like I was going back to do some sort of routine, though how such an amazing job could become routine, I don't know. I was going to visit some old friends on the route again. I was looking forward to seeing Chicory, Patrick, Betty and Harry. To my surprise, I found out that Chicory was actually in Beijing. I'd talked to Rockhard and Lyn, both of who had got jobs working for the Beijing Olympics and they told me that Chicory was also working for them. The tourist season in Sichuan had been particularly bad, the earthquake, the knock on from the Tibet restrictions, westerners not getting visas had all added up and she had decided that it was better for her to come to Beijing to earn some money during the Olympics and employ somebody to do local guiding for her around Chengdu when the trips came through. We met in the hostel bar along with Bruce who was in town. I hadn't realised that Chicory didn't like Bruce for two reasons. The sacking of Cherie still hurt a lot of old leaders and she also told me a story of when Bruce came to Sichuan to view hotels and she had to cover all his bills and expenses.

So, I started with another group of twelve. Most were under 30. I had two couples, two girls travelling together, one of whom was a celiac (a new one on me) two Aussie women around 50 and Sid, from the US aged 63 and dying of cancer. He didn't want anybody to know, so I didn't let on. He was travelling whilst he could. He liked a beer, as did the British couple, Mark and Carly. This worked well as Steven was in town for a day. It took me a while to figure out the celiac thing. Not being able to eat anything with wheat was going to be a big problem as this included wheat in sauces, of which there were many in the average meal. I also met up with Eugenie and a couple of other leaders for lunch. After this we went to a cake shop to organise a cake for Carly's birthday. Eugenie excelled herself with one of the shop staff, who, after telling us some incorrect information about a cake, went quiet. "If you don't want to talk, you can go and work in the kitchen" said Eugenie. When I tackled her about this later, she said that this would "improve" the shop assistant and that she was only telling her this to be helpful. She will never change; all I can say is "look out Birmingham" when she arrives in September. We managed to get the birthday cake, slightly squashed, onto the train for a mini celebration. This had the potential of a good trip again.

Xi'an failed me for the first time, in that there was some construction work outside the South Gate and no singing and dancing, but we still managed nights out. In Chengdu, most went to the Cultural Show and a group of us went on to the Irish bar for a good night. It was free margaritas for girls. It was good to go back to Emei Shan and see Patrick, Betty and Harry at the Hard Wok Cafe and Mr Li, the manager at HCP monastery who is always pleased to see me. I also managed to pop in to see Nathan. Whilst out on the hike, I showed some of the group that the "ancient stone carvings" were fake. "hit it with your monkey stick" I said to Carly, thinking she'd bash the base of one of the statues. Instead, she whacked the neck of one of the bird sculptures, which instantly broke. The rest of the group, not knowing that it has only been created a few months earlier were horrified. We were also told that there was a visit of the Olympic torch to Emei Shan. Just like my visit to Zhongwei a month earlier we hoped to get a glimpse of it, but just like a month earlier we were forced to abandon these plans. I was told directly that we would have to change our departure time so that we would not be in any vicinity of the town when the torch passed through. Chinese paranoia and security were on red alert for foreigners.

There was a change to our itinerary. There had been a terrorist attack foiled earlier in the month. Instead of going to Chongqing for the boat down the Yangtze, we had to get a train to a place called Xing Feng arriving at 5am. Then a bus would take us to Yichang. The Yangtze boat cruise was now a two days excursion up the river and turning around and returning to Yichang. I'd never been to the transfer town before and the local guide was a few minutes late, that sent panic through the group as we were hassled by local taxi drivers and hotel touts. When James arrived, he said "what do you want to do? We have nothing planned for today, no hotel, no activity until we get on the boat at 9pm." We had to do a hasty phoning around to get two day rooms at the hotel and agreed to do the Dam tour in the afternoon. Hopefully, the company would cover these costs. We arrived at Yichang at 08:30 and James gave us a quick walk around my least favourite place in China, then it was "free time" and the group actually found things to do. The girls found shopping, what more can I ask for. We boarded the boat in the evening behind a group that had an average age of 70, all over weight and were piped aboard the "Victoria" by a band. I was so glad that I was not with them. Our boat was smaller than usual, about 170 passengers and it had a bar/karaoke lounge that we put to very good use over the following two nights.

This time we were having a visit to Shennong stream. The itinerary mentioned a boat ride, similar to that through the Three Little Gorges, but at some point, the river would be too shallow and we would get "boat pullers". These were traditionally men who worked along the Yangtze in the days before the Dam and before the last reefs and shoals had been dynamited. Boat Pullers would work in a team of six or more and literally, attach a rope to the prow of your boat and pull you up the river, over the rocks. This was to be one hell of a feat of man against the elements and it was now part of our excursion and tourist entertainment. I picked up the tickets for the excursion and on the front of the ticket was a photograph of the traditional boat pullers. They didn't wear any clothes.

From where the photographer was sitting in the boat, all you could see was a queue of bare behinds doing a reverse tug-of-war. I'm glad that we didn't have the picture from the front angle. Once again I thought of my group and having another experience that you just wouldn't get back home.

Off we went in our long-boats and through the mini gorge scenery. After an hour, we stopped at a "new village" which had a market area for us tourists and we were also directed to a theatre. We were going to get a performance of traditional song and dance. Into a large theatre we all filed, all the tourists from all the small boats that come from all the multi decked Tourist cruise ships, so there must have been over a hundred of us and from the way we were being ushered in, as other boats left, this was like a conveyer-belt of performances. The performers filled the stage, beginning with a traditional song from the boat pullers that I'd heard before. But that didn't grab mine, or any of my groups attention. It was the naked arses, or to be more precise, the same picture as on the tickets is the larger than life backdrop for the show. So, as you sit watching the performers, there is the static picture of the arses of the boat-pullers behind them and every once in a while, a performer will place himself directly between the legs and underneath the naked arse cheeks of the picture of the naked boat-puller. Somebody else apart from me must have realised this and pointed it out, as I did, to the un-impressed lady next to me.

After some more performances and unfathomable "1970's Summertime Special" jokes from our co-hosts, we had our finale. A shout went out to the audience for a volunteer and there were enough rowdy groups to push forward a couple of drunks. Then two girls enter from back-stage, both wearing veils. The idea is that the male volunteers have to out-bid each other in order to marry one of the unseen girls by auction. There is some traditional element to this, but I was not so sure what it was, but the winning groom has to prove his strength with his new wife and carry her on his back around the stage to end the ceremony and with it our performance. Then, we are hurried and cajoled by the mega-phone touting boat guide back to our launches. Up to 15 boats full of 20 tourists each.

Further upstream we came to a village. Locally it was known as the village where the most beautiful women lived. They were a Minority people called the Tujia and until recently had lived in isolation from the rest of China, but now with the increased river trade, the dam, tourism they were now just another village struggling against the changes that modernity had brought.

This is where we were met by the boat-pullers. Teams of men who were all over forty, there was no one young, this was hardy work and work had dried up until the Tourist Agency began to employ these men again. They lashed a rope to the prow of our boat and they pulled. Chinese in other boats were chanting "Jia you" or "add oil" in encouragement. Have I ever seen people work so hard for "entertainment?" After a ten minute haul up-stream, the boats are cut free and speed back down past the other boats and we are on our way back to the Yangtze and our life of relative luxury on the cruise ship.

Somebody asked about The Yangtze Dolphins. This had been mentioned on a few of my trips, guides had never been very forthcoming with any information, but always knew someone who had seen one. My sceptical groups would put them on the spot, but none would admit that they were extinct. The government would only announce that there was another study underway, but events had caught up and now the lack of sightings of the Yangtze Dolphin had been in the news. Whilst in Hong Kong I had heard that they were officially extinct, as had all the interested tourists on the way to the Yangtze. This news had not been released, or rather, was not allowed to reach the ears of the Tour Guides in China. However, even as my group talked about the Dolphins demise, the patriotic guides were resurrecting the animal, saying that it was western anti-Chinese propaganda again, as we were always trying to pull China down for one thing or another and we were just jealous of their achievements along the Yangtze River.

Whilst catching some television time, on my trip through Vietnam and Thailand, I had seen a programme on Nat Geo, or Discovery, called "Visions of the Yangtze". I'd managed to catch a couple of these episodes and saw how a family had lost their farm and house as the river rose. The daughter had got a job on one of the tourist boats, but as she had never had a good education, or any grounding in social skills or the etiquette of the service industry, or even a regular job before, it wasn't long before she was struggling. The boat companies had to take on some local employees, but they had never served at tables before or had to keep to a routine and they soon returned to their families. There were arguments, demonstrations and even fights about who had gained compensation, who had been allocated the best new housing, or land or jobs in the new towns. Some people had been given a little compensation, spent it expecting more and now had nothing. Some families had been told that they were not eligible to compensation because their houses or farms were not correctly registered, or they had arrived in the valley illegally from somewhere else. Money was given to people as compensation in small instalments as the first people that got compensated gambled it all away. Some people refused to leave, then didn't have enough money for a new house. People were rehoused in high rise when they are old or disabled. Other people were separated from their local community as the towns that they were moved to were often five to 10 times the size of their old towns.

We were back in Yichang again two days later. There wasn't much to do, but it was the day of the opening ceremony of the Beijing Olympics. Lyn texted me "my dream has come true". She was taking a group to the Birds Nest and would be there for the spectacle. We stood in front of a big screen in Yichang town square, with a couple of hundred locals and watched. It was spectacular. I had some weird sense of pride about being in China and somehow connected with all this. Was I turning just a little bit Chinese? We stayed whilst the teams came out. The crowd was attentive and for Japan had a sharp intake of breath and some muttering. Taiwan was roundly applauded as was Hong Kong and then Russia and India, both countries that had recently supported China. Afghanistan was applauded. When the U.S. team came out there was discussion about how large the contingent was, but as Bush was shown on the screen, there was applause. He was one of the few important world leaders that had turned up. Every time a Commonwealth country came out, with the union jack in the corner of the flag, I heard the comment "England" and I tried to explain that none of these countries was England, or Great Britain. The Chinese had no concept of the world outside their own doorstep, the legacy of great empires and European colonial rule was literally "foreign" to them. That all these countries, including Australia and New Zealand were tied to England, meaning that this other country for centuries had a much greater importance on the world stage than China was something that they just couldn't understand. Then the Chinese team came out. Covering the running track with its far superior number of competitors. The shout started, sounding like "Junguo Ji-yo, Junguo Ji-you". There was a lot of that over the following few weeks.

Next stop was Yangshuo again. We packed as much in as we could and had a couple of good nights out as usual. Pierre was in town, always good value and it was his and Ton Tons birthdays. I watched the first events of the Olympics. China was winning Gold in event after event. Notably, every time that there was a judging decision, it looked to go Chinas way. The diving was definitely suspect, but so were many others. The locals were glued to the T.V. screen, oblivious to anything but China winning and the chants of Junguo, Ji-yo. The two Australian women left us in Yangshuo, one was off to do an acupuncture course. Then the rest of us went on to Hong Kong. My schedule had me looking at seven weeks off, mainly because the trips were not allowed to go to Beijing whilst the Olympics were on. Other leaders had holiday plans, or had gone home and there had been the intent of a few of us meeting up in Ulaan Baatar, but those plans had come and gone and I just couldn't afford any of this, so when Zef called to ask if I'd do Vietnam trips again, I had to say yes. My negotiation tactics was to ask for a few weeks off first, then an interesting China trip before going back to Vietnam. He agreed; nobody else would take the trips. We had a good time in HK for once. I had found Sticky Fingers on a time off and so we went there when we had had enough of the Irish bar and danced through to the early morning. A conversation came up about the prostitutes in the bar and got on to Sid, who had been seen taking a girl into the Yangshuo hotel a few days earlier. I quizzed him about this. The trip was over, so there wasn't anything I could do or say to him, as he confessed. His cancer and medication had meant that he'd not had sex for a long time. He said "I didn't know if I could do what I could do"', but he did.

I'd been asked to pick up another group at the China border as the leader; Mack didn't have a Hong Kong permit. This was a pointless 24 hours with a group of strangers. Yolanda was in town, but wasn't coming out because her best friends' husband had killed himself after only two days of marriage. The pressures on the Chinese for getting married was so great, there seemed to be so many unhappy ones. I'd made a decision as to what to do over the following three weeks and bought a ticket to Bangkok. I reckoned that I could travel overland from there, through Laos, a country that I had long wanted to visit and return to China to activate my next 30 day visa. Then spend a few days going from the Chinese border in the South West, back to Beijing, hopefully visiting a couple of new places on route as I had a "new trip" on my schedule for after the Olympics with towns that I'd not been to before. It seemed like a plan.

My cheap ticket to Bangkok had me on an Ethiopian Airlines flight to Addis Ababa, via Bangkok. I'm glad that I got to the airport early, as there were already dozens of people there, all African, all with lots of large packages. Cardboard boxes gaffa-taped up. Canvas bags stacked high on the baggage trollys. 2, 3, 4, and more bags and boxes per person. There was no orderly queue. The airport staff had sectioned off an area near the desks as a holding bay with 30 or so people already in there, then there was a queue of sorts, outside, waiting to get in. Every time the airport staff left the holding bay gate to deal with yet another argument of "you have exceeded your baggage allowance, you can't take all this on the plane", somebody would open the barrier and wheel another 2 or 3 trollies into the holding bay. I followed one of these trollies as Africans shook hands around me, people joined, left and re-joined again. There was no way of knowing which line (because there wasn't any) fed which counter. Some trollies were brought up on the outside of the holding bay. The intention was for them to be wheeled to the check in desk at the same time that their friends got there. This was never going to work. The airport staff devised another plan. They found the few actual travellers who were travelling without stacks of bags and opened a desk for us. This didn't stop the Africans from trying to join that queue, until one bright lad said that it was only for luggage that was physically being "carried".

I arrived in Bangkok at 11:00pm, I've done this trip many times before and was on Kho San Road before 1am, however, the cheap hostels were all booked up and I didn't fancy paying over the odds for just a couple of hours sleep. I intended being on the first bus out of Bangkok. I called Esmeray, she was still in Khoa Tao, working as a diving instructor and too far away to get to for just a quick break. There was a bus to Pattaya, first thing in the morning and after visiting Thailand eight times, I'd still never been to this notorious resort. It was time for me to take a look at what all the fuss was about. I spent a couple of hours in the internet cafe and got the morning bus to the coast. I shared the trip down there with a Chinese couple, who I don't think knew what they were heading into and six men. Nobody chatted much apart from the two German friends and I could just about make out what they had planned for in Pattaya in between the expectant guffawing. This place is not the sort of place where you get chatting to people about where they're from, what they do, where they're going, why they are there etc. The others all had accommodation, I asked to be dropped in the centre of things, so, that's where I ended up, somewhere around Soy 23 and Soy 24. I walked around, lots of closed, or empty girly bars. I tried a couple of hotels, which were very expensive. I also noticed that some of the bars also advertised accommodation. I picked one that looked a lot like a British pub and got a very nice room for 500 Baht.

I had a wander around, it was still very early. So many bars with Union Jacks, football scarves, "The Royal Green jackets" bad graffiti and English breakfast, it was obvious who was here. I suppose for a lot of people, this is a piece of paradise, or was 30 years ago. People sold up and moved here for the sun and the nightlife. For a divorced bloke with half the profits of a house sale, or ex-army sapper coming out with money, this place would be very tempting. There were bars full of Americans too, mainly ex-Vietnam vets who had taken a liking to the lifestyle. There were some Europeans and the Russians were definitely coming. By late afternoon, some of the massage parlours were doing "2 for 1 happy hours" or a "4 handed massage" (with probable happy ending) now that's a marketing plan and a half. Along the beach, there were other bar areas. These were open air courtyards with maybe 10 wooden, open bars. Each had a few girls waiting there, saying 'hello' as you passed. By 5pm they were staring to get customers, lots of old men. I mean really old, the sort you'd see at this time of day in a Wetherspoons back home. They were chatting to each other over a beer. I decided that they were residents, retirees. I reckon that the girls didn't offer too much interest for them anymore. There are western women here too, but most must have been here by mistake. On some cheap package holiday to Thailand, then find that they're in Girly Bar Central. Lots of Essex, tacky bling, sports wearing, overweight and complaining. They were shopping. Pattaya, in an attempt to legitimise itself as a 'resort', sells itself as the place to shop in Thailand. There is also the world's largest pearl market. They have a sort of Disney-land/waterworld as well, just in case you were daft enough to bring the kids here too.

That night I started by having a drink in the bar downstairs. I was immediately latched on to by one of the four girls in the bar. She hardly spoke any English, but seemed suitably impressed with me and within a few minutes wanted me to take her back to England. She was 29, from North East Thailand (as are so many of the girls) and had only recently come to Bangkok. I didn't find out much more, it was time to move on. I walked around the area, picking up a few beers in what looked like the better bars. Around 11pm, I was back at my lodgings and the girl from before was sitting next to me again. Time to move on again. A few doors along, there was a real girly bar. There were a few girls sitting outside, waving, saying hello as I'd passed by earlier, "very friendly" I thought to myself, but what would happen if I actually went in to one of these places?. We have all heard lots of stories of you getting ripped off as soon as you enter, or unable to leave without getting robbed within an inch of your life. You can't see what is going on from the outside, the girls are sitting on the veranda, smiling, waving, saying "hello". In these places, you have to actually open the door an go inside. You can't see in them until you actually go in and you never know quite what to expect. There is the saying that "curiosity killed the cat" but I decided to take a look. On first impressions this place was a nice enough bar, well lit, air conditioned, fitted out like any other bar could be. It was quite empty with only another two western blokes, each chatting to a girl. I tried to chat to the girl who had escorted me into the bar and was sitting very close to me, almost on me. I was obviously, now hers. Before too long, the subject cropped up about business. I found out from the Madame, that you pay 300 Baht, or 400 Baht to take the girl away. I then found out that you pay the bar a further 700 Baht for their "room" or what is commonly known as a "bar fine" service. "Every farang knows this" she told me. Well I didn't, it's not like I frequent girly bars. I left, with the madam thinking I was a cheapskate whilst I was feeling a bit out of my depth.

Not to be deterred with my new adventurous plan to find out what else went on in Pattaya, the night continued. I found "The

Schoolyard" and in I went. There was an obvious theme, all the girls dressed in miniature tartan skirts and white blouses, until the blouses were removed. Here, as in many of the other bars the girl has a number, pinned to whatever clothing she is still wearing. The drinks prices were openly displayed, on a school blackboard no less, ranging from B100-B150, or £2 to £3 for you to buy the girl a drink. I ordered a cheap beer for myself and I didn't experience any hard sell, any scam, any rip-off and I was mostly left by myself as I finished my drink. I took in a couple more places, including the open air bars where there was a Thai Boxing ring in the middle of the courtyard. The idea was to get smashed and watch someone get smashed, but the mainly, very smashed clientele couldn't see beyond the rim of a beer bottle. The Essex wives would appear with truckloads of shopping and the husbands would try to make out that they'd not gone to see a live show. In the early hours and suitably drunk I returned to Schoolyard, just as it was closing. The Madame approached me immediately, asking if I wanted a girl. Not tonight, I said, as I was far too tired and drunk. However, tomorrow, would it be possible for you to arrange two girls for me? She looked at me quizzically "two . . ." she cupped her hands in front of her face "so that they do this?" she proceeded to tongue the inside of her cupped hand. She continued. "You would have to pay maybe 1500 and maybe the girls will not want to do this". So there you have it. I have to ask these things, otherwise we would never know.

I slept in until 11am. My first proper lie-in for a long time. Then I set off in search of the bus station, to buy my ticket back to Bangkok for the following day. I was immediately pounced upon by a girl with a questionnaire. I filled it in. "Wow, you have won the Star Prize", she said. Come with me to collect it. Now, 20 years ago, I may have been taken in by this scam. 5 years ago, I would never have even done the survey, thinking the worse. These days, I do the survey and I go to collect the prize. Why? I suppose I'm far more confident in my ability to deal with any situation now. Nobody will actually scam me, I haven't got anything "to" scam. What's more, I'm curious to find out what all this is about and the girl herself seemed pretty genuine and I am usually a good judge of character. In a large business and hotel complex I met Guy from Canada. I was told I had won either, a holiday, a digital camera or $500. All I had to do was listen to his presentation. He was going to try to sell me "Time Share". No problem. He talked a bit about himself. He'd taught English in South East Asia before marrying a Thai girl and had moved into Time Share. Not really the "Big Time", but for most Brits abroad, it sounded like the ideal life. I had the measure of him. Then he had to find out about me. I worked as a Tour Leader in China, Vietnam and possibly anywhere else I wished to travel to. I had no permanent base out here, but I have a flat in London, that I will go back to, when I get a holiday. I have no dependents; my Chinese wage is so low that it didn't register on his computer. My next planned destination for a holiday, also wasn't on his computer. (I want to complete the rest of the Silk Road, Kashgar to Istanbul, through the Middle East and all the 'Stans'). Guy was not one of the world's success stories, today was not going to change that. So, what had I won? Surprize, surprize. I'd won . . . . a 1 week holiday in 1 of 3 resorts in Thailand (or Lanzarotti, or Hong Kong) owned by the same company. I checked it out later. It's genuine. Anybody want to come?

I got to the bus station at last, ate pies (yes, there is a pie shop) on the way home, looking at the sun setting over the Gulf of Thailand. Back to my room past the girls beginning to loiter with intent along the esplanade. Then went out on the town again. This time I went up "Walking Street". I don't know why I'd not got here the night before, but this was even more intense than the Soy's I'd been drinking on. Most were doing offers for drinks at B50 or less. I decided to take advantage. Once inside the first one, I was overwhelmed. Naked girls doing a slow wiggle on a stage, 1 or 2 girls in a bath. In another bar were two girls doing the most disinterested, brain dead oil rub down of herself that they didn't look like they had a spark of humanity in them. I was generally left alone again, having 1 beer in each place then moving on to the next one that caught my eye. There was a "ladyboy drag show", there was a Russian bar with Russian strippers and a whole load of Russians hanging around. In all the bars I went in there was "no smoking". I thought to myself, "what is the world coming to when you can watch two girls playing with a dildo in a bath, but you can't have a cigarette?" Finally I found "Hot Tuna", now I know what you are thinking but to my relief this was a genuine rock bar. A band played, I was served beer by real people and no girlies. The band struck up AC/DC's Highway to Hell. I just had to sing along, revelling in the experience and the irony. I remember seeing a girl holding a sign out to dine in a French Gourmet Restaurant. There weren't many takers. How difficult is it here to make a go at a business that isn't part of the sex scene. How difficult is it for the girls to keep away from it? The next day I was in Bangkok and I caught the overnight bus, with a load of other westerners to the Laos border and Vientiane.

The Capital city of Laos is a very strange place. The centre of town looks like a suburb of somewhere else. With the international cafes and guesthouses it's a little like an Embassy district of some larger capital city, but that is all there is. As I walked around, it looked like most countries were sponsoring projects there. A German school. A French community centre. The Japanese had paid for a road. These projects were attached to each Embassy or Consulate building and there was usually a cafe attached to that, as if the Ambassador, with nothing else better to do, had decided to moonlight as a restaurateur. I headed to the 2 or 3 places of interest. First, was the "Arc d'Triumph" called the "Patauxy" that the Lao people had built. Money had been donated to build an airport, but they built this instead. It was a large, concrete arch, at the end of a long straight boulevard heading north out of the city. Ten minutes' walk further on was the "National and Spiritual Centre of Laos Culture", the Tha That Luang palace and temple. It is the large golden elongated stupa that you find on all pictures concerning Laos. Around the main stupa is a nice enough cluster of buildings which are temples and chanting halls and restored palace buildings. The main golden stupa of That Luang was closed for lunch when I got there. You had to pay to get in. It would cost foreigners 5000 Kip to enter. For nationals it was 3000. As I waited for this Centre of Laos culture to open, I used the toilet, it cost 2000. I pondered on which one was expensive, which one was cheap and the relationship between the toilet and the centre of Laos culture and religion.

That evening, I wandered around this charming, sleepy place again then found the river bank, where there were dozens of make-shift, wooden structures that were serving as restaurants. Sandbags surrounded the area as the Mekong often flooded, often because the Chinese further up-river would open the dams every once in a while. The restaurants were all decked out in lights and from the high river bank, looking over the dark Mekong slipping by below, the scene was wonderfully calm. I wandered around town again, there were a couple of bars recommended, I'd looked for one earlier without luck and the other wasn't getting going yet, if indeed it ever would. People seemed pleasant enough and I got talking to a girl. She seemed a bit quirky; always fidgeting, but I like quirky girls. Before too long, we were off to a bar, or so it seemed. I gave her some money, a dollar or so, to get some beers in, or so I thought. Then, we didn't seem to go anywhere as she darted from place to place, without a great deal of joy. She wanted a smoke, I offered her mine and she took the whole packet. Cute, very cute. Then we were standing in one of the side streets, a lot of people coming and going. A man offered me opium, well, I wasn't expecting that. My drug taking days have been over for 10 years now. Then he asked if I wanted a girl, I pointed at the girl I was with. "her? . . . . ha ha ha" he laughed. She was talking to one of the other men. I was starting to take note a little bit more of what was going on. The man came over to me again. "She wants two, 60 for you and 60 for her, that's 120". I still hadn't got it, as she sidled up and doing that cute thing she was always doing, fiddling with her hair. "Yellow, you know what that is?" No, I didn't, but it was all too obvious now. As I stood there, one of the fellow travellers from my bus ride from Bangkok recognised me. He came up, said hello and asked me what I was doing. I couldn't quite say that I was in the middle of a drug deal for a crack whore, but with that, it was all too clear. I've only been away from London for 18 months and I didn't recognise her for what she was, or what I was getting into. This life had changed me, for the better, and as a better man, away from all that at last, I just walked away. I found a bar, sat there wondering what would become of the girl. Could she be rescued? cleaned up? There was nothing that I could do.

In the morning I set off again. I met the tourist from the previous night again, a German bloke around my age called Andy. He also was going to Vang Vieng, so we waited at the place where the bus had dropped us the previous day. Nothing happened, even though we both had, well "tickets". Small pieces of paper and that's all they were right now. Just as the heavens opened, Andy and I hopped into a tuk tuk to the bus station and boarded a waiting bus to Vang Vieng. This was a local bus in every sense. Wooden floorboards, curtains only down one side (facing the sun on the northbound, or southbound trip, twice daily), no windscreen wipers, but a man, furiously rubbing the inside of the storm drenched window. Once the storm cleared, we had the most marvellous mountain scenery of winding roads through the hills. Villages of wooden huts on the side of the road, children playing in the dirt wearing the barest of clothes. Cooking pots steaming, chickens running. A tough six hour journey, then we were at Vang Vieng. We decided to follow a bloke to his hotel and hit the jackpot. There were bungalows along the river front and a bar with a veranda. Opposite was the Karst scenery which had initially attracted the tourists. I could stay here a couple of days. Unfortunately, with my tight schedule, getting back up to Beijing, it could only be a couple of days.

I took a look around town. Tourism was definitely taking off. Dozens of stalls selling "sandwiches", actually "subs" filled with all manner of things western including cheese, bacon, tuna, and chicken. Now that was a surprise. Other stalls advertised "pancakes" with fillings and as well as the obvious backpacker favourite of "banana pancake" there was chocolate, honey and everything else from the sandwich menu that was bad for your diet. They were cooked and wrapped in a crape from a hot plate. Larger cafe/bars had T.V.'s showing "friends" or "family guy", this in a village of what was still mainly converted wooden shacks. Everyone spoke English, some westerners even looked like they were working in some of the bars. Shops sold tours, elephant riding, cycling out into the countryside and "Tubing". This has become a backpacker initiation; everybody comes here to do it. You get a big tyre inner tube and float down the river. Makeshift bars have sprung up every 200m or so and the real "hard-core" stop off at every one and get completely smashed. You can dive from swings into the river from platforms extended out from the bars. A number of people have died doing this. Then I found the island. This has the feel of a hippy commune. You get to it across shaky plank bridges and there are a half dozen bars, all lit up and pumping with music. One girl with a "mockney" London accent and new tattoos was saying "yo, blood" as I crossed the bridge. You know the type. Later, I overheard people slagging each other off, then saying what they were going to "do" to someone. A lot of people had been partying for far too long. I'm not too sure if they knew who, or were they were anymore, it was all so fake. That night when I was out having a drink in my exploration of the island it rained and I got trapped in "Bucket Bar". I watched one lad argue with the Laos D.J. saying that "an Englishman's word was his word, do, you understand that?" There were around 30 westerners trapped in the bar with me. This is the closest I've been to so many westerners for a long time and I didn't like it. Some, were quite fun, like the Spanish who started off by just singing songs, but the loud and the boisterous soon took over. All the conversations were about how fantastic they all were, all having a party in somebody else's country. I talked to one of the 4 or 5 local girls who were there. One asked me if I was going to another bar afterwards. That's as far as the conversation went. The rain stopped, I walked home

Andy and another lad from our initial Bangkok bus ride went tubing the next day, and they loved it. It was the fun and alcohol fest that everyone raves about. Lots of free shots, swinging into the river, party games in some of the bars and very little actual "tubing" down the river. I met them after dinner and we went out to the island again hoping for better things. In another bar, things seemed to be much more fun and the electric storm that descended around 11 o'clock made it an amazing sound and light experience, dancing on a tropical island, in the Mekong River, lightning flashes and thunderbolts in time to the music. I decided, once again, I could have stayed longer, but time was pressing on and I left the next morning for Luangprabang. This was another arduous journey through stunning scenery. Luangprabang bus station is a few miles out of town, so you get set upon by the touts as soon as you arrive and there doesn't seem to be any other way of getting to the centre. One tuk tuk with a hotel card was as good as another so off we went. At the hotel I'd agreed to stay at, the passengers from the tuk tuk in front of me had discovered that the place was full. Fair enough, I had a wander around, got money out and found a cheaper place to stay, closer to the main street. Luangprabang is another very charming town. Built on a headland between the Mekong and another river, there are loads of temples and houses built in the colonial French style. It's a picture postcard of a place. A fair amount of western tourists had made it there and the main street was all cafes and travel service. There were lots of places along the main street selling tours to H'mong and hill tribe villages, everywhere advertised elephant rides to waterfalls, even the songthaw tuk tuks had signs advertising trips there. I was a bit surprised when I checked the price though and I didn't fancy an expensive excursion to anywhere by myself. I was remembering why I'd given up backpacking in favour of group travel in my early thirties. There were places also selling art, traditional wares and monks wandered around the neat and clean town. On the river, there were the cafes again. These were all of a higher standard than the ones in Vientiane. All had waiters in uniform, table clothes, a vase of flowers. It was all quite sophisticated and you could tell the French influence. Totally mad how much of the rest of the country is still very third world. Not once on this trip had I had a problem with language, and western food was available everywhere. What's more, it looked and tasted like western food, not the guesswork that you get in China.

I was planning my next move, further into Loas, before crossing the border, when I got an email from Zef at work. They were asking me to return to Beijing a.s.a.p. in order to get my Vietnam Visa processed before my next trip. My next trip had been moved forward. The email said that they would do this visa processing for me. Now, I remember the last time this happened and it ended up with me bribing officials at Hanoi airport. I was more than capable of getting the visa myself but now they had decided that I didn't have enough time between my following two trips to sort this out. When, I'd sent them all this information weeks ago there had been no reply. Nevertheless, this all involved a change of plan. Luckily, a new bus route had just opened up from Luangprabang to Kunming. It would take around 30 hours and from there I could arrange a flight back to Beijing. Not what I'd wanted and the cost was an issue too, but there wasn't anything else for it. Andy who I had last seen in Vang Vieng had now caught me up and we had a last night out. The only place in town open late is the Ten Pin Bowling Alley; this is because Laos with its mixture of Communism and traditional Buddhism doesn't want to encourage excesses, decadence and vices of the west. No one had bothered to tell this to the people in Vang Vieng. The bowling alley was literally that, and it is odd trying to have a party in a cavernous and brightly lit hall, but there were westerners determined to give it a go. They were all congratulating themselves on all the places they had been to, what they had done, where they were going to next. They had really begun to annoy me. Maybe it was time to go back to China anyway and the real experience of being in a foreign country, not this westernised tourist trail with it back-packer bars and burger stalls.

It was an early morning start. The bus stop was at a Chinese hotel and everything was in Chinese. What's more I could read it and the surprise on the faces of the agents was all too evident when I spoke to them. The bus was also a big surprise. I was expecting the same style of sleeper bus that I'd had in Xin jiang Province and the Silk Road. Yes, it was similar, but with one crucial difference. The beds were double beds. We had to share. Nobody was too happy about this, even those who were friends, but I was to share with a young lad from Shanghai who was studying in Kunming and spoke a little English. I never asked his name. For some reason, this seemed appropriate. Not knowing or remembering the names of random people I have shared beds with has become a common theme throughout my life. Also, he was only going as far as the border. Then I would get the bed to myself. The road quickly deteriorated. A couple of hours out of town and we hit an area where the hard surface was now just a muddy hole. There were a gang of locals there too. I'd heard about this from other travellers. The locals, often paid to repair the roads, would sooner work at a go-slow and extort money from vehicles in order to pull them through the unrepaired road. Here, they'd gone one step further and had actually removed some of the stones that our driver had put in the hole on his recent journey into Luangprabang. We had to get out and walk. Then we watched as the bus, churned its way through the mud and across to the other side. Back on the bus again for another half hour or so and the same thing happened again. This was costing us time. What's more, the border closed for foreigners at 4pm and nobody had mentioned this when they sold me the ticket. The driver said that he was going as fast as he could, but if we missed the deadline, I would have to stay in Laos, somewhere. There was a pre-border check that took ages as someone was taken off the bus for a search and we left him behind. We got to the border at 3:50. I dashed, ahead of the Chinese (quite a feat) to the front of the queue. I got my exit from Laos stamped. A tuk tuk driver was waiting to take people across the no-man's land. He wanted to wait until his tuk tuk was full, so I had to pay him for the empty seats. We got to the Chinese side, no time to spare. The border guards practised their English with me and asked about the Olympic Games in London. I could truthfully say that the Beijing Olympics would be far better than ours. Then they let me through. My bed companion left at the first town across the border. We stopped for a while at the bus station for the travellers to get some real Chinese food. I always find that strange when the Laos food was not so dis-similar, especially with so many catering for the Chinese. Here I was approached by a man who spoke English who asked how old I was. He was disappointed that I was 39 and proceeded to show me a letter and photograph from his 24 year old daughter who wanted to marry a foreigner, but I was just too old. I couldn't help but wonder what the circumstances were that had gotten a father hanging around a bus station trying to find a husband for his daughter, who evidently spoke English and had worked in a hotel in Dali. Then it was back on the bus, with a bed to myself and a morning arrival in Kunming.

I walked to the Camellia Hotel. Pauline had organised me a flight to Beijing the following day. I had a wander around town, my first real chance of exploring the city in my 11 visits here and I was pleasantly surprised with the centre of the City having some old buildings and nice pedestrianized squares. That night I went in search of The Hump for a few beers hoping it would be a place to take the group next time I was coming through. The Hump was both bar and hostel. Unlike most other provinces in China, Yunnan has a steady influx of western travellers, off to discover the delights of Li Jiang, Dali, Tiger-Leaping gorge and on to Tibet. Kunming is the major transport hub and stopping off point. Though the city has been pretty much modernised over the last thirty years, it was the centre for a number of ethnic minorities, so some aspect of their culture survives in the local restaurants. More recently, there was a western presence in Kunming and there are a few western style colonial buildings in the centre of the city that have all been refurbished. These are next to an "ancient street" of traditional houses, that the city planners have allowed to remain in a cleaned up, but historically quaint locality. This area along with the bird market that we had explored earlier in the day is centred around "The Hump". I took it to mean the road in the centre of the city that "humps" out of the uniform, rectangle of street when you look at it on a map, but there is more significance than this. "The Hump" was the terminology used by the Second World War air pilots when referring to the Himalayan Mountains. When the Japanese closed the Burma Road in the spring of 1942 the only way that the Chinese forces could be supplied was by flying missions from India to Kunming, over The Hump. The missions were initially thought to be too dangerous and unflyable. One quote was that the only thing tougher than The Hump, was the pilots who flew them. These men became known as "fei hou" or "flying tigers". There were only 80 missions flown but they kept the supply line open to the Chinese Guo Min Tang armies against the most impossible conditions. Upstairs at the Hump hostel, there are photographs and information documenting these men and their missions. You really get the feel that this place is a place proud to be a western enclave in Kunming. I got talking to one guy who was working on golf courses across China, another who was doing motorcycle tours over through Tibet and into Nepal. Kunming had gone up in my estimation. With my flight to Beijing the next morning it meant that I was going to miss out on visiting Datone and Pingyao before the start of my next trip, so I'd be visiting them with my group, blind. Still, it meant I had a week in Beijing. This would be the most time I'd spent in the city in 18 months. In a way, I was quite looking forward to it.

I spent the first couple of days in the City Centre Youth hostel, but didn't see anyone. I organised mandarin lessons, the first opportunity of doing this for a long time and picked up the Beijinger and Time Out. My intention was to get to at least some of the places that i felt I'd missed out on whilst being elsewhere in China and Vietnam. It didn't really turn out that way. When the crunch came, I just didn't fancy going half way across the city, to sit in some bar by myself. I did get to the Lama Temple and the Confucius temple though. It was my first time visits to both of these places which are high on the tourist agenda and both in the same area.

The Lama Temple as you may guess is a Tibetan temple. The street that it is on has rows of shops selling incense sticks and Buddha charms and looks interesting as the Chinese tourists and pilgrims haggle over the copper and jade amulets and candles. I remember somewhere in my notes on Beijing it said "see a fortune teller" though what a fortune told to me in Chinese would be useful for, I didn't know. The temple itself was converted from a place in 1744 in the Tibetan Buddhism style that was all the vogue in the Qing court and holds one of the two vases used for determining the re-incarnation of the Dali and Panchen Lama. It is now the official residence of the Panchen Lama when in Beijing. It was a beautiful day in Beijing, a real blue sky day, not only an official one and the crowds were out in number. The government measures the "blue sky" to tell you if it is a "blue sky day" or not. Officially there are many more of these "blue sky days" now than ten years ago. Sometimes you can't believe your eyes in China. The temple courtyards were being raucously tested by the baseball cap wearing and flag following groups. There was a large bronze incense burner with a sign saying "do not throw coins" pinned to it that was being constantly bombarded under a hail of one Yuan pieces. The temple itself was full of marvellous buildings with their high gates, higher halls and the tiled, elongated eves of the overhanging roofs. In each there are Buddha statues, long drapes. The Hall of Harmony and Peace (Yonghegong) is the main palace of Yonghe Lamasery and inside are the traditional religious three bronze Buddhas are displayed—Sakyamuni in the middle, Kasyapa-matanga on the right and Maitreya on the left. There are 18 Arhats or statues of Buddha disciples, positioned on both sides of the hall. The last grandest hall is Wanfu Pavillion and there is an awe inspiring sight as you enter, and look up and up, following the long white flowing scarf towards an out stretched arm and finally the face of the Buddha, 18m above you. He is supposed to be carved from a single piece of sandalwood and pilgrims were attempting to throw more of the Tibetan white scarves or "Khata" as a blessing around the giant statue.

Having enough of the crowds, I crossed over the main road and headed to the parkland setting of the Confucius Temple. Far fewer people in this temple complex dating from 1302. There are statues in amongst the trees and as I neared the staircase to the main pavilion I overheard a tour guide telling his group a story about one Cypress tree known as the "Touch Evil Cypress" (Chu Jian Bai). Its name derives from a story from the Ming Dynasty that when a famously corrupt official was passing by, the tree knocked off his hat, and since then people have thought this particular tree could distinguish between good and evil. Around the temple are the stone tablets, mounted on turtle backs, inscribed with the names of those who passed the imperial examination or historical documents and court pronouncements. There are 190 steele recording the Confucian classics. Much of the Temple had just been re-constructed from the rubble left after the Cultural Revolution. It had become a favourite place to torture those with a high educational background or those in the arts would witness book burnings, or opera costumes being incinerated and they would have to admit their anti-Revolutionary crimes. For a long time Confucius was on the Communist hit list, though they were quite adept to using his philosophy of an ordered society when they needed to.

Inside the main pavilion was an exhibition on Confucius and his life. He was born in 551BC and became a philosopher and political advisor. He edited the "pre-Confucian classics". The Book of Changes, or I Ching, concerned with how the unlimited universe gave rise to the dynamic, changing world formed on the basis of two forces, yin and yang. Within the yin and yang force there was a subdivision of two opposing forces, different degrees of yin and yang as represented by a trigram of different combinations of the yin and yang lines. Altogether, the eight original trigrams could be combined into sixty-four hexagrams. They were used to indicate changes in the world, from seasonal, to personality. The Book of Songs was first major collection of Chinese poems. Documents/Classic of History: early Chinese prose. The book of Documents is a history book by today's standards that records the words and deeds of lofty public figures such as the ancient sage kings. The Spring and Autumn Annals was the first annalistic history in China, of the state of Lu before 481 B.C. and The Book of Rites is description of court rites and ceremonies.

Confucius himself worked profusely. "Great Learning," "Doctrine of the Mean," "Analects" and "Mencius" were all written from his philosophies or by his students and covered the aspects of "The Way" that is prescribed by a heavenly mandate not only to the ruler but to everyone. They heavily influenced the philosophy and moral values of China and later other East Asian countries especially through The Imperial examinations, education and order in society.

I met Rockhard and Stephanie, but that was all and after a couple of days I decided to move to the apartment because it would be cheaper. The map and directions that the Tour Company gave to the apartment were bad. Why was I surprised? It led me to an area of the city that I was unfamiliar with. Twenty story high square concrete towerblock housing complexes. I was definitely not where I was used to going with the tourists in China. It made me realise that I'd been living in a sort of bubble even thought I'd been in the country for over a year. This was the first time that I'd actually been in a residential block and not a hotel or guest house. I had to enter into one of these, set around a courtyard. Grimm, foreboding, looming and blocking out the sky. The sort I'd left behind in England a long time ago. I was filled with repressed memories and for the first time in a long time I felt like I was on my own, a stranger in a strange foreign city. There were sounds of singing and dancing that rose with me in the elevator that took me from graffiti covered lobby to dimly lit deck access corridor. From the 13th floor, I looked out, over a city of towerblocks, all with red neon signs on the top of them, all shouting in Chinese Characters. Shouting something that I could not understand. Yes, I was in a stranger in a strange land.

There had been a big change in Beijing with the addition of the new subway lines. It is a big city and the network of only two lines, one a 30 kilometre loop, left most of the city untouched and inaccessible. Taxis were notoriously difficult to get. Now the addition of five new lines meant that there was access to the Olympic area and the loop of line 2 had been bisected by line 5. The subway stations were all modern, gleaming affairs with polished stone floors and this is where I started to think that they hadn't thought through the issues again. Time after time I would see the Chinese descend the escalators and go into a trot, always pushing past each other on their way to the train. Then, slip on the polished stone floors in a heap. The next issue was the security check. All the stations had been built, then the government must have decided that they were prime sites for a terrorist attack. Now, there was an x-ray machine squeezed in between the ticket offices and the ticket machines. The older subway entrance halls simply didn't have enough space for these and there would be the usual pushing and shoving crowds. I also noticed one other oversight, which the government was hastily trying to put right. All these "underground" facilities had no disabled access. What's more, the Para-Olympics were in town. By the staircases, wheel chair lifts had been "tagged on" as an afterthought, but there was no way to operate them. Supposedly, if you wanted access, you could call the station attendant and he would come and operate the wheelchair lift to the next level. However, it was obvious to me that the next level was the only place that the disabled travelled would get to because the escalators and staircases inside the subway station had no disabled access at all.

Having time off in Beijing gave me my first opportunity in a long time to take Mandarin lessons at Frontiers language school. My Chinese teacher was Lui, a man of around thirty who had taught me occasionally before on my infrequent free days in Beijing. We had a strange relationship because he could never understand why I only ever did a couple of lessons, before disappearing for months, then come back and had forgotten what we had covered earlier. My Chinese language was progressing slowly and it was my biggest frustration about being in the country and in doing my job. I had arrived a year earlier with no more than the basics of counting and "hello", "thank you", "how much?", "sorry". I had a C.D. for listening practice that had got me the basics in hotels, restaurants, street directions and from my time with Eugenie I had practiced food over and over again. But I felt that I had progressed little further. It doesn't help when you are listening on the train and after five or so minutes one of the group comes up and starts asking "what is the name of the village we just passed." There is no un-interrupted study time. I was still learning my way around the country with only trip notes to refer too, there were all the historical and social things to get my head around too. My language lessons were suffering. Bruce had often told me "talk to your local guide", but I found that the local guides always reverted to English, that is what the rest of the group wanted to hear. I had bought another language C.D. which to my surprise didn't have any English translation on it, so I understood so little that I learned nothing. What I had picked up, was the language from my phrasebook to get me by at work. I bought tickets; I could ask the driver where the bank was and then change money there. I had even confirmed bookings with hotels and restaurants over the phone. But when it came to my classes with Mr Liu, he started with the classroom basics. I still could not pronounce the words for "school" or "to study", they were new to me.

Being well travelled, I am quite used to people from other parts of the world speaking English, most of us are. Other nationalities will mis-pronounce words, use incorrect grammar, but we can figure out what they are trying to say because we are sort of accustomed to it. It is not like this in China. Firstly, there are just not many foreigners around and most Chinese people have never heard a foreign accent trying to pronounce a Chinese word. Secondly, the words are "tonal" and only a slight difference can completely change the meaning. I quickly learned that I could not just say one word, maybe with an action (like stupidly miming the use of a knife and fork for eat when they use chop sticks) and expect to be understood. I also saw people try to communicate by drawing pictures in the air, but the Chinese assume that you are drawing a "character". I had committed a whole load of phrases to memory, many of which I was mis-pronouncing, but as they were entire sentences, which had a context, I was being understood, at least some of the time. Liu said that I should start from the begging again and learn "pin yin", along with the tones, otherwise progress would always be this slow.

Pin Yin was devised and adopted in the 1950's in order to educate the illiterate Chinese masses. It is still used in the kinder garden class at school before the children are able to recognise the characters. It uses the Latin alphabet and helps you pronounce the words correctly, as long as you know what each letter sounds like. The first hurdle is pronouncing the "q" as a "ch" sound, the "zh" is a bit like a "j", "x" is more like an "s" but there is also an "s" as well. "e" is flattened "i" is like "ur", especially in the Beijing accent and then you start getting "ao" and "ou" and "uo" all with rising or falling tone lines above them. I could go on.

My lessons with Liu covered "a day trip to the Great Wall" and then "a trip to Xi'an", finding directions and going to the restaurant. He was happy with what I knew. Then he asked "how are you?" then "how do you feel?" and "what are you doing?" and I had no answer. I also could not answer the simple question "where do you live?" Why would I know the answer to that when I don't live anywhere? On the positive, I was starting to recognise some of the characters. From the initial "beef" and "chicken" I could now read things in a menu that were more complex. I had bought a pack of playing cards called "what's in a Chinese character" and they had 52 characters with the stories of how they developed, then how they combined to form other words. Hardly any Chinese character is a word in itself and most single characters are built up of other simpler characters. For example, the characters for male child and girl, once combined together form a single character for "good". One of my favourites is the character "fu", we used to practice it in the calligraphy class at Beijing Huiling and it means "good luck". It is built up of a set of clothes, a mouth (character "kou") and a field (character "tan"). The description is that if you have one set of clothes, one field and one mouth to feed then you have enough and you are lucky. Turn the character up-side-down and it becomes "fu dao" which means "good luck coming back to you".

Over the next couple of days I met Erin and Efrat, two of the last remaining western leaders in the region, and they were mainly doing Russia trips. I had two hours of Chines lessons a day and hung out in the office with Zef, Ching, Li, and Bora, the only people that I now knew. Li had been right in her assessment of the office, it had changed and lacked atmosphere. Lyn arrived, by chance. I knew she was here, but with her boyfriend, so I hadn't seen it fit to try and arrange meeting up. As it happens, she was in the same situation as me, not knowing anybody anymore in Beijing and desperately trying to meet up with people to hang out with. Amy arrived the next day, so we all tried arranging a night out. In the end, everybody cancelled, even Lyn after not being able to find the restaurant. But Amy and I made it to the Red Rose, a Xin Jiang restaurant, full of music and dancing and we feasted on far too many kebabs. The next day I met up with Eugenie for dinner. We walked around chatting about her imminent move to Birmingham, then had dinner with Suzy, who after quitting as senior leader had been co-ordinating some of the travel to and from the Para-Olympics for the competitors and honoured guests. We ate Manchurian this time. Then we headed off to Zefs' bar. He's had this up and running with his girlfriend for a year now and regularly packs out the 12 sq m which is supposedly the smallest bar in Beijing. Loads of people arrived. Stephen, Stephanie, Bora, Amy, Erin, Lyn and her boyfriend, Cindy called, she'd also just arrived in town and came over and it was Terry Li's birthday. Before too long we were having rounds of tequila shots, it was just the night that I needed, but all too soon it was over.

The next night I went for Korean with Amy, Cindy, Terry, Mack and Peter. The following morning before Mandarin class I listened to Cindy practice the Guzhou, a cross between a harp and a slide guitar; it's a large sting instrument that lies across your legs. This girl never stops surprising me. She said that when she was with her previous boyfriend, she never went out and got bored, so bought a second hand Guzhou and 1 lesson a week and started to learn. There are just so many things in life that I've wanted to do, but never got around to it. I look at my Northern working class upbringing as an excuse, but here is a Chinese farmers' girl, doing things, so there can't really be any excuses. I readied myself for my next trip. It was a 'Nomadic China'. I got a phone call at 7am from the Harmony Hotel who couldn't understand the booking sheet again, or hadn't even read it. This trip was supposed to go into the Tibetan Grasslands, but was re-routed. Not only Tibet was closed for the year, but the grasslands were closed too. I was expecting a tough start trying to explain all this. I would be visiting some new places, so a little bit of flying by the seat of my pants again as well, but I would also be seeing my good friends in Emei and Chengdu again and that would always mean a good trip. From then, I'd be back doing the Vietnam trips again and heading south for the winter.

Chapter 7.

SOUTH FOR THE WINTER

"Congratulations!

Today is your day.

You're off to Great Places!

You're off and away!"

"You have brains in your head. You have feet in your shoes.
You can steer yourself in any direction you choose.
You're on your own. And you know what you know.
You are the guy who'll decide where to go."

Today is your day! Your mountain is waiting.
So . . . get on your way.

Dr. Seuss. Oh, the Places You'll Go!

My full group of twelve on the Nomadic China turned into one of the best trips I've ever had. Full of fun, full of incident. The first hurdle was to get them to accept that the trip had been re-routed and to my surprise, there was no complaint. They were quite a young group and although most had done a little travelling before, there was a big element of "first time in Asia" and four of them were off on the Thailand and Australia jaunt, so China wasn't actually the main attraction. Jimmy and Sarah were a couple of emigrating schoolteachers from Liverpool. Fellow Liverpudlians Michael and Michelle were a brother and sister, him over to travel this leg with her before he went home and she travelled on. Bruno from Brazil was fun from the start. Rita and Jay from Australia were also on for a party. Rebecca and Sarah, English girls and Diana from Wales made up the group as such. Then we had Natasha, a trainee doctor from Estonia, studying in London. A sensible head amongst all the frivolity but we also had Margaret. 58 year old lecturer from Sydney. The age difference and background was very at odds with the others. I enjoyed the sensible questions, the discussions about politics but I was so thankful to Natasha, who acted as a bridge (and as a buffer) with the rest of the group, but as a whole, it was a struggle meeting the two parties and giving a valuable experience to all 11 of them.

This was the first time that I had been to the Forbidden City since the Olympics and I noted the "improvements". I mentioned earlier that the Chinese had evidently forgotten that the Olympics come in a pair with the Para-Olympics. Here, there was more evidence of the work that had been done for "disabled access". Part of the courtyard of bricks had been re-laid to provide a smooth path for wheelchairs or those with difficulty walking. I was pleased to see this. Then I also noticed that the areas around the raised Temple of Supreme harmony had also been smoothed out. But as my guide Kevin pointed out, there was no way for the disabled people to actually climb the steps on to the raised platforms. He said that during the Olympics, a wheel chair lift had been installed, but it didn't go all the way to the top and there had to be staff on hand all the time to assist. Now the Olympics were over, even this Heath Robinson affair had been removed and the wheelchairs were left to circle at the base of the temples.

On the great Wall, The younger ones shot off at a fast pace and Margaret struggled. At night, the younger ones went out and I dined with Margaret. I also joined them all in the bar at around 11 and there was a crazy party in Jay and Rita's room that kept us all up until 3am. I was 5 minutes late checking out. I can't remember having a start to a trip quite like that before. We had a train to Datone (a new place for me) that arrived at 6pm. By the time we'd checked in it was dark and we went looking for food around the station. There didn't seem to be much around, which for a station in a city the size of Datone was a bit of a surprise. I'd asked the local operator where to go. He'd suggested eating in the hotel and also said that all the sites in Datone (namely a couple of temples and a nine dragon fresco wall) were all closed. I rang Eugenie, who'd done the trip a month or so earlier and she said she'd not found anywhere and ate at the hotel. We went one better and ate at Mr Lee's California Beef Noodles. The only place big enough to take a group of 12 and it had picture menu too, so all I had to translate what meat it was. Back at the hotel, Margaret wanted a drink. This became a recurring theme for the trip. She wanted a white wine. I explained that this would be hard to come by in China, as would a Scotch and coke. She settled on a bottle of red. As the conversation unfolded, she confided in me "from one alcoholic to another" (I didn't take the bait, just nodded) that she would usually have a bottle of wine in the evening.

We had our own bus from Datone to Pingyao, stopping at a couple of sites on the way. The first was Yungang grottos. This was a cave system, similar to the Magoa Caves at Dunhuang on the Silk Road. This place impressed me greatly. It's been a couple of months since I last visited a site that I thought was truly awe inspiring and this place definitely hit the mark. For the whole group, it felt like we had arrived in real China. Carved Buddha's, some looking out through caves, some seated on the cliff face. Other caves contained artwork from different periods of the caves construction. This spanned from the 5th to the 11th Century's and had influences from India, other parts of the Buddhist world, different dynasties and different styles. Compared to the Magoa caves, the restoration work was in keeping with the surroundings and the whole place shot close to the top of my "must see" places in China. There was also a local market outside the caves and the group could have shopped there for a lot longer than I could allow. One bought a pictograph representing sexual positions. I've seen these before (no smutty jokes now please). On a girls wedding night, her female relatives would give her these engraved bamboo scenes depicting men and women, so as to show her what was going to happen. A sort of sex education. Next stop was the Hanging Temple. This is another "must have" photograph from China. The temple is half way up a sheer cliff face. It is propped up by long poles driven into the cliff face below. We went up, pushed about by local tourists with no care to the vertigo that we all felt. The temples' wooden floor creaked as we walked on it and we peered over the hand rails into the void below.

At around 7pm we arrived in Pingyao. We were met by Julia, our local contact and Peter, the hotel owner. They ferried us in "golf buggies" inside the walled town (no cars allowed) through the backstreets, lined with red lanterns, to our hotel. One of the girls completely forgot to take her bag from the bus to the "golf buggie", so we had a minor drama contacting the driver who was heading back to Datone. Like so many passengers, she assumed that somebody else would be moving her bags in and out of transport for her. This hotel was a fantastic surprise. A traditional house with courtyards. The rooms all wooden and straight out of a Qing period drama. Even the beds were traditional big doubles, where the idea was to place a table halfway, to create two separate sleeping areas. Julia asked if we wanted to go for food, being 8pm there was hardly anywhere open, but she organised a place in another courtyard. After this, she asked if we wanted to go to a bar. Once again, she found the only place open and watched as we started knocking back the drinks. At midnight, we were all singing kare-oke, Julia and Peter were still there, ferrying the early leavers back to the hotel, then returning for the rest of the group as the bar closed. Now how's that for service? It was a slow start in the morning and a very slow breakfast. This was the first time that the group had experienced a Chinese version of "Western Hostel" style food and service. I'd told them it wasn't South East Asia, but would they listen? It's the same every time. Then we all split into groups and went exploring.

The town is the last surviving Ming and Qing Dynasty walled city in China. When the Empire fell, the banking houses that had once made Pingyao wealthy, moved to Shanghai and other places. Pingyao fell on hard times, so much so that in the 1960's when every other place in China demolished their town walls in a strive for modernisation, Pingyao could not find the funds. So the wall stayed and so did the Ming and Qing houses that it protected. It is real China as depicted in the movies. It is what people come here to see. Wooden houses with tiled, upturned roofs, courtyards, lanterns, alleyways. It's all here. From up on the wall, the town may as well have been frozen in time. A Chinese Brigadoon that we were privileged to witness. The town wall was designed in the shape of a turtle, the banking houses that it protected are now museums and all worth checking out along with the splendorous mansions and preserved temples. All too soon, we had to leave and we were on our way to the train station. This was an elaborate affair as it is too difficult to get tickets from Pingyao to anywhere, so someone had bought our tickets from the previous big city, Tai Yuan. All we had was hand written pieces of paper but Julia did the talking and we were on the train and in cabins to Xi an.

Xi'an was excellent as ever. The only down side was that I lost the note-book that I was keeping and along with it all the poems and observations that I had scribbled down on my trip through Thailand and Laos a month earlier. However, it was Mid Autumn Festival, "mooncake day" and the city walls were even more brightly lit up. The crowds outside the wall were dancing and my group started dancing with them and carried on from bar to bar and right through the night and on to the Loco Nightclub until the morning. One of the group; Jimmy, had played as a drummer in a band, so when we went to Moonkey bar, he got an invite to Jam up on stage. Another fantastic memory, this is the stuff you will tell your grand-children. "The time I played drums in a band in China". The following day was similar and once again most of the group ended up going out until the early hours of the morning. Some never made "check out" and opted for the 4pm day rooms and that was still too early for them to see the light of day. Then they still had a wait because our train on the final day was at 10pm. As I left the transfer bus, I said "goodbye" to our driver, Mr Nui, saying in Chinese, that I'd see him next year. In the station, one guard came over to us. He couldn't explain what was happening, but we were ushered downstairs. Here, I was told that the train was not going to Emei Shan. Quick thinking, I said that I would get off in Chengdu instead, but they said I couldn't do that, even though I could read the timetable enough to see that it went there. I called Ren Ming. Bearing in mind that it was the equivalent of New Years Eve, I was surprised when he offered to come and help. He showed up 20 mins later with his date in tow. It turns out that the train was being completely re-routed. I would have to get tickets for another train and the options for Emei Shan weren't good, so I decided to go with the Chengdu idea and rang Chicory and Patrick to see if they could help me with a changed itinerary. They both said "no problem" and Ren Ming organised accommodation for us for the night. It's at times like this that I really appreciate the people I work with. Patrick and Chicory are friends, but Ren Ming is a business man with a certain reputation. He told me that he should have been singing karaoke that night, but, no-matter, there was always tomorrow. He didn't really need to help me as much as he did, but I'm glad of it. We boarded the bus and Mr Nui had a good laugh at me "see you next year? I see you are here in 1 hour, ha, ha!" Nobody else understood the joke and I wasn't going to translate it for them.

The itinerary change had left me with a bit of a financial problem because it meant that we had spent one extra night in a hotel. At the office, Zef said that the company would not pay for this and I had to work within the budget. This also made for a hectic few days with additional travel, but we had a night in Chengdu, then in the morning went to the Pandas and then on to Le Shan and Emei Shan. At Le Shan I was trying to do some negotiations with the locals concerning lunch and the ticket prices for the boat compared with the entrance fees for the Da Fo. One man was staring at my chest hair, protruding above my T shirt collar and laughing. I could understand that he was trying to say that I was like the monkeys on the mountain. I said that it was a sign of strength and that he didn't have any, but he was too quick for me and just continued to laugh and pointed at his groin area. I'd given the group the option of "boat or climb" to view the Big Buddha and came in with a saving as the boat was the cheaper option that they all chose. Patrick was also a bit of a star. He knew of my dilemma and said that he didn't mind if I used the large monastery rooms as "dorms" putting more than one couple or twin in each. It facilitated the "party atmosphere" of the group and they were non the wiser as they'd expected nothing more from a stay in a monastery. Patrick also told me that some of the Chinese leaders were doing this on a regular basis to make cash, which I was more surprised about. This got me just about on to budget again and off we went up to Hung Chun Ping monastery for the night with the young, fit, ones in the group racing ahead from Margaret who was getting very pissed off with their attitude, lack of consideration or knowledge of culture and just about anything else. It was also obvious that Jay, in his drama "queen" best was doing as much to wind Margaret up with some underhand remarks that were becoming more open insults. I was wondering how to deal with what was a situation coming to a head, but fate stepped in. This is where I had the most serious incident so far working as a Tour Leader.

As we descended the mountain, there were a lot of monkeys. I was at the back, as usual, with Margaret. She was determined to take some photographs and I was trying to hurry her along, but she wasn't taking too much notice of me. A large monkey circled around us "oh, he's a big one" she said, took a picture and scanned around for some more to photograph. "hurry up" I said, looking at the still circling large Tibetan Macaque "come on, he's going to get you". She was still fiddling with her camera when the monkey jumped on her back. I heard her scream out. Then she was on the floor as the monkey tried to wrestle her backpack off her shoulders. I lashed about with my monkey stick and he moved off, but not far enough and was still eyeing the bag. Margaret looked down at her ankle and it was obviously dislocated. The first thing she said was "you'll have to pop it back in". Well, I wasn't prepared to do that. At least at this moment she wasn't actually in pain, which was one bonus, but all I was thinking about was getting her carried down the hill, away from the gathering monkeys and to hospital as soon as possible. The other tourists and the monkey police started to arrive. I got on the phone to our guide, Nathan, and he arrived along with Natasha and Michael who was a physiotherapist. He said he'd popped dislocations back in, but only where there was an ambulance standing by to take them to hospital. Both he and the trainee doctor agreed that she had to go to hospital. All three of us knew that her holiday was just about over but it would take days for it to sink in for Margaret. They strapped up and splinted her leg and we got a sedan chair to take her the two hour journey down the mountain to a waiting ambulance, which by chance had just arrived from the town, two hours away.

The hospital was basic. The X-ray theatre was just a bare room with a bed and the machine hovering over it. Sort of like when you see "Star Trek" and the Enterprize has brought some futuristic equipment to a Medieval world. Natasha was impressed with the actual technology though and we saw that the ankle was broken in two places. Not to "pop it back in" was the right decision. Zef at the Beijing office advised me that it was still Margaret's decision to leave the trip and at this point she was intending to travel on with us. This would be possible, but very impractical. Patrick and Nathan were brilliant in getting me receipts and translating the forms and medical terminology. We had to go shopping to buy a few cartons of top quality cigarettes for the doctor to start putting his name to anything, but that was all it needed. A doctor wrote that the break would need medical attention in Australia (which should swing it for the insurance) and another made a plaster "back-slap" cast. Then we took her to "Teddy Bear Guest House", because there was no way she could have made it to the monastery. Over the next 24 hours, she slowly came around to how impractical it would be to travel on. Originally, she assumed that I and the others would be around to help, but when I explained that she would need getting on and of trains, carrying her bags and that I would be keeping to the itinerary, and that my priority was for the group and not for the individual, she wavered. When I said that she would be left in hotels all day as we went out exploring, she finally decided that she would leave. Then it became a crazy run around for me, faxing info off to her insurers, producing the receipts and advising on travel in China. Patrick and Nathan said that they would get her to the airport in a couple of days time. I did all this before we left for Chengdu again. I was very relieved for that chapter to be over.

There is of course the alternative story, which goes a little bit like this. The whole group were finding Margaret difficult. She had commented about their lack of knowledge and respect for the country, whilst at the same time demanding bottles of wine or other impossible drinks from the bars that we ventured to. She was putting a downer on the trip, she was definitely the odd one out. At some point on Emei Shan, close to the monkey area, a banana was strategically placed on her back-pack . . . .

We had another crazy night out in Chengdu. Those who came for hot pot loved it and the old woman who regularly serves us. Then it was the Irish bar, where I left them whilst many of them went on to a club. At around mid day as we were checking out, Michael came up to me. He said, "put this in your note book. Make sure that everybody has a hotel card before you leave . . . ." "hold on", I said. It's your responsibility to pick up a hotel card. I asked if you all had one when we left and it was on the very first note that I left for you all in Beijing". It turns out that they spent from 5am to 11am walking the streets trying to get back from a nightclub. They were surprised that no-one spoke English, that no one knew how to read their map. They had had a very sheltered trip so far, simply because they were always all together and I'd sorted out just about everything for them. Only now did they realise what a strange and different country they were in.

We had a day in Hua Long Xi. This was the village used in the set of "Crouching Tiger Hidden Dragon". I've never seen the film, but it's an ancient Qing village with a riverfront. The houses are all wooden and the streets pedestrianized. It's a tourist place and one of the main activities was to hire costumes of Qing outfits, or ball gowns, soldier uniforms or just about anything else for having a picture taken. A very nice side trip. Then we were off to the airport and a flight to Yangshuo. The flight was delayed and we were staying at Outside Inn, only arriving at 8pm. I said I fancied going into town, eight of the group followed and this turned into a party again. In bar 98 there was Snow, Ton Ton, Bruce, Terry and Z. She was covered in scrapes and bruises from falling off a bike but it hadn't stopped her coming out for a beer, she was quite a girl. She also questioned my drinking, saying that every time she saw me I had a bottle in my hand. "Is the bottle stuck to your hand?" she asked me, implying that it was grafted to me, funny girl. There was a strange incident that night as we all drank and joked together. Terry said that Bruce was getting fatter in his leisurely life in Yangshuo. Bruce responded with sharp Aussie humour "it's because every time I fuck your mother, she gives me a cookie". Terry was shocked. "What did you say?" So Bruce just repeated himself again, laughing as he did so. "What?" Terry still couldn't believe it, and couldn't get the reaction out of Bruce that he wanted. Bruce was none the wiser for this grave insult and carried on with his beer and another conversation. Terry left. Nobody thought anything more of it. As for my group, it was two days of utter mayhem, especially once we had changed hotels to the Morning Sun in the centre of town and they were all dazed with the effects of alcohol and no sleep when we had to leave. I also met up with Amy as we crossed paths, her arriving, me leaving. Her and Sam, a local guide went for noodles and didn't offer me any. I asked why and she said that I wouldn't like it. I persisted, until she told me that she was eating pig brains in noodles. When it comes to some things we are just worlds apart. Here she was, just about the sweetest girl I know and she's munching on pig brain.

The final night in H.K. was an odd one. After all their partying and shopping, I was very surprised that they all thought Hong Kong was too expensive. After dinner, they all went to Jay and Rita's room for drinks and only a few were interested in going out afterwards. We got to Sticky Fingers late and there was mainly just older men and the bar girls. Michelle was horrified. She'd never seen anything like this before and a few of them soon left. Michael chastised me for bringing his little sister to a bar with prostitutes. Considering that they were off travelling to Bangkok and South East Asia next, they would be in for a rude awakening.

I had a couple of days off, met Terry in the Apartment, collected my visa and prepared for my next trip. This was a basic Hong Kong to Hanoi with 15 passengers. I'd already met some of the group in Yangshuo and checked passports. I had six people from a basic Beijing to Hong Kong run by Bing, three from an "Essence of China" run by another Chinese leader and the rest were new arrivals in China. Also a result of the pre-trip passport check I was picking up one girl in Shenzhen who didn't have a multi entry visa. I also found out that another girl had changed her passport since booking the trip, so we had to get Li in the office to re-book her flight tickets too. All not so easy on 1st October, national holiday. This was a tough group right from the start. As I talked to them in the lobby, one lad asked why they should come to the group meeting? Why they should pay a local payment? Or why couldn't it have been paid at the first part of their trip? He said that the last tour leader hadn't done any of this, so why was I? It turned out that he wasn't even on the trip. Then they said that most of them had left their bags at the other hotel and needed to get them. We also had to walk to The West Hotel for the meeting because the YMCA wanted to charge me $250 for the room. At the West, I saw Bing and asked him if he wanted to say "hi" to his old group. "No way" he said. "You have them now, they were the worst" then started to tell me how they had never listened to him, walked off and got lost. One girl wanted money back for her knickers being dis-coloured in the laundry in Xi'an. "She wants $100 for three pairs of panties, who owns panties worth $100?" He hadn't paid up.

Not everybody turned up for the meeting and those that did were not listening. It quickly became a case of me telling them how this trip was not like the trip they had done in China already, it was much harder. There would be long travel days, 3 days of hiking and very basic accommodation. When they started asking about breakfast and all the other things they wanted, it just became a case of saying "no, we leave from here at 7:30am, if you are not ready, I will leave you". That evening, after checking visas I noticed that Jackies was in-correct. I went to her room to point this out and she said "no it isn't!" as if I was trying to accuse her of something more than a mistake. It transpires that she'd realised her visa was not valid, so had gone to the Vietnam Embassy in H.K. and had had a stamp added to authorise her to travel on the correct day. I'd never seen one of these before and told her that the border police probably hadn't either, so she may have some trouble. She had a bit of a rant about not being the one with an incorrect visa, so we left it at that.

The first day went exactly as planned and although the hiking was tough on day two, the group coped with the many river crossings. The homestay had improved on last year too. The family had built a new guesthouse where the pig-sty-toilet used to be. There was also a new toilet and shower. The down side was that there were only 10 beds and 16 of us, so a couple would have to bed down on the floor and others were taking the beds from people in the village. The rice wine soon arrived to take the edge of it, but although most of the group were drinking, Jacky and a couple of others were notable exceptions. On our visit to the Li family guest house in Xi Jiang, the group started being difficult again. I said that we usually ate at the Li's guest house, but the group of six from the basic trip said they would find somewhere else and started asking about internet cafes. Others also agreed to eat "in the village" though I told then there was little option. When we arrived I took them around the village and there had been big changes and I thought I'd have to eat my own words. Along the river front, where there had been some local houses, there had been a re-development and a new town square built surrounded by new, traditional style building that looked like ornamental pavilions and shops selling tourist goods and snack food. On the other side of the river, facing this was a monstrous construction along the river bank, which turned out to be an open grandstand of a wooden seating. The whole centre of the village had been turned into a performance arena. So much for traditional culture when it comes to Chinese tourism. There was enough time to do some teaching of Mah-jong and Chinese chess, before dinner and the others in the group came back too. They had not found anywhere to eat; the "hostel" didn't have a menu or internet, so now they wanted to eat with us. All we could offer them was noodle soup. It was too late to go to the market, buy more food and start cooking again. Then mostly it was about the rice wine welcome and the cultural performance in the village square. Nearly all of us got involved and even sang songs and made a human pyramid, mainly organised by Ian, who was a self-appointed leader for the six from Bings basic group. But once again, there were exceptions. Jacky had travelled with the Essence of China group earlier and her two fellow travellers from that group, James and Clare, had already described her as difficult. At one point, on the Yangtze boat, she'd phoned the captain to tell him to turn off the engines because they were too loud. She also admitted to having anger management issues. Coping with her as well as the group of 6 from the basic trip was a lot to ask. Especially when things don't go right.

At the end of the Miao villages trek, we went to get bus tickets to Guiyang, but they wouldn't sell advance tickets. After a couple of hours in the day rooms, we returned to the bus station to find that the only tickets available were for 4:40pm. This was far too late for us to get the 7:30 train. I went with Fox to see the station manager, who was being badgered from all sides, passengers and drivers, trying to organise transport. We explained our predicament, showing her the train tickets and I got as far as asking whether we could hire a bus or pay for another bus to run, anything to get us there on time. She said to buy tickets and that she would change them. The group, which already had shown itself to be difficult, were not impressed as I told them our predicament, but that it would be sorted. "Why hadn't we already got a private bus," they cried "the other leaders had always done that". It wasn't going to help to say that was not part of the company policy, we were supposed to take local busses wherever possible, not private hire and that was exactly what I was doing. When I finally got tickets for two busses and told them that I would take one group and Fox the other, they didn't want to split up the groups as some of them "had been travelling together for 4 weeks". It was either that or missing the bus, but they still continued to be difficult. Once on the bus I explained that I'd tried everything, even bribery to get us onto these busses. This seemed to have the effect of placating much of the group. I'd just got us out of a very sticky situation, by the skin of our teeth. We all met up outside Guiyang train station and were on time for the train to Kunming. I had a spare train ticket to Kunming, so Fox had decided to come too in order to do a bit of travelling on his own. He wants to be a leader, but will need to travel more in order to get that position and my giving him the ticket was my way of helping him do that.

It took ages to get taxi's from the station. More complaining. I ran into Steven in the lobby of the Camellia, quite a surprise. Fox was glad to see him too and Steven suggested he join him on his trip. Some of the group just stayed in their beds in Kunming, I took the others for a look around and they weren't impressed. Well, that's Kunming. We did a dinner that went down well and said goodbye to Fox, who they all loved, (possibly at my expense). I leant him some money for his travels through Yunnan Province. The next day it was 12 hours to the border. My Vietnam sim card wasn't working, so there was a lot of fumbling trying to re-contact the Mountain View in Sapa. Then we crossed. As predicted, the border police hadn't seen Jackys Visa stamp before. They weren't going to let her pass. I can speak enough Chinese to explain these things, but the Chinese can't read Vietnamese. It took a while to get it confirmed, with Jacky looking like she was about to explode at any moment. She didn't appreciate any of what had transpired. In hindsight, I don't know why I bothered. I wish I would have left her there. We got the 1 hour bus up to Sapa, I gave them a run-down on Vietnamese etiquette, souls of feet, touching heads, stuff like that on the way and we split into the usual groups for dinner. Us in the hotel, them spending time to look for a place and returning to the hotel as it was only place that I said would be open. The following morning was the same for breakfast, after my orientation walk. I took the usual group straight to lunch and Ian led the others off until one of them finally split and joined the other group and me in Sapa Smile. My favourite little cafe in Sapa.

Mr Dan, Mr Ding and Miss Quin were still at Mountain View Hotel. We had Ham as a guide again. He's a lot of fun and we did the homestay, rice wine and karaoke again. He played his part, flirting with the girls, asking if they had boyfriend. One of my group, Ruth said she didn't and necked a shot. This was news to me. Evidently, she had dumped her boyfriend during the trip and hadn't bothered to tell me anything about it. Abruptly, it all stopped at 10pm. Jacky and a couple of others had poured water on the party and it was off to bed. The cards came out, but it was two tables. At least I was sober enough to do the trek in a record time of 1hr 20 mins. Most of the girls actually took motorcycles from the village rather than walk. I had dinner in the English pub, with a small mixture of the group, the first time the barrier hadn't been put up over the whole ten days. Even though, there was general discussion between the two halves about where to go and it definitely wasn't with me to the "expensive" English pub. We arrived in Hanoi early. I pulled off a real coup by negotiating the hire of a bus that was in the station car park. The hotel was actually expecting us for once. I'd needed this to go right so much. Still, on the orientation walk, they still weren't satisfied, when Ruth piped up to ask whether I could give them any information about the French St Josephs' Cathedral. I was so glad to be getting all this over with. They complained about the service being too slow in Highway 4 where we had final night dinner and nearly missed the Water Puppets. We finished in Hair of the Dog, where I bought James a drink and thanked him for being about the only normal person in the group. I didn't stay late. This was my worst group and I was glad to be starting a new trip the following day.

Even before I'd begun these trips in Vietnam I'd started to look at them as something to get through. I wasn't looking forward to the winter. The isolation on these trips, especially with so many people not working, can get a bit much. The trips are definitely not the easiest. Also, mentally, I'd achieved what I originally set out to do when I got this job. I'd worked for 18 months. That was a goal I'd set myself and out of the 23 people who started with me I was the only person who'd worked through the whole period. I was still annoyed by how little I'd progressed with my Mandarin, but if that was my only frustration, it is a small one. The job had far exceeded my expectations in terms of fun and enjoyment. I suppose what I was doing now was what I'd originally expected would be the day to day work of the job. Taking groups of people around China. With the added bonus now of visits to Vietnam. My previous group had left me a little wary about what to expect next. They had been my worst group and no-matter what I had tried, they'd begun the trip, prejudiced, closed minded and not liking me and left the trip no better than they had started it. Still, I had another group now and I reckoned that there was no way that they would be as difficult as the previous lot, even if 4 of them were German. Yes, two pairs of German girls, travelling independently. Two lads around 21 years old, Richard from England and Gavin from Ireland made up the group. Maybe a little small for it to be a great group, but definitely manageable. Or at least it should have been.

Sam and Anna were vegetarians and found the sea food on the boat a problem. Then, they dropped out of the card game abruptly, the rest of us didn't know why, but something had already started. The next morning I found them on deck. They'd moved out of their cabin because they could hear a rat in the walls. They slept the day in Cat Ba as the rest of us went for a Hike. This culminated in an hour of kayaking on the sea to an island. The water still warm enough to put a toe in and I watched as the sun started to set behind the karsts as I paddled back to the mainland. The last sun on the warm sea. This was the last real day of summer. Mr Hai was not there, he was in Singapore studying English as part of his school board job, so Old Mr Tuan was taking care of things. This meant that I wasn't subjected to one of his sea-food dinners and rice wine frenzys. The place just didn't seem the same. Butterfly valley went without too much of a hitch, but Sam hadn't told me that she didn't want lunch, so they prepared it and charged us. It turns out that Sam was not only vegetarian, but would only eat pizza back home. In Liuzhou I tried to Find Pizza Hut on Five Star Street. I knew there should be one there, but with the rest of the group getting restless we went for an option suggested by Jim and the leaders from last year. They'd told me it was a restaurant where you point at a dish, but it wasn't quite what I was expecting. Inside, there were a number of counters, all with plates made up. The idea was that you sat at the table and one of the group would go around and pick a few of the plates. It was difficult to see what was vegetarian. It was difficult to see what most of the things were or what they would taste like. First we all sat down whilst I went around with Sam asking what was vegetarian, or what she would eat. The rest of the group, now very restless also got up and started ordering. Some things arrived and got eaten by the wrong people. In the end it sort of came together, but Sam made a point of only contributing 5 Yuan for the small portion that she'd eaten. Things in the group were going downhill. I took them to Soho bar and the night was somewhat revived, but there were still a couple of incidents, namely, when Gavin spilled a drink on Sam, but only wiped down the seat, saying to me "my mother told me not to touch what you can't afford" all this was completely lost on the girl and she took it as an insult. We still drank and danced, but the group was splitting.

In Chenyang, Sam and Anna ate in the village at the new hostel that served pizza. That evening they didn't join the rest of us to play cards or "who am I?" Admittedly, the second game was very Anglo-centric and Simone had spent years studying in England so had a real advantage. But it's supposed to be about joining in, even if you don't know who you are all the time. That night there was a frog in the girls room. They screamed and videoed the frog as they screamed. Then video'd themselves screaming some more as the frog jumped onto them. They'd had another sleepless night. The second night in Chenyang was no better as they found as spider in the bathroom that admittedly was bigger than my hand as I trapped it in a colander and took it outside. We talked about how unfortunate they'd been on the trip and they brought the subject up about the other two Germans, Simone and Sandy. They had decided that because they were from the former East and Bavaria, the other two, who were very well educated, sophisticated and from the West, were looking down on them. I was gobsmacked. The wall had come down 19 years earlier to unite these people and here I was with girls in their early 20's telling me that they couldn't get along with each other.

I had always thought that our accommodation and "host family" arrangements were odd. The Wu family had owned a guest house close to the wind and rain bridge, but the government had demolished it two years earlier for being "old and structurally unsound". It also blocked the view for the ever increasing numbers of paying tourists to the town. This had left the Wu's as hosts without a guest house. So they moved into Mr Ma's place. Mrs Wu continued to cook, although this must have caused friction in the kitchen with Mrs Ma. Tim continued to guide and as the only English speaker his role was secured, whilst Mr Wu; well, he was Mr Wu. At some point he had held a position of importance in the village. I was told that he would often bluster his way into meetings and tell the village elders what to do. He was that sort of man, larger than life, always in control. But now they lived in Mr Ma's house.

So when we arrived at the Chen Yang guest house, there would always be an over the top welcome from Mr Wu, repeating the half dozen words he knew in English along with flamboyant gestures whilst Mr and Mrs Ma and their handyman "young" Mr Wu looked on. At meal times Mr Wu would get involved again with the rice wine and playing mah-jong. The Ma family had been watching this all summer and where-as once, there were only ever western tour leaders who may need translation, even bad translation from Mr Wu, we now had a number of Chinese tour leaders who just saw Mr Wu's antics as needless, interfering buffoonery. The Ma family had also cottoned on to this. Now, whenever I went up to Mr Ma or "young" Mr Wu to ask a question, change a light-bulb, fix the air conditioning or tell them about mealtimes, Mr Wu would grab me to one side "no, no, no" and indicate that "he" was the boss and they were irrelevant. The Ma's also saw this.

So we had a ridiculous situation in the "Fawlty Towers of Chen Yang" with the Wu's and the Ma's all vying for importance. Sometimes Mr Ma would wear an official "security" uniform, sometimes "young" Mr Wu would. Sometimes they would all wear suits of a better quality than Mr Wu's old jacket and trousers. Mr Ma would ask me when I would like to have dinner. Taking Mr Wu out of the equation until Mr Wu would hear about what had happened and chastise me for answering. It was hilarious to watch, but unsustainable.

The German partition in my group continued into Long Ji and Yangshuo, where I ended up duplicating all the activities for both parts of the group, even down to having two orientation walks. I was complaining about this in bar 98 to Snow. Her and Scott were back from their third wedding, this time in Mongolia province. A lot had happened in their lives this year, the problems with the marriage being only the tip of the ice berg. Scott's dad and half-brother had been over since the wedding, they were never a close family, Scott leaving home when he was a teenager, but over the last year it had come to light that dad was ill, so they had buried the hatchet so to speak. The wedding had been a way of bringing them all back together, but the pressure of actually being able to get married plus dad's declining health had put a lot of strain onto Scott. He was also trying to run the Bike Asia business as Snow was trying to run Bar 98. They had a lot on their plate. There was also the problem of Scott and his fathers' reconciliation not going down to well with his mother. Then they had got the news that Scotts mum was also ill. Then within a couple of months, she died. Scott had been going to and from Australia over the last few months, that is why I'd never seen him around. He now had the issue of what to do with dad, who was thinking about living out his days in a hotel in Yangshuo. No Chinese would allow that on account of there being a ghost to deal with. There was no easy solution.

Amy was in town again, so we went to a Chongqing restaurant that I knew had just opened and we caught up with Terry, who was avoiding Bruce after insulting him last time through. Lacy was also around and it was good to finally meet her. She was also doing the Vietnam trips and had been in contact with me for advice after reading my extensive trip reports. The group had to postpone the bike ride because of the torrential rain. I met Mei Li at Moon Hill, who had my next group with her and I went through the visa/passport thing with them, just like last time, just so that there wouldn't be any problems. Once again, one person would be staying in Shenzhen and meeting up at the airport. It's amazing how many people have the wrong visas. What the hell would they do without me? and do they appreciate it? Obviously not, because as I was in Yangshuo, I received the worst feedback ever from my previous trip. There was a general "he didn't know anything" vibe from the feedbacks, even though they'd not asked any relevant questions. Ruth had complained, saying that it was the local guide who had answered the questions, well, that's their job. Then Jacky gave me nothing but a character assasination. Accusing me of kicking locals off the bus, taking taxi money off the passengers, slagging off the other leaders and the company. I think we were on two completely different trips. I hope I never meet anyone so twisted again. It knocked me for six. Got me wondering what was going on, what I was doing. I was already tired, already thinking of home. I was wondering about what the Company had in store for the following year with all the changes and no guarantees. It just makes the job all that harder.

We finished off in Hong Kong as usual. Quite amicably, with a few hand-shakes. No drinks though and we slowly all lost ourselves in Temple St Market. I was waiting on Amy arriving the following day. We finally got together around 4pm. She had also had a difficult group and was feeling the pace. She had called me three days earlier, whilst on a train, on the top bunk, crying. She didn't even know why. These trips have taken so much out of her and I was quite stunned that after all the shit she gets from foreigners that she would chose me as the person to talk to, in English. I was talking to her about how British Hong Kong was, with the three pin plugs, the mix of ethnicities and how people acted differently from the mainland Chinese and of course the double decker busses. She didn't like the double decker busses, as she thought they might unbalance as they went around a corner and tip over. Well, they didn't in

England, so they shouldn't do here" I joked. We talked about the differences between Britain, Hong Kong and China and aspects of our culture. Somehow she was telling me about the shoes they wore during the Tang Dynasty that looked like little rockers, all curved. I was asking how people walked in them and mock staggering around the road. "The height of Chinese culture and civilisation and you had to balance on curved soles? No wonder the Tang was defeated, they could hardly go into battle on rocking shoes" I said. We were talking about different trips and the people we had met and for some reason got on to the Donald Duck Tree in Emei Shan. I said "of course someone trims the branches ever few months, how else would a tree grow like that for years?" We laughed about so much together. We met up again after her last night dinner and went straight to Murphy's Irish bar, leaving her group behind. Liverpool beat Chelsea, but I never saw any of that. We talked late into the night.

We covered all the subjects only close friends talk about and for the first time she talked about her parents' divorce and got upset. She was nine when it happened. There had been a fire at her father's warehouse and as he was out of town, her and her mum had gone to investigate. When they got there, amongst the charred buildings was a back room, obviously turned into a bedroom and living quarter and there was the belongings of her father and another woman. Amy and her mum knew who this woman was, they even visited her and Amy played with her daughter. This was the defining moment in Amys life. She told me, she could never trust anyone after this. I got on to how she would deal with getting married. I knew her mum was still putting the pressure on and I also knew how much I felt for her. She surprised me with her answer. "I won't marry for love, it will be easier". She continued that there was no way that she would want to go through anything like that again. I knew she had already split up with one boyfriend last year. Previous to that there had been another boyfriend who had broken up with her; maybe her first love and she had resolved at that point that she would never fall in love again. She'd decided to

289

cut him out of her life, just like she did the next one, who was no-longer contacting her. She would not trust anybody; she would not be hurt again. I tried to talk her through it, putting something positive into the mix, a sort of "what if" scenario, because I said that she was still young and she couldn't just live her life like this. It had to get better, but no; she said she would deal with it. She then said that she had fallen for somebody else a few years earlier, but she had the last boyfriend at the time and he had a girlfriend, so nothing had happened. He had been another tour leader. Then they had not seen each other for a long time, she had split up with her last boyfriend and didn't know that he had split up with his girlfriend. When she found out, she was going to contact him, but before she did, he emailed her with the pictures from is wedding. Things move very quickly in China. She felt cheated again, no point in even thinking about falling in love. Instead, be practical about things and just forget about the bad things. It all just sounded so hopeless and sounded like my own echo. As if it was coming from me, someone who has spent long periods believing that I won't find true love. Strange, that in such strange synchronicity I'd find somebody with the same thoughts, but how cruel can fate be that you find somebody with the same feelings as you, just when you thought you might be able to change? Just when you thought that this was the person who you could trust. We were so similar, but she was an echo of what I had felt until I had met her.

I took the spare bed in her room. We continued to talk and I did what I'd been wanting to do for ages and got into her bed and held her. We talked a little more until I fell asleep. The following morning I awoke alone, she was in the other bed, nothing much was said and after check out we transferred over to her next hotel. She was starting another trip the same day. She hadn't recovered and said she felt stiff and ill, a pain in her neck and just completely run down. I took her for a curry in Chungking Mansions, her first ever authentic British style Indian curry. As a Chongqing girl she said that she could eat the spiciest food, so I put that to the test and she was choking on her words and the different kinds of spice in an Indian curry. Personally, I too can eat spicier Sichuan than I can eat Indian or Thai, it is all a matter of taste. I left her in the afternoon to get on with things, met Bing at the West Hotel, where he was taking Richard from my previous group. We arranged to meet up in the morning with Amy. She said that she was feeling no better when she arrived. Her neck and back were painful and she hadn't slept. We did a spot of shopping, it's good to have a girl around when you need new clothes and boots, but being Chinese, I just don't think we are matched when it comes to individual style. My 80's retro-rock thing doesn't work over here. She invited me to spend Chinese New Year with her, but I had to decline because, as a foreigner, I would definitely be working. The Chinese all wanted Chinese New Year off. Then it was goodbye again.

A day later and I was meeting my next group. A full 16 again, loads of British gap year students and all I could think about was the nightmare I'd had a trip ago with the entire group hating me. At least according to the schedule, this was to be my last one of these and once again, it was highly unlikely that I'd have a whole group as bad as that time. They all got to the group meeting and discussed the following weeks. It looked like it might rain at some point in the trip, but I assured them, that we would probably miss most of it. We all ate together on temple Street. 13 of the group had already travelled together from Beijing; there were only three new people and me. Odd in a way, being the leader and the new one in the group, but from the outset, they seemed accepting and inquisitive about the next part of their trip. In the morning I headed down to meet them for our 7:30 departure. Then the lift stopped. I pressed the emergency bell, then pressed it again and finally somebody came. They apologised and said they would get an engineer. It was getting close to 7:30, I shouted to them that I had to get out quickly, because of my group, but they didn't understand at all. I phoned Tom, one of the group, telling him what was happening. I could hear them laughing as he relayed the message. We wouldn't be laughing if we missed the bus, then the plane.

Around 7:40 I was out, as the staff apologised and I was trying to check out and leave with the group at the same time. We ran on to the bus stop and were in time. We were at the border a couple of hours later. Crossing was pretty quick, but as I looked back, they weren't letting someone through. This was Elaine She was one of those fly by night sort of girls who has an opinion on everything and has done everything. When everyone else talked about boyfriends back home, she said that she had two. She had travelled to more exotic locations and had a far more interesting experience than anyone else had, and she was a high flyer in the corporate world too. What she hadn't done, is get the correct visa. It transpired that on the previous trip she'd had to leave China early because her visa was not as long as the trip. It also turns out that her entry date for this second entry has already expired. I'd asked them all in Yangshuo if they for-saw any problems and non had been flagged up. Admittedly, I should have clocked this one when I was checking all the visas the previous night, but I was concentrating on the Vietnam Visas and had found three that were in-valid for entry as it was. I never expected someone not getting into China. Well, there she was. "What shall I do?" she said. All I could do was shrug my shoulders. There were flights to Kunming or Hanoi that she could get to catch up, but that was all I could suggest. The rest of us were waiting to catch a plane. She asked for her Local Payment of $300 back, which I can't do. Then I left with the group, met another of the group with visa issues; Melvin at the airport and flew to Guiyang.

We met Fox and had dinner in the usual cafe. After this, most of the group fancied trying the rice wine. I was a little concerned for myself, drinking so early in the trip, but I have little to no will-power. We finished off around 2am in one of the rooms. The next day it began to rain. Not too heavy, but almost constant. I was on the bus to the start point of the trek when Amy rang. It was difficult to hear, but she said that she had been to see the doctor in Yangshuo and was now going to finish the trip when she got to Chengdu. The doctor had x-rayed her neck and there was something not right with it, which was giving her pain and along with the constant bag carrying it had been aggravated. This meant her finishing the season early, as it was probably going to be her last trip anyway before taking time off for Winter. She asked me again if I could go to her house for Chinese New Year, but all I could tell her was that as far as I knew, I would be working it. We couldn't talk for long, we were about to start the trek. There were a couple of older ones in the group, who hiked at the back and before long we struck up some excellent conversations. The river crossings were all more difficult than last time and we were in the water immediately rather than crossing on stepping stones. I thought of calling it off, but the young eager crowd seemed ok with it all, so on we went. They were also ok with the homestay, sharing beds or going into the rooms in the older houses, complete with warning about rats.

It was New Year in the village. I have to explain. Each village has its own New Year, depending on when the rice has been harvested. For this village, it was today. The family were mainly out visiting. We had another rice wine session, playing "21" and Seb, a new arrival was the star of the show until his wife took him to bed, too drunk to do the action sequence or down another drink. In the morning, he and Richard went off exploring and got an invite to lunch in the village. Before we left, the lady of the house came in. She told Fox that she'd seen a couple in bed together. Here is another local custom. Although there are not enough beds and we have to share, men and women can not share the same bed. Victor and Elise, in their 40's had decided to cuddle up in the morning. The next part was a little tricky. Because of Victor and Elise, the room was unclean and would have to be blessed by the sacrifice of a chicken. A holy man would have to do this and the whole ceremony would cost. Around 50 Yuan. Victor was happy to pay. He now had a good story to tell.

Another four hour hike in the rain and we were in Xi Jiang. Everyone was soaked, so we tried to use the washer drier and even borrowed a hair-drier as some of us sat around in underwear and duvets. We had the cultural performance inside the guest house and some of the girls tried on some of the local clothes afterwards. They were thankful for the rice wine. The next day, the weather still hadn't improved and ironically, when we got to the hotel in Kaili, there was no water to shower. We got wetter and wetter walking between hotels. There was a couple of pissed off, tired out girls by this time. Before too long, we were on the bus and the train to Kunming and the sky actually cleared whilst we were there. We also had a night out, going to "The Hump" bar, getting back a little late and I was thinking about Amy a lot, she'd not replied to my texts or calls since we were cut off at the beginning of the hike a couple of days earlier. So, just like the month previous, I sent her a "Goodnight Kisses" text, but unlike the previous month when she "kissed" me back, this time, I didn't get a reply.

59. From Chongqing to Chengdu 20/11/08 (China).

Two hundred miles, I'll travel, to be with you
Two hundred miles, I'll travel, to be with you
Two hundred miles, Two hundred miles
Two hundred miles, from Chongqing to Chengdu

You take me to Flora land and we go spinning around
Stroll through Paris in springtime and European town
Pictures of you on the carousell
An artists impression in the park
And then you're gone again and I'm wondering
What does this all mean

Two hundred miles, I'll travel, to be with you
Two hundred miles, I'll travel, to be with you
Two hundred miles, Two hundred miles
Two hundred miles, from Chongqing to Chengdu

The lights in Chongqing city, can be pretty, that's true
But there's nothing quite so pretty in Chongqing as you
You keep me spinning around
Untill we meet again
It keeps me wondering, if were more than friends
Wondering, where this will end

You ask me home,
You say you'll come away with me
And I start to dream
About what could be
From the streets of London
To the banks of the Yangtze
The bright lights of Chongqing city
Aren't a patch on you, and me

All the lanterns in China
Could be raised up high tonight
all the lanterns in China
Don't compare with you tonight

And here I am, spinning around again
From one month to the next, I don't know where I am
And you keep me spinning around again
And I don't know where I will land
So, it leaves me so confused
Cos I was falling in love with you
Are we still stuck on the Mery go round
Or one day will we both stop spinning around

60. Temple Street Market 26/10/08 (Temple St, H.K.).

The ticket barriers beep
The sound of the subway
Like "The Chemical Brothers"
"Sounds Like D.J.'s"

The jumbled market
Spilling out over the street

Navigating around the people
Gettin nowhere fast, getting under my feet

The whirr of a toy
as it rises into the neon sky
Past the air con units on grey apartment blocks
Artificial rain from the slit of a nights sky

The parade of market stall fashions
A wu hu si hai at each stall front
Languages and people mix with
Styles, colours, clothes and ornaments

And plastic tables, outdoor resturants
Plates of noodles and soy sauce condaments
The smell off the cooking the slap and dash
The washing up, piling up, the basket full of cash

61. Goodnight Kisses 03/11/08 (Camellia Hotel, Kunming)

Goodnight kisses from Kunming again
I hear that piano playing a song
A best friend sends me a long email
Saying how they are all getting along
I think of home
And you're the nearest thing to me
And I'm alone
Clutching at you as I drown in a foreign country.

Tomorrow I cross another border
Your last chance to reply
But so many messages I've sent
You don't answer and I don't know why

I love the world I'm living in
And I don't want it to end
I'm not sure where to begin
and I love you as a friend
But I'm starting to go under

And I need a helping hand
For a time will you brave the water
Would you let me be your boyfriend?

62. Bus Kunming to He Kou 4/11/08 (He Kou).

It rained so hard as I crossed the border
Leaving you behind, heading South for Winter
Wipe away my wet face, tears in rain
I felt like it was going to rain forever and ever again

I'm heading south for the winter
Following where the birds fly
Come south with me for the winter
Why don't you, why

I hear them playing a sad song
I think it will rain all winter long
So follow me south, towards the sun
Please come with me, just come.

The bus to He Kou and the Vietnam border was the same beaten up wreck that we'd usually got, so I wasn't surprised when it broke down. The pneumatic suspension had burst. This took a couple of hours to fix, meaning that we wouldn't make it to the border in time to cross. I got on the phone to Pauline and she booked me additional rooms in He Kou (I was already going to have to leave two people there overnight who didn't have the correct entry date, now it just meant that we were all staying). I got in touch with Ham in Sapa and he contacted the Mountain View on my behalf. Elaine had already made it there, even though her train had been delayed 10 hours due to flooding and landslides. Going into Vietnam didn't look like the best option either. Amidst all this mayhem, Lyn phoned. It was her last day in China and she wanted to say goodbye. Strange how we'd not met up in months and were still at opposite ends of a vast country like China, but it is still important for us to pick up the phone and say goodbye. She'd missed saying a real goodbye to so many people because we are just scattered across the country. I felt bad that I was in the middle of another problem on another trip and couldn't give her the quality time for even a decent phone call. But we know the job too well. We got to He Kou for 10:15pm where we stayed overnight and crossed the following morning. We were in Sapa by 10 am

Our trek the next day turned into quite an ordeal. It rained again, making the path very slippery. Everybody fell, some over a dozen times. This also slowed us down considerably and we did the last half hour in the dark, sliding down the pathway to the village as it was the only way to get there. Once again, we took advantage of the rice wine. Melvin was smoking a bong and then challenging the men of the house to arm wrestling competitions until he threw up. Some of the others weren't in a much better state and of course there was the Karaoke.

Back in Sapa and I rang the Sunflower hotel and the bus to pick us up from the station. Mr Ding helped me and it was all confirmed. At Hanoi station at 6am the following morning, the bus was there and the driver knew who I was. But when we got to the Hotel, it was the same old problem. There was no booking for us. It took 40 mins of me going through the Hotels booking sheets and telling them that the people sitting in front of them were the people on the next trip. My trip from Hong Kong to Hanoi, the next trip from Hanoi to Saigon, all the same people. The manager finally found me another hotel just up the road. Our trip finished off, as you would expect on beer Hoi corner and the Hair of the Dog. Some of them were up to going to Soulas, but when we got there, the police were closing it down so we moved on to Funky Monkey, then Roots Bar. By this time I'd more or less exhausted my knowledge of underground and shuttered-up bars in Hanoi, but the group were impressed. Then, in the morning I was off again, to the Victory hotel, to meet my next group.

This became another strange trip. There were three couples. Paul and Judy, in their 60's from Canada. Neville and Brigitte in their 40's from Canada, travelling on Australian passports and living in Alaska, working on the engineering side of the mines and pipelines. Then there was Markus and Sonja, in their 30's from Switzerland. Sonja was the only one never to have been to China before. All were well travelled, seemed ready for the trip and on paper it looked good. But for some reason, that I never quite fathomed out, Paul hated Nevile. From the very start, Paul said that he liked doing his own thing, rather than group things. He then told me that his hearing problem, namely being deaf, also went super-sensitive at a certain pitch. This just co-insided with Nevilles laugh. So Paul and Judith began to eat separate from the group. They walked at a different pace, or Paul would just wander off. This was fine, if a little eccentric and it didn't affect the trip as the others didn't know his real feeling.

In Butterfly valley, which is supposed to be a retreat in the countryside, we shared the guest house with over 50 locals on a "training trip" from a company that involved them getting riotously pissed and singing karaoke. This wasn't what the group were hoping for on a trip through rural China. In Chenyang, I'd brought Mr Wu a bottle of Vodka from Vietnam that he had requested on the previous trip and he was extremely gratefull. Mr Wu invited me to eat dinner again with Mr Ma and the teachers from the art college that were also staying there. Whilst I was sitting on the terrace writing my diary, I heard a terrible squeal. There had been an accident on the road behind me and a dog killed. Mr Wu was running past me as fast as his stubby legs could carry him and then I saw him running back to the guest house, holding the dog. I could guess that he was heading to the kitchen and preparing for our evening dinner. I had an invite along with the teachers to the Wu family table along with Mr Ma the actual guest house owner, and some important people from the village. There were a few other random choices of guests too, but I didn't think too much about it. There was the usual overflowing cups of rice wine and Mr Wu was on fine form. As he pointed at the dog meat stew in front of us, he would bark at me and everyone would laugh. His "table charades" got more intriguing as he went from focusing on the food, to the drink, then to the girl sitting on his right. He would point at her, look at me and do a quick "finger inserted between thumb and forefinger in the shape of a circle" motion. Then another round of rice wine. Then more barking and another "finger in hole" suggestion again, this time followed by his favourite "money, money, money" with the associated hand gesture. He was suggesting that for some money I could sleep with the girl on his right. I was obviously missing something, so I finally received a text message from Tim, saying that the girl had been provided for me, if I wanted her. It then became my turn to explain to Tim, that if he wanted a job with the company as a leader, we couldn't do this sort of thing, even in our time off. I was also thinking of myself here. Though tempted by the pleasures of the flesh, I was constantly thinking more and more about Amy and what was worrying me was that I had not been able to contact her. The phone line out of Vietnam had been dead and although messages said "sent" I had not had a reply. I tried "facebook" and she had been deleted, this had me so puzzled and I looked for her in other people's profile, using the "stalk book" for its alternative purpose. I got to thinking that with her quitting the last trip, maybe she's been laid off and as a result was not talking to anyone about it. Losing her job was "losing face". I had to get into contact with her and it was only now that I finally managed a hurried conversation with her. She was at home, doing things with her mum and resting a lot. At least I knew now that she was O.K. and the doctors medicine had taken some effect and her neck was on the mend. I also knew now, how much I had fallen for her and the more I thought about it, the more I started to believe that Amy was "the one"

63. At Blue Note Bar 11/11/08 (Blue Note Bar, Cat Ba).

I'll never forget about you
My best friend in China
You travelled from Chongqing to Chengdu
Spun me higher and higher

And when there was only me and you
I thought we could be together
Somehow, some way
We'd manage to do this forever
Somehow, between two worlds
and against the force of gravity
We'd fly away like in Flora World
and make something of this fantasy

But you're somewhere out of reach to me
Beyond text, or call, or internet, some closed off country
So, before winter sets in
And you're snow bound and hibernating
While I've still chance for communicating
Please reply, I'll be waiting
Cos you're more than my best friend in China
If you'd let me love you, I'd be your lover
Oh, spin me around, again, in fantasy
Talk to me, come to me, be with me

64. A passport to Paradise 11/11/08 (Blue Note Bar, Cat Ba)

A passport to paradise
A visa for heaven
From my land trapped in ice
My snowbound kingdom
Don't let it be winter again
The summer went so fast
Put me on that airplane
Leave behind this icy past
Running across the sand
Running into sea one more time
Into that vast picture of summer
Into that world that can be more than a picture

65. Madness 15/11/08 (Nanjiang Hotel, Liuzhou).

Madness like a slippery wet mould
Starting to coat my brain
Thinking that there is a grand plan
Or a God out there again
Calculating all my actions
To trade with karma and superstition
I edge my bets in this game
Do things happen for a reason?

Am I writing for a record
and rhyming for a reason
Am I a quill feather riding the wind
Each new place and situation
Have I no control at all
Some acolyte, some pawn, so small
A bouncing, random, human, ball
Through every city and every season

A god rolls a dice
And I face another foe
Action packed, romance comedy
Or so the story goes
I am filled with a majic force
That I just can't quite see or touch
In a split second I see I'm above the rush
Then I'm back in the world below

66. Just for a second 27/11/08 (H.K. apartment)

For just one second
There was the glimpse of a future
Like a world set out beneath me
Or to see my place amongst the stars
A little prayer, a wish to wing away
Bouncing off heaven, a glancing blow
Sending ripples across space and time

A breath across fortunes dice
And just for 1 second, the futures mine

A summers day in another country
As yet undiscovered, waiting for me
A place in the world, maybe a home
Where the heart is where I rest my bones.

Paul had decided not to join the rest of the group for Tim's guided walk around the villages, but he opted in for Farmer Tang in Long ji. On the morning that we were leaving Da Zai, I saw that he had met with Neville and Brigitte. It turns out that he'd told them that "there were still another three days left" and to stop what they were doing. Neville and Brigitte were puzzled, but he'd also told them that I knew what they were doing and that they should listen to me. I was all at a loss on this one. I didn't know what they were doing that must be upsetting him so much. I then talked to Paul, but he didn't elaborate beyond saying that they were always talking and that they were too Americanised. Then there was the incident on the bus. It was a very crowded bus and I was sitting on the back seat. The man next to me leaned on me, Chinese style and his hand rested on my leg. This is pretty commonplace, but I shook him off a couple of time and he kept coming back. Then I half remembered Farmer Tangs story from a year ago, saying that he'd had his pockets slashed and money taken whilst on this bus. I had a closer inspection of what was going on and it was obvious that the man next to me had cut into my money belt and was in the process of taking stuff out of the front pouch. Luckily for me, this was just receipts, but I stood up and called on the bus driver to stop the bus. I couldn't risk manhandling the local, with so many other locals around, it would just look like a westerner having a spat. As a result, the bus stopped and he ran off. I then showed the conductor my slashed money belt and everything fell into place. He'd also tried to rob one of the locals and the conductress and the bus driver ran off after the thief. I think she caught up with him, but a girl on her own couldn't do much. She chastised the passengers when she got back to the bus for being so useless, but she definitely knew who the thief was. We were ushered back onto the bus and off to Guilin and Yangshuo.

How much did I need a good night out in Yangshuo. I ran around town twice with the split group again then went in search of a good time. Well, I definitely got one. It was Bruce's birthday. First I met Beata. With Tibet being closed all year she had been doing trips in China. She told me that the start of the year had not gone well, with her hanging around in Beijing for months, always on the "next trip" but the next trip to Tibet never came. Other leaders had left at this point. She had been offered work at GAP but turned it down only when Tracey had decided to put her on trips in China, just to keep her with the company. Then Steven rang, he was coming to town. After a quick visit to Monkey Jane we went to bar 98 and ended up singing and dancing with Bruce and the rest of the pub up until 3am. In many ways, Bruce had changed over the last year. His drop down the company ladder had him considering is actions a lot more. He was starting to talk about giving the groups a real Chinese experience, and not ripping them off in the process as he saw so many of the new leaders doing. He had got into travel and later tourism because he wanted those things and the company that we worked for had always prided itself on delivering exciting trips, real life adventures, responsible travel, but with the new Chinese tour leaders he saw a change to formulated tourism and the local guide mentality of "get as much money out of them for the least possible work". Bruce said that it looked like it might only be us three, along with big Chris and maybe one other as the surviving western leaders for 2009. Many had left due to the lack of secure work, many of them to GAP. All of us had ended the night covered in Bruce's birthday cake and rubbing up against each other whilst we were dancing. We would never have done that a year ago. In amongst all the merrymaking, Bruce had shown me an x-ray of Amy's neck, with the unusual growths of bone fragments. I'd said how concerned I was, especially when she didn't return my calls or emails and he told me that she had asked him to delete her from Facebook when a difficult passenger had replied to a thread on it. Now she didn't want to have contact with anybody on it any more as all her friends were on QQ the Chinese Instant messaging site. Back to my strange group and I still had 24 hours to go with them. This meant just getting through the train journey with all six of the group having to share the same cabin. Paul asked if it was too late to change the tickets, but of course it was. I thanked the other Canadians and the Swiss for their patience in dealing with Paul and in H.K. I had two last night dinners. Once again, I was glad when the trip was over.

I settled into the apartment for a couple of days. After talking to the new boss, Julia who had been promoted from her role as manager of the Russia region, it looked like I was going to do one more trip, then get a new passport in Vietnam, then do another sequence of Vietnam trips. So much for Zef promising me that his would not happen. However, Julia also said that they were desperate for trainees for Vietnam. I called Amy and asked her if she would be my trainee in January and she said yes and emailed Julia. Within a couple of days, she was there, on the schedule, as my trainee. Something definately worth looking forward to. Pierre was also in the apartment so we went out for a couple of beers and I tried to get some more travel insurance, which is impossible without a credit card. (Mine expired months ago). Pierre had a new girlfriend. Last year he talked about quitting the Company and starting a paint ball company in Yangshuo, then when that fell through, getting a job in the newly opened Venetian Casino, Macao. The last time I saw him he was talking about setting up a hotel or something in Vietnam. Now he had met a Vietnamese girl who had a family business in construction and he was going to quit the tour company again, learn Vietnamese and go into some sort of business with the girl and her family. Something is always happening for Pierre. In typical style he'd chatted up a girl on a beach and he was off doing something else. He also told me about an incident in Maoliu, the Miao village homestay. If you remember, I had Victor and Elise who had got into bed together in the morning for a cuddle and got a 50 Yuan fine. Well, Pierre, being Pierre, on his training trip with Qing, had slept on the living room floor with a couple of others and had sex with one of the passengers. Not only that, but he was encouraging one of the other lads to join in for a three-some. This lad had run off back to his girlfriend and had been spotted in bed with her by the family in the morning. They had tried to fine the couple for sleeping together when the story came out that he was only in bed with his girlfriend because Pierre was having sex in the living room. In the end Pierre paid a 200 Yuan fine. He said it was worth it.

Pierre left and I settled into learning Mandarin and getting some rest. Then Lacey and Steven walked in through the door. 'No" I said, with a smile on my face. I held off until 5pm before I cracked and had my first beer. Later in the evening, Lacey made us dinner. We'd been joking with her about her cooking, but she actually prepared a banquet for us. Then we went off to Wan Chai for a good night out that had me dancing with some Pilipino bar girl in the early hours. Steven said that he couldn't remember the last time that he laughed so much. We got in around 4 or 5 am and slept to around to 4 or 5 pm. The next day I was off on a flight to Hanoi again and another group.

67. Sapa 05/11/08 (Sapa).

Filled with magic
Swirling tunes and video clips
The scenery on the bus trip
The stories and the histories
Places to go, places to see
Rice wine dancing
Karaoke singing

68. Hanoi 4/12/08 (Bus to San Jiang).

Hanoi rain and the street floods
Complete with the perfume of the laundry suds
Wading through the traffic, ankle deep
Pictures of this country, memories to keep
Like the girls carrying the baskets on poles
The conical hats and the bicycles
In the art shop pictures on every wall
All come to life and what a life as Hanoi rocks and rolls

69. Superhero 28/11/08 (H.K. apartment).

A superhero in a comic book
Some meaningful dialogue
and I can turn the world on its axis
Stopping time, just for us
Whilst I ask you what you want to dream
And we'll make our home on the brightest star
If somebody grants my wishes
Why should I wonder how or who they are
I should take this magic moment
And live it to the full and live it now
We are the stuff that dreams are made of
So our dreams can become true if you try and believe

70. This most beautiful view 1/12/08 (Cat Ba Beach).

This most beautiful view
I can't wait to share it with you
Stars in the sky, boats on the sea
Alone in paradise, be alone with me

Let the magic of this place
Speed to you across the ocean
And connect us like we were face to face
Bring you here, holding my hand
So that we can both walk along this beach

Share the sunset as it tries to keep
the day from ending. One last burst of the sun
The sky awash with colours, and the colours, run
This should be our sun set, don't let night descend
Don't let the sun go down, don't let it end.

This was supposed to be the last of my Vietnam trips, my 8th Hanoi to Hong Kong trip, some sort of record. I arrived at Hanoi Airport around 4pm, called the Victory Hotel to say I was running late and booked KOTO's for the group dinner. I arrived 6:16 and the front desk rang up the passengers. Two arrived. It turns out that with all the trouble in Bangkok airport, The Yellow Shirt Occupation of it, one passenger had cancelled in the week and two others were stranded there. So we had a group consisting of John, me and Mary. They had both travelled with our Company in China before. It should all have been so easy, but that's exactly what I thought last time. John and Mary were like chalk and cheese. Mary didn't drink she worked as a maths teacher in a University and was married to a professor. She didn't eat pork, but soon after we also found out she didn't eat chicken with bones in it either, or sea food if it consisted of calamari, or prawns with heads. In Butterfly valley she declared that she would turn vegetarian. She couldn't understand why she couldn't get a pot of tea with her breakfast. She didn't understand breakfast. Our three way conversations were truncated. By 9pm every evening we had usually exhausted pleasantries and Mary would head off to bed. If the opportunity presented itself, I'd have a couple of beers with John. He was a salesman. Salt of the earth type of bloke who said what he thought, but I'm glad to say, didn't say what he thought of Mary in front of her.

As we travelled from Butterfly Valley to Nanning in Grass' husbands car, Mary commented that his windscreen was dirty. So he stopped and cleaned the car. Mary, coming from drought ridden Melbourne was horrified at the amount of water being used, all in the name of giving her a better service. Later, she asked if he wasn't going to stop for a toilet break, so he did a detour for her towards the airport, the only toilet stop for miles. The nights were cold in China and bed was the only option. Mr Wu and Mr Ma invited me for dinner again in Chenyang and it was dog again. I must be their favourite. Mr Wu had had to do the guiding as Tim was in Liuzhuo renewing his license. I promised Mr Wu I'd bring him Whisky and Vodka for the rest of the staff when I returned in six weeks time. Ann had also said that she didn't tip, so it looked like I was going to be buying presents to make up for it. Then we got to Long ji, where Mary said that she didn't like walking up hills. She'd done the Active Trip with Steven the previous year and admitted that she'd complained all the time. If only I'd have known. I was a bit of a celebrity in the Bus Station where the Manager wanted to talk to me. The attempted robbery of three weeks earlier had been big news and they had actually managed to catch the thief. He was now in prison in Guilin.

Once again, I was needing that little bit of respite in Yangshuo. All the time I'd spent with the two passengers had meant that I'd done hardly any work. Bruce was in town as ever. There was a major discussion concerning our new rates of pay, getting paid whilst I was getting my new passport, contracts ending, being renewed and loads of other stuff to do with the job. Everything was changing, little of it for the better. Cindy was there and we discussed meeting up in Vietnam whilst I was renewing my passport. For some reason she would not be going home to her family over the Christmas period, which seemed rather strange for me knowing how much it was a traditional time for meeting family on the run up to Chinese New Year. Z also made an appearance on the first night, so we had a late one. In the cold nights, bar 98 is the only place in town with heating, so it was quite a good atmosphere. Snow and Scott were not there. They'd gone on honeymoon and Scott's dad had died, so they had temporarily moved on to Australia. It's been such a bad year for those two and in a country where I have very few actual friends they're as close as anyone is to me. From Yangshuo it was Hong Kong again. A last night dinner in the surprisingly warm weather. Mary still made a comment about the price of things in H.K. even though she'd spent such a lot on shopping. She did actually tip me, which was a surprise. John and I rounded off the night and the trip on Temple Street market with a few beers. He told me stories of other trips he'd been on, none were like this. He'd been to the Philippines with his mates on a "root-fest". He turned the conversation around to asking where he should go on his last night in Hong Kong. I pointed at the girl who was sitting on the fire hydrant, then another few further along on the pavement behind the market stalls. All he had to do was walk back to the hotel and he would be propositioned. I left him, as he wanted another beer and I had an early start again. The next day I was flying to Vietnam again. I had to get a new passport, Cindy was heading there too and we were going to spend some time travelling, then Amy was going to arrive for her training trip. We would spend some time together before the trip started. Things looked good and I couldn't help but wonder what was going to happen. I felt like I was about to undertake the biggest adventure of my life.

Cast of Main Characters in order of appearance.

Me—A Tour-Leader in China and Vietnam

Mary—Irish girl from Belfast who I travelled with once before

Monkey Jane—Owner of the guest house and roof top bar in Yangshuo

Jim—Tour Leader from the U.S. interested in "active trips" doing the Vietnam trips

Mr Hai—Tour Operator on Cat Ba Island

Grass—Tour Operator in South West China

Tim Wu—Local Guide in Chen Yang

Mr Wu—Host in Chen Yang

Farmer Tang—Tour Guide for Yangshuo and Long Ji rice terraces

George Chan (and Richard)—Tour Guides and brothers, in Yangshuo

Snow—Chinese ex-Tour Leader and owner of bar 98 and in Yangshuo

Scot—Australian ex-Tour Leader and owner of Bar 98 and Bike Asia in Yangshuo

Pam—Owner of the Yangshuo Cooking School and ex Tour Leader from Australia

Tamsin—Passenger on my second trip

Claire—Passenger on my second trip

Kelly—Passenger on my second trip

Jay—Tour Leader originally from Singapore

Fox—Local Guide around Kaili

The Li family—Guest house owners in Xi Jiang

Pauline—Local Operator in Kunming

Doung—Local Guide in Sapa

Gift—Thai Tour Leader working in South East Asia

Joseph and Joan, Mark—Passengers on my third trip

Jane—Tour Leader from England

Miss Nham—Friend of Mr Hai

Esmeray—Experienced Tour Leader from Turkey

Lewis—Friend from London, travelling in South East Asia

John and Karen—Friends from London visiting Thailand

Tony—Ex Tour Leader now a manager with GAP

Aaron—Tour Leader from U.S. moving from our company to GAP

Keith, Mike, Les, Astrid, Kim, Bronwyn—Passengers on my fourth trip

Ching—Ex Tour Leader now a manger in the Beijing office

Yi Ben—Guest house owner in Ping An

Tang—Tour Leader from Yangshuo

Mill—Tour Leader from the U.S.

Cherie—Chinese Tour Leader

Tracey and Max—New managers in Beijing

Bruce—Manager in Beijing and Yangshuo

Sarah and Helga, Zeb, Mike, Alan 28—Passengers on my fifth trip

Janie—Tour Leader from the U.S.

Estelle—Friend from London travelling in Vietnam and China

Sho—Tour Guide in Sapa

Steven—Tour Leader from Australia

Pam, Alice, Frances and Nigel, Hannah and Corina, Carolina and Elsa—Passengers on my sixth trip

Amy—Tour Guide on the Yangtze River Boat

Lyn—Tour Leader from U.S

Liz, Anthony, Ann, Mike and Tim, Alison and Eion, Rita—Passengers on my seventh trip

Ham—Local Guide in Sapa

Cindy—Trainee Chinese Tour Leader

Candy—Passenger on my eighth trip

Chris—Tour Leader from Australia

Ting Ting and Ada—Tour Leaders from my intake

Mei Mei—New Chinese Tour Leader

Z—New Chinese Tour Leader

Chicory—Tour Operator in Chengdu

Patrick—Tour Operator in Emei Shan

Qing—New Chinese Tour Leader

Pierre—Tour Leader from Canada who had previously been living in China

Li—Office assistant. Chinese girl

Suzi Li—Senior Tour Leader

Zef—Australian Tour leader, now a manager in Beijing and the owner of 12sqm bar

Rockhard—Australian Tour Leader

Tina—Belgian Tour Leader mainly doing trips in Russia and the Silk Road

Eugenie—Experienced Chinese Tour Leader and my trainer

Xiao Feng—Local Operator in Beijing

Terry, Mack, Peter—Chinese Tour Leaders

Kevin—Tour guide for the Forbidden City and Beijing

Momin John—Tour Guide in Turpan

Kim, Jo, Gordon, Gen—passengers on my tenth tour

Yue—Chinese Tour Leader

Margo—Tour guide in Tiger Leaping Gorge

Bataar—Tour Leader from Mongolia, who was operating Mongolian trips

Bolo—Tour Leader from Mongolia who worked for Bataar

Henry—New Chinese Tour Leader

Andy—German traveller in Laos

Mr Liu—Teacher of Mandarin in Beijing

Jimmy and Sarah, Michael and Michelle, Bruno, Rita and Jay Rebecca, Sarah, English, Diana, Natasha, Margaret—Passengers on my eleventh group.

Julia—Local Operator in Pingyao

Ren Ming—Local Tour Operator and businessman in Xi'an

Nathan—Tour Guide for Emei Shan

Jacky, Ian, Ruth—Passengers on my twelfth trip

Sam, Sandy, Anna, Simone, Gavin, Richard—Passengers on my thirteenth trip

Melvin, Seb, Victor, Elise—Passengers on my fourteenth trip

Paul and Judy, Neville and Brigitte, Markus and Sonja—Passengers on my fifteenth trip

Lacey—Chinese Tour Leader

Beata—Tour Leader with experience of tours in Tibet, from Hungary

Julia—Manager in Beijing